UNDER THE EAGLE

Jenny Pearce

Foreword by Richard Gott

U.S. Intervention in Central America and the Caribbean

Latin America Bureau

From the Library of [signature]

First published in Great Britain in 1981

Updated edition published in Great Britain in 1982 by

Latin America Bureau (Research and Action) Ltd
1 Amwell Street
London EC1R 1UL

Published with the assistance of:

Trocaire, The Catholic Agency for World Development, Dublin.
WOW Campaigns Ltd, London
Latin American Working Group, (LAWG), Toronto.

Written by Jenny Pearce
Design by Jan Brown Designs
Maps by Michael Green
Typeset, printed and bound by the Russell Press Ltd, Nottingham
Cover illustration by Chris Welch

Contents

Foreword

In the late 1970s an area of the world whose struggles had previously passed unnoticed and unsung suddenly brought itself forcibly to international attention. The tenacious battles of the people of Nicaragua, led by the Sandinistas, brought about the overthrow of the Somoza dynasty and set in motion a tidal wave of revolt throughout the Central American isthmus. For nearly fifty years the United States had relied on the Nicaraguan regime to keep the area safe for the Americans. Anastasio Somoza, father and son, had acted like a Godfather to the evil satrapies of the region. Stiffened with American military aid and training, the Central American armies (far from any international enemy) concentrated on their self-appointed task of keeping rebellious peoples in check. And the world firmly looked the other way.

For decades Central America was *terra incognita*. No international newsagency bothered to keep reporters even in the capital cities. Few foreign journalists made the trip. Repression and struggle went virtually unrecorded. The splendid histories of the individual republics were ignored or forgotten. Past and present were reduced to the level of a joke — the capital of Honduras described as *Tegucigolpe* to mark yet another military coup, the war between Honduras and El Salvador dismissively referred to as 'the football war', the countries collectively and contemptuously called 'banana republics'.

From this historical oubliette, the area was rescued by the Sandinistas. Their victory gave new meaning and new vigour to the struggles elsewhere. For the first time in living memory there were signs of hope and a belief that change was possible. Ripples of rebellion spread westward. Within months the revolutionary embers in El Salvador and Guatemala had sprung into flame. Before long the entire area was awash with journalists, cameramen, and instant pundits. Suddenly Central America was front page news. The Americans started to panic.

Meanwhile, to the east, the hitherto quiescent Caribbean was beginning to rumble. The Cuban Revolution of 1959 had never been repeated elsewhere, though not for want of trying. For twenty years the slow process of decolonization took place in the Caribbean lake under the watchful eye of American gunboats. But in spite of a degree of surface prosperity — a patina of tourist-induced wealth for the benefit of an elite — the islands large and small were vulnerable to every economic ill-wind that blew through the region. And with the end of the colonial era the countries began to be open and receptive to an entirely fresh set of ideas. The islands began to discover what they had in common. The most advanced political thinkers and activists soon realised that the most significant common denominator was that the Americans were marching in to the vacuum left by the departing European powers. If decolonization was to have any meaning, dissent and rebellion were on the agenda.

It is important not to underestimate the difficulties facing the inhabitants of Central America and the Caribbean as they begin to tackle their immense historical legacy of neglect and exploitation. An astonishingly varied amalgam of peoples — the descendants of Aztecs and Mayas, the Indians of the jungle, the children and grandchildren of slaves brought from Africa, the heirs to the settlers and planters from Spain, France, England and Holland — they have all to overcome immense problems of history, culture and language in order to embark on a joint successful struggle.

And their battles are taking place in the shadow of the most powerful nation in the world. Not for them the easier option of rebellion against a distant imperial power the other side of the world, with friendly neighbours to lend assistance. The peoples of Central America and the Caribbean are isolated, atomised and alone.

For this reason, this book is extraordinarily important and timely. As the battles grow in size and significance — and in El Salvador and Guatemala the guerrilla struggle is already far advanced — it will be vital to have an informed and sympathetic public opinion in Britain, Europe and the United States, capable of refuting the stream of official lies with which the American government (and much of its press) seeks to cloak its activities. This book sets into context the most recent developments, and rescues from oblivion the history and origins of the epic struggles that are gradually and necessarily impinging on the consciousness of the western world.

Richard Gott

Richard Gott was for many years the Latin America correspondent of the *Guardian* and is now its features editor.

Preface

Our intention in publishing this book is to provide an analysis of and background to the present crisis in Central America and the Caribbean and especially of the part played by the United States in creating and perpetuating this crisis. It is written for human rights and solidarity organizations, trade unionists, church groups, teachers, students and others concerned with both broad development issues as well as the specific problems of the Caribbean basin. Above all our aim has been to present as clear and coherent a picture as possible of this important and complex subject.

While much painstaking research has gone into this book, we have tried to avoid making it too detailed or academic. Nevertheless, some will no doubt feel that they would like to know more about certain events or aspects and for this reason we have included an annotated bibliography of major sources and further reading. This bibliography also lists the most important sources used for the book; we have therefore not included footnotes which, we feel, would have burdened the text.

In focusing on the role of the United States in the region we are not unaware of the part played by other external and internal forces in shaping events — e.g. Spanish, French, Dutch and British imperialism, as well as national class structures and dynamics. But, for reasons of space and the dominant role played by the United States in the region today, we have only touched on these in passing.

For the purposes of this book we have looked in particular at US involvement in Guatemala, El Salvador, Honduras, Nicaragua and Panama in Central America and, in the Caribbean, Jamaica, Trinidad and Tobago, Barbados, Guyana, St Lucia, Grenada, St Vincent, Dominica, Puerto Rico, the Dominican Republic, Haiti and Cuba.

A word of apology is due to all those Americans, North, South and Central, who may justifiably object to our treating the word 'America' as a synonym for the United States. We reluctantly chose to do this for stylistic reasons and beg their indulgence.

Finally, we extend our grateful thanks to the organizations and individuals, too numerous to list individually, in Central America, the Caribbean, Britain and the United States who gave us invaluable information and advice.

Latin America Bureau
September 1981

Central America and the Caribbean: Political

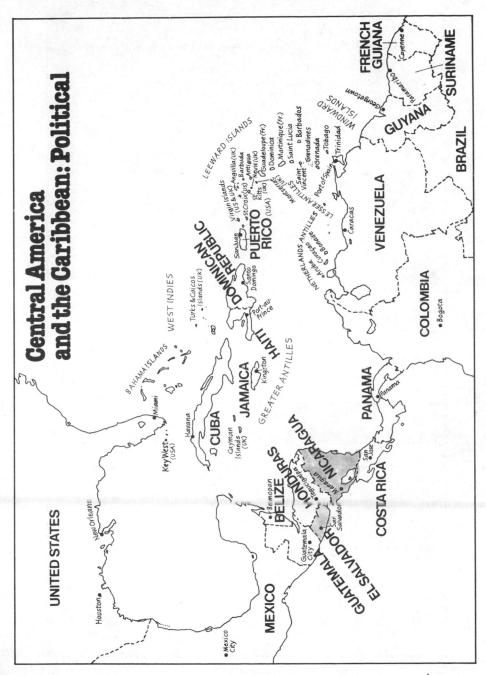

UNITED STATES

Houston

New Orleans

MEXICO

Mexico City

Guatemala City

GUATEMALA

EL SALVADOR

San Salvador

BELIZE

Belmopan

HONDURAS

NICARAGUA

Managua

COSTA RICA

San José

PANAMA

Panama

Key West (USA)

Havana

CUBA

Cayman Islands (UK)

JAMAICA

Kingston

GREATER ANTILLES

BAHAMA ISLANDS

Miami

WEST INDIES

Turks & Caicos Islands (UK)

HAITI

Port-au-Prince

DOMINICAN REPUBLIC

Santo Domingo

San Juan

PUERTO RICO (USA)

Virgin Islands (US & UK)

St Croix (US)

LEEWARD ISLANDS

Anguilla (UK)

Barbuda

Antigua

St Kitts (UK)

Nevis (UK)

Montserrat (UK)

Guadeloupe (Fr.)

Dominica

Martinique (Fr.)

Saint Lucia

Saint Vincent

Grenadines

Grenada

Barbados

Tobago

Trinidad

Port-of-Spain

WINDWARD ISLANDS

LESSER ANTILLES

NETHERLANDS ANTILLES

Aruba

Curaçao

Bonaire

Caracas

VENEZUELA

COLOMBIA

Bogota

GUYANA

Georgetown

SURINAME

Paramaribo

FRENCH GUIANA

Cayenne

BRAZIL

Statistical Profile of Central America and the Caribbean

Country	Population (millions) (1) = 1979 (2) = 1980	Population Growth 1970-79 (%)	Urban Population 1980 (%)	GNP per capita (1979 dollars)	Exports (millions US$)	Imports (millions US$)	Main exports (%)
Costa Rica	2.2 (2)	2.5	43	1,820	923 (79)	1,392 (79)	Coffee (34) bananas (18) meat (9)
El Salvador	4.8 (2)	2.9	41	670	1,029 (79)	1,024 (79)	coffee (40) cotton (10)
Guatemala	7.3 (2)	2.9	39	1,020	1,192 (79)	1,504 (79)	coffee (35) cotton (15)
Honduras	3.7 (2)	3.3	36	530	733 (79)	830 (79)	coffee (24) bananas (23)
Nicaragua	2.7 (2)	3.3	53	660	774 (78)	848 (78)	coffee (35) cotton (23) meat (15)
Panama	1.9 (2)	2.3	54	1,400	292 (79)	1,185 (79)	oil products (25) bananas (23) shrimps (15)
Barbados	.26 (1)	0.6	46	2,440	—	—	sugar
Cuba	9.8 (1)	1.4	65	1,410	4,456 (78)	4,687 (78)	sugar nickel tobacco
Dominica	.08 (76)	1.9 (70-76)	—	400	—	—	sugar coffee
Dominican Republic	5.9 (2)	2.9	51	990	822 (79)	1,062 (79)	sugar (23) coffee (18)
Grenada	.11 (2)	—	—	620	16.1 (80 est)	49.9 (80 est)	cocoa (44) bananas (21) nutmeg (28)
Guyana	.9 (1)	2.2	46	580	685 (76)	927 (76)	sugar rice
Haiti	5.8 (2)	1.7	28	260	184 (79)	221 (78)	coffee sugar
Jamaica	2.2 (1)	1.6	50	1,260	769 (79)	1,010 (79)	alumina } (46) bauxite }
Puerto Rico	3.2 (1)	1.7	—	1,990 (76)	3,346 (76)	5,432 (76)	sugar tobacco
St Lucia	.11 (76)	2.0 (70-76)	—	780			bananas cocoa
St Vincent	.11 (76)	2.8 (70-76)	—	330 (76)			bananas arrowroot
Trinidad & Tobago	1.2 (1)	1.3	65	3,390	4,895 (78)	4,721 (78)	oil

Sources: *The World Bank,* World Development Report, *1981.*
Inter-American Development Bank, Economic and Social Progress in Latin America, *1979.*
CEPAL, Statistical Summary of Latin America, 1960-1980, *1981.*
Unity is Strength, *LAB, 1980.*
Intermex Guide to 18 Latin American Countries, *1980.*

Includes underemployment.

Country	Unemploy-ment (%)	Percentage Labour force 1979 Agriculture	Industry	Literacy (%)	Population provided with drinking water (%) 1977	Infant Mortality (age 0-1) average 1975-80 (per 1000)	Life Expectancy at birth 1979
Costa Rica	4.6	30	23	90 (75)	80	45	70
El Salvador	35 (77)	51	22	62 (75)	55	79	63
Guatemala	45	56	21	47 (75)	40	89	59
Honduras	10	63	14	60 (79)	42	95	58
Nicaragua	45 (80)	40	14	90 (80)	74	96	56
Panama	25	34	18	80 (79)	82	38	70
Barbados	—	—	—	—	100	—	71
Cuba	—	24	31	96 (75)	60	24	72
Dominica	—	—	—	—	—	—	—
Dominican Republic	40 (78)	50	18	68 (78)	57	74	61
Grenada	—	—	—	95 (80)	—	—	69
Guyana	33	—	—	—	98	—	68
Haiti	70*	74	7	4	10	121	53
Jamaica	24.5 (75)	22	25	—	82	—	71
Puerto Rico	25 (77)	—	—	—	—	—	
St Lucia	40-50 (est)	—	—	—	—	—	—
St Vincent	—	—	—	—	—	—	
Trinidad & Tobago	12 (78)	16	36	95 (75)	89	—	70

Introduction

Today international attention is focused on El Salvador where a civilian-military junta, kept in power only by massive inflows of United States military and economic aid, has been responsible for the brutal deaths of at least 25,000 people in the past two years. But American intervention in El Salvador is only the latest example of the United States' prolonged and intimate involvement in the daily lives of millions of people in Central America and the Caribbean.

Over the past century and a half the United States has built up an impressive collection of weapons and techniques to maintain and promote its interests in its 'backyard'. These have ranged from direct military intervention, the threat of force ('gunboat diplomacy'), the use of surrogate troops (indirect military intervention), clandestine 'destabilizing' operations against radical regimes — including assassination attempts of 'unfriendly' political leaders — to economic blockades and sanctions. Although at any particular time one or other of these methods might be the most favoured instrument of United States foreign policy none of them has ever been completely abandoned. There is a high degree of continuity in United States foreign policy towards the region and the United States has preferred to keep the widest possible range of options at its disposal.

But United States influence in the region cannot be seen purely in terms of the political dimension. American foreign policy is intimately connected with its economic interests and these have had a profound impact on the socio-economic development of the Central American and Caribbean countries. While, economically, these countries may be less important to the Americans than other Third World regions, the economic impact of the United States on them is immense. The United States dominates the economies of the region, shaping them to its needs through investment and trading policies in a way which has left a lasting legacy of dependency and underdevelopment. At the same time the United States has ensured that only a small minority of the population of these countries can benefit from its involvement. The history of United States foreign policy in the region is also the history of its support for local elites favourable to its interests. The close alliance between those who control political and economic power within the region and the military and economic might of the United States has resulted in some of the most extreme forms of exploitation and repression anywhere in the world.

Such attempts by one country to dominate others are usually called 'imperialism'. Not surprisingly, the United States portrays its interventions otherwise, as Van Alstyne, an American historian has written:

American foreign policy has a vocabulary all its own, consciously — even

2

ostentatiously — side-stepping the use of terms that would even hint at aggression or imperial domination, and taking refuge in abstract formulae, stereotyped phrases and idealistic cliches that really explain nothing. Phrases like 'Monroe Doctrine', 'no entangling alliances', 'open door', 'good neighbour policy', 'Truman Doctrine', 'Eisenhower Doctrine', strew the pages of American history but throw little light on the dynamics of American foreign policy. Parrot-like repetition of these abstractions and other generalities produces an emotional reflex which assumes that American diplomacy is 'different', purer, morally better than the diplomacy of other powers.

The United States will thus go out of its way to present its interventions as defensive operations against external aggression. At various points in history the external enemy in Central America and the Caribbean has been Europe, Nazi Germany and the Soviet bloc or 'Communism' and the United States has always intervened to 'protect democracy' or the 'freedom of the individual'. Indeed the rhetoric of United States foreign policy has altered remarkably little in the course of history, so that its real nature and impact on the impoverished people of Central America and the Caribbean has frequently been obscured. This book aims to explore both the history and motivations behind United States policy towards the region and how it has affected the struggle for socio-economic justice. It also looks at the present crisis in El Salvador and the United States' attempt to prevent the people of that country determining their own future. The objective is not to speculate on the likely outcome of that particular struggle but to use it as the most recent illustration of what it means, in the words of Jose Marti, the Cuban revolutionary, to live 'in the Bowels of the Monster'.

PART 1
The Eagle Rises

Contents

1823	Monroe Doctrine pronounced
1835	Clayton Bulmer Treaty
1898	Spanish-American War
1898-1902	US troops occupy Cuba
1901	US acquires Puerto Rico
1903	Panama becomes independent from Colombia
1905	US marines land at Puerto Cortes, Honduras
1906-1909	US troops occupy Cuba
1908	US troops sent to Panama
1909	US-backed overthrow of Zelaya in Nicaragua
1910	US troops land in Honduras
1912	US troops sent to Panama
1912	US troops occupy Cuba
1912	US troops briefly occupy Puerto Cortes, Honduras
1912-25	US marines occupy Nicaragua
1914	Panama Canal is completed
1914-34	US marines occupy Haiti
1916-24	US marines occupy Dominican Republic
1917-23	US marines occupy Cuba
1918	US troops sent to Panama
1919	US marines occupy Honduras' ports
1926-33	US marines occupy Nicaragua and set up National Guard under Somoza. Sandino defeated and assassinated

1924	US marines land in Honduras
1932	US warships stand by during El Salvador *matanza*
1933	Franklin Roosevelt declares 'good neighbour' policy
1944	Bretton Woods conference sets up World Bank and International Monetary Fund
1947	The Truman Doctrine signals the beginning of the Cold War
1948	Organization of American States is founded
1954	CIA-backed invasion of Guatemala
1959	Cuban Revolution
1961	Abortive CIA-backed Bay of Pigs invasion of Cuba
1962	Cuban missile crisis

'Fate has written our policy . . .'

In 1823 President Monroe of the United States declared that interference by any European power in newly emerging Latin American republics would be considered an unfriendly act towards the United States itself. This became known as the Monroe Doctrine. It established the right of the United States to 'protect' Latin America and it was based on the assumption that the two regions shared common interests which the northern power had the right to interpret.

During the nineteenth century an aggressive expansionism was added to the defensive paternalism of the Monroe Doctrine. It was rationalised at the time by the phrase 'manifest destiny'. The United States came to believe that it had been singled out for a special mission: to carry its particular brand of economic, social and political organization initially westwards within North America and later throughout the Western Hemisphere. Westward expansion was completed by the end of the nineteenth century at the expense of the Indian population, which was decimated, and neighbouring Mexico, which lost nearly half of its territory (Texas, New Mexico and California) in a war deliberately provoked by the United States.

In the mid-nineteenth century the United States gave a foretaste of its future role in Central America and the Caribbean when it began to challenge British power in the region. At this time British naval superiority and commercial dominance were considerable, and, in addition to its West Indian colonies, Britain controlled part of the Atlantic coast of the Central American isthmus including Belize and the eastern coast of Nicaragua.

As the United States pushed westwards and became a Pacific as well as an Atlantic power, its desire for a cheap route linking the two oceans came into conflict with Britain's own wish to control such a route, for which Nicaragua was a favoured location. In 1850 the United States signed the Clayton-Bulmer Treaty with Britain. By this agreement neither power was to hold exclusive control over the Nicaraguan route, but this only temporarily resolved Anglo-American rivalry. Tensions between the two nations mounted in the 1850s and 1860s, particularly after the United States had recognized the short-lived 'conquest' of Nicaragua by an American adventurer, William Walker. In 1867 the United States violated the 1850 treaty it had signed with Britain and made an agreement with Nicaragua granting it exclusive rights of transit across the country.

By 1890 United States westward expansion was almost complete and 'manifest destiny' came to include wider dreams of empire. It was a period of great change in the United States. By 1870 more people were working in the cities than on farms, half a million immigrants a year came to the United States between 1880 and 1893 till its population (almost 70 million by 1890) overtook that of any single European country. In the 1890s the United States began to outpace Europe in the production of steel, coal and iron and giant monopoly firms emerged with surplus capital for export and in need of raw materials and markets. The strong links between United States big business and the country's foreign policy were forged in these years.

In 1890, following the publication of an influential book which suggested that sea power was the key to greatness, the United States built its first battleship. Expansion overseas seemed the logical next step and Senator Albert Jeremiah Beveridge reflected the mood of the times when he stated in 1898 that

(American factories) are making more than the American people can use . . . Fate has written our policy . . . the trade of the world must and can be ours. And we shall get it, as our Mother England has told us how . . . We will cover the ocean with our merchant marine. We will build a navy to the measure of our greatness. Great colonies, governing themselves, flying our flag, and trading with us, will grow about our ports of trade. Our institutions will follow . . . And American law, American order, American civilization and the American flag will plant themselves on shores hitherto bloody and benighted by those agents of God henceforth made beautiful and bright.

The nearest shores, and those most likely to be granted the privileges offered by Senator Beveridge were in Central America and the Caribbean — the 'backyard'.

'The Great American Archipelago'

The first target was Cuba, which, since the 1840s, had been considered a prime objective of the United States' southward expansion. Unfortunately it was still a Spanish colony and the Spanish refused to agree to United States proposals to purchase and annex the island.

By the 1880s United States capital was heavily involved in the Cuban economy, particularly the sugar industry: 'It makes the water come to my mouth when I think of the State of Cuba as one in our family' wrote an American financier in 1895.

In 1898 the Americans decided they would rescue Cuba from Spanish despotism and they went to war with Spain in support of Cuban independence. The contribution of the Cuban population to the country's war of independence, which had been going on for some time before the United States entered it, was subsequently written out of history and the United States declared it had 'liberated' Cuba. The United States then took responsibility for Spain's other colonies. It invaded Puerto Rico and purchased the Philippines for US$20 million. Guam and Puerto Rico were later ceded to the United States by Spain as 'spoils of war'.

Cuba was not officially annexed but it was occupied by American troops from 1898 to 1902. In 1901 it became technically an independent republic, but only once the United States had introduced the Platt Amendment to its new constitution. This gave it the right to intervene in Cuban affairs and to establish military bases on the island, including a naval base at Guantanamo Bay. The United States was to manipulate Cuban political and economic life from then on until 1959, sending troops to occupy the country between 1906 and 1909, again in 1912, and from 1917 to 1923.

Cuba emerged as a model for United States imperialism. American economic and political domination had been secured without the seizure of a colony. The United States could continue to boast its anti-colonial traditions and beliefs despite having transformed Cuba into a virtual dependency. 'Sphere of influence' became an internationally palatable euphemism for neo-colonialism.

It was less easy for the Americans to explain the status of Puerto Rico which in 1901 was defined as a 'non-incorporated territory which belongs to, but is not a part of the United States'. But there is no doubt that in all but name Puerto Rico became a United States colony and one of considerable strategic importance for the emerging United States empire in the Caribbean. An editorial in the *New York Times* in 1898 made this clear:

There can be no question of the wisdom of taking and holding Puerto Rico without any reference to a policy of expansion. We need it as a station in the great American archipelago misnamed the West Indies and Providence has decreed that it shall be ours as a recompense for smiting the last withering clutch of Spain from the domain which Columbus brought to light and the fairest part of which has long been our heritage.

One of the most important results of the Spanish-American War was to turn the United States into a world power with strategic frontiers in the Caribbean and interests across the Pacific Ocean. The scene was set for the American eagle to spread its wings still further. Jose Marti had foreseen the danger as early as 1895. Although he was at the time engaged in a struggle against Spain he saw his duty also 'to prevent the United States with the independence of Cuba extending itself through the West Indies and falling with added weight upon our lands of America'. Early in the twentieth century the Nicaraguan poet, Ruben Dario, speculated on what 'that Cuban (Jose Marti) would say today in seeing that under cover of aid to the grief-stricken pearl of the West Indies, the "monster" gobbles it up, oyster and all'.

The Big Stick

Theodore Roosevelt had been the United States' hero of the Spanish-American War, it made his political career and in 1901 he became President.

Roosevelt's particularly truculent use of power in Central America and the Caribbean — invasions, threats and treaties made at gunpoint characterized his presidency though they were not exclusive to it — has associated his period in office with the use of the 'big stick'.

Roosevelt stressed the strategic importance of the region to United States interests and frequently expressed his impatience with the unstable governments which threatened them. Behind his impatience was a thinly disguised racism which maintained that the Anglo-Saxon was duty bound to help backward races who were incapable of governing themselves. Such views clearly lie behind Roosevelt's famous 1904 addition to the Monroe Doctrine known as the Roosevelt Corollary:

Chronic wrongdoing or an impotence which results in a general loosening of the ties of civilized society, may in America, as elsewhere, ultimately require intervention by some civilized nation, and in the Western Hemisphere the adherence of the United States to the Monroe Doctrine may force the United States, however reluctantly, in flagrant cases of such wrong doing or impotence, to the exercise of an international police power.

Once again the pursuit of national self-interest was disguised by appeals to moral obligations and United States destiny.

It was military and commercial self-interest which motivated the United States' acquisition of the Panama Canal Zone. A transoceanic canal would drastically cut the cost of United States trade with Latin America as well as facilitate trade between the east coast of America and United States interests in the Far East. Direct control over the canal and United States bases on Cuba and Puerto Rico would enable the United States to defend its commercial interests militarily, principally against Europe.

Once it was decided that the Panamanian isthmus was the best place to build such a canal the United States rapidly overcame the problem that the area concerned belonged to another country: Colombia. The Americans encouraged and helped finance a Panamanian independence movement and the new Panamanian government immediately signed a treaty with the United States when it came to power in 1903. This gave the Americans the right to build a canal on a strip of land leased to it in perpetuity. The United States also guaranteed Panama's 'independence' and assumed the maintenance of public order in the country. It sent troops into Panama in 1908, 1912 and

11

1918 in fulfillment of its obligations.

The Panama Canal was completed in 1914 and became an important symbol of growing United States power in the Western Hemisphere. But the United States was not the only imperial power in the Caribbean. Rivalry between the United States and the European powers for control of the Caribbean was intense in these years. Great Britain, France, the Netherlands and even Denmark, until it sold the Virgin Islands to the United States in 1917, all had colonies in the region, and in these years America had to assert its right to defend its 'backyard'. It would often portray its interventions as well-intentioned acts to prevent more sinister European incursions and in this way tried to conceal its own imperial objectives.

Most of the interventions at this time involved the collection of debt by gunboat. Many countries of the region had borrowed heavily from European and United States creditors in order to build railroads and ports, pledging their customs duties as security. When a country defaulted on interest repayments and the creditors were unable to collect the customs duties they would call on their own governments to help. Thus in 1904 the government of the Dominican Republic defaulted on its payments to a United States financial company. The United States took over the collection of customs duties before any European government who was owed money could do likewise and then distributed the proceeds amongst foreign creditors. At the same time it imposed the United States dollar as the national currency thus opening the door to American business interests. In 1912 the US National Bank was established in the country.

In 1909 the Liberal government of Jose Santos Zelaya in Nicaragua defied the United States by negotiating a loan with a London syndicate and opening negotiations with the Japanese over a canal through its territory. The United States backed an insurrection against his regime and once it was overthrown appointed its own representative to collect and retain customs revenues, while US bankers Brown Brothers and Seligman negotiated new loans. The Americans were particularly anxious to secure control over rival canal routes in the region.

Sugar Satellites and Banana Republics

The humiliations which so many countries were to experience in these and future years were part of the legacy of colonial rule in the area. One by one the islands of the Caribbean — Barbados, the Leeward Islands, Trinidad and Tobago, Guadeloupe, Puerto Rico, Haiti, the Dominican Republic, Cuba, Jamaica and, on the mainland, British

Guiana (now Guyana) — had been incorporated into the world market by their colonial masters as exporters of one single crop: sugar. The wealth from this product, originally based on slave labour, promoted industrial development in England, France, Holland and the United States but devastated the economies of the Caribbean. At least until the Second World War and in many cases beyond, these countries came to depend almost entirely on the fluctuating fortunes of sugar.

Even those countries which gained their political independence in the nineteenth century — Haiti from France in 1804 and the Dominican Republic from Spain in 1844 — were in effect countries 'born in ruins', with little control over their own economies and the majority of the population condemned to absolute poverty. A corrupt local ruling class emerged in these countries which enriched itself through its ability to raise loans from the United States which were frequently used to finance their internal power struggles. The United States took advantage of the endemic political instability and economic vulnerability of these nominally independent republics to promote its own political and economic interests. United States companies soon came to control sugar production in Cuba, Puerto Rico and the Dominican Republic.

Coffee and bananas were to Central America what sugar was to the Caribbean. As European and North American demand for coffee grew towards the end of the nineteenth century changes took place within the region which would lock it into a system of dependency on the export of one or two crops. The needs of the indigenous population suffered total neglect as the local landowning elites — often referred to as oligarchies, for indeed they were — were encouraged to produce solely for the consumption of Europe and North American markets.

The so-called Liberal reforms of this period paved the way for the expansion of coffee production by permitting the further concentration of land ownership, mostly at the expense of communally-owned Indian lands, and by creating a labour force. As Indians lost their land they were forced to work on the coffee plantations in conditions of semi-slavery. In El Salvador, Honduras and Nicaragua the land itself remained mostly in the hands of the local elite though the processing and marketing of production was in foreign hands. In Guatemala German immigrants as well as the local oligarchy came to own land, and by 1914 nearly 50% of Guatemala's coffee production was grown on German owned lands. In Costa Rica the large rural estates or *latifundios* characteristic of the other countries in the region did not emerge, mostly due to Spanish lack of interest in the country during the colonial period as it lacked both Indians and mineral resources. However

13

Portrait of a Banana Republic

In Honduras tens of thousands of acres of some of the richest virgin soil in the land were going begging, and its particular attraction to foreign investors lay both in its proximity to US ports, and its extremely low labour costs, which it was foreseen could be kept under control with the co-operation of bribable local bosses. Finally Honduras, like all its neighbours, was poor, weak, and militarily negligible, with a feeble government that could be easily suborned or browbeaten into giving the banana companies all the concessions they needed. The US war correspondent Richard Harding Davis took a ride on one of the first banana trains and after returning full of euphoric visions from the experience, he probably spoke for the nation. 'There is no more interesting question than what is to be done with the world's land which is lying unimproved . . . whether it shall go to the great power that is willing to turn it to account, or remain with its original owner who fails to understand its value.'

Theodore Roosevelt clearly thought it should go to the great power, etc. He has just scored his greatest personal triumph in creating the puppet state of Panama, and detaching it from its parent Colombia, and his appetite was whetted, for more easy conquests. He saw Honduras as a place which could be conveniently exploited without actual American intervention, although he issued a stern warning as to what it might expect if, in its dealings with the US it failed in any way to respect 'the primary norms of civilized society'.

The national mood of optimistic expansion contributed to a general desire to assist in the improvements of which Davis had spoken, and a horde of adventurers, Mississippi gamblers and soldiers of fortune, descended on Central America, the more intelligent of them to find enlistment in the services of the fruit enterprises. A corps of Diamond Lils received instruction in the basic Spanish essential to their calling and were let loose on the Honduran politicians and generals, and seduced by dollars, whisky and soft smiles. Presidents threw away national territory as a big spender at the tables might hand out ten dollar bills. One president, taken by his clients on a spree to New Orleans was given a ride on a cigar-smoking circus elephant, then taken to the town's leading bordello where he bought a night of love with a quarter of a million banana plants. These the lady of his choice promptly traded off to her next customer for a case of champagne. President Gutierrez was induced to lease out the best land in Honduras for a rent of one dollar per acre per month. In this period of open-handed gifts of territory United Fruit was able to acquire 175,000 prime acres without the payment of a single dollar. The Hondurans were dazzled by the technology of their day. It became a normal practice for a government to hand over between 250 and 500 hectares for every kilometre of railway line constructed by a fruit company. In consequence the companies built 726 miles of rail — all designed to carry the companies' bananas to the companies' ports — out of the 788 miles of railroad possessed by the Honduran nation. Tegucigalpa remains the only capital in Latin America not served by a railway.

Sometimes a president drew back shamed by the outcry from below that he was giving his country away, in which case he was promptly removed. Such a man in 1910 was President Davila, deposed by the efforts of a US citizen Sam Zemurray. This man recruited a boatload of mercenaries — under General Lee Christmas — renowned for his habit of biting pieces from the rim of his drinking glass in emphasis of a point of view. General Christmas and his band captured the port of Trujillo, Honduran government troops in the area having received orders from American warships to offer no resistance. The uncooperative Davila was replaced by a grateful and subservient Manuel Bonilla who had written to Zemurray, 'I will make you rich, give you place and power once we have taken the Capital.' He did. Zemurray was allowed to gorge himself with the pickings, and Lee Christmas with his pearl-handled pistols and 'the many watches with which he adorned his person', was appointed commander in Chief of the Honduran Army. Cuyamal Fruit, later to be merged with United Fruit took over all the land they could handle, with no payment of any kind to be made for twenty-five years. When Zemurray and Cuyamal came to power half the banana production of Honduras was still in the hands of small local farmers, but under the new dispensation nothing was easier than to dispossess them. The operation was mounted by Christmas' lieutenant, Machine-Gun Maloney — who herded the uprooted farmers into the company plantations at the point of the gun. *Latifundia* were created of land forcibly cleared and left ready to be turned over to bananas as and when they thought fit. Thus by 1946 the Tela Railroad Company, known outside Honduras as United Brands held 410,000 acres, of which only 82,000 acres were kept in production

Norman Lewis, and The Observer 1981.

the opportunities offered by the coffee export trade enabled the wealthiest agricultural producers to enrich themselves and this elite consolidated both its political and economic power in this period.

Banana production unlike coffee was gradually concentrated in the hands of United States capital, in particular one company: United Fruit. United Fruit's penetration of Central America began in the late nineteenth century with its construction of railroads and port facilities in the region. The company came to own, either directly or indirectly, nearly 900 miles of railroad in Guatemala and El Salvador, the major railroad network in Costa Rica and Honduras, and Guatemala's only Atlantic port. At the beginning of the twentieth century the company signed contracts with local banana producers to transport their produce to guaranteed markets in the United States, but gradually, through grants and purchases of land, it began to control production directly. United Fruit eventually owned half a million acres of the most fertile land in Guatemala and 400,000 acres in Honduras. The company became particularly important in those countries and Costa Rica but it also established a huge network of plantations throughout Central America as well as in Cuba, Jamaica and the Dominican Republic.

The company plantations were export enclaves within backward economies and they made little or no contribution to the host country's development. Their links, particularly in the case of Honduras, were almost entirely with the developed countries to which they exported. The railroads which United Fruit built in the region linked the plantation zones to the ports leaving the rest of the country without any system of communication. The wages paid to the labour force were spent in company-owned shops and the companies enjoyed lucrative benefits in the form of tax exemptions and profit remittance. In Guatemala for example, United Fruit's contract with the government gave it unlimited use of the country's best land for 25 to 99 years, exemptions from stamp, port and other taxes and import duties and unlimited profit remittance.

But the impact of the banana companies goes beyond the purely economic. The countries of Central America became known as 'banana republics' because of the companies' profound influence on political and social developments within the region. They participated in local intra-elite power struggles contributing to the chronic instability in the region and let their own rivalries spill over into local politics. The most notorious example of this was in Honduras where the competition between United Fruit and the Cuyamel Fruit Company provoked a civil war in 1923. In Guatemala and Costa Rica the banana companies played a key role in the election of every President and throughout the region they allied with the local oligarchy and the military against any threat from the workers and peasants.

The early twentieth century thus saw on the one hand the emergence of the United States as an imperial power in Central America and the Caribbean, prepared to back up its authority and protect its interests with brute force. On the other, it saw the beginnings of the penetration of United States capital into economies which were already weak, export-oriented and dependent. The effect on political and social

16

developments in the region was as profound as the economic impact.

Dollar Diplomacy

William Howard Taft who followed Roosevelt as US President is said by one historian to have replaced bullets with dollars in his policy towards the region, although use of military force was never, in fact, totally abandoned. The basic objectives remained the same, however, as Taft himself made clear in 1912: 'The day is not far distant when three Stars and Stripes at three equidistant points will mark our territory: one at the North Pole, another at the Panama Canal, and the third at the South Pole. The whole hemisphere will be ours in fact as, by virtue of our superiority of race, it already is ours morally'.

Taft's policy of safeguarding United States financial interests and promoting United States investments, partly to counteract European penetration of the region, was reinforced with even greater vigour by Woodrow Wilson. The United States was now seriously challenging British capital within the hemisphere. In 1914 the United States held 17% of all investments in Latin America; by 1929 the figure was 40%. Between 1914 and 1929 United States investment in Central America and the Caribbean tripled, though the majority was still concentrated in Mexico and Cuba. On the Central American mainland United States investment was greatest in Guatemala and least in Nicaragua (see Table, page 18).

The growing United States economic stake in the region received United States government protection. In the 1920s the Evart Doctrine developed under President Coolidge justified intervention in the internal affairs of Latin American countries to protect the foreign holdings of United States nationals.

The marines were sent into Cuba in 1917 and they stayed until 1923 putting down strikes and protecting United States property. A United States governor virtually managed the finances of the Cuban government and representatives of American sugar interests became leading political figures. The United States was thus able to ensure that the Cuban government pursued policies such as free trade, which suited its own needs for markets for its manufactured goods and cheap sugar imports, at the expense of Cuban national development.

Using the pretext of a civil war the United States occupied the Dominican Republic in 1916 and stayed until 1924. It claimed it was responsible for maintaining order in the country and it established martial law and a United States military government. Shortly afterwards two American companies set up business in the country: the Central Romana Sugar Refinery and the Grenada Fruit Company; and in 1917 the International Banking Company of New York arrived.

US Direct Investment in Central America 1897-1929
(in millions of US dollars at year end)

Country	1897		1908		1914		1919		1924		1929	
	Amount	%	Amount	%	Amount	%	Amount	%	Amount	%	Amount	%
Guatemala	6.0	52.2	10.0	31.4	35.8	46.6	40.0	41.5	47.0	39.4	58.8	29.2
El Salvador	—	—	1.8	5.7	6.6	8.6	12.8	13.3	12.2	10.3	24.8	12.3
Honduras	2.0	17.4	2.0	6.3	9.5	12.4	10.4	19.1	40.2	33.7	80.3	39.8
Nicaragua	—	—	1.0	3.1	3.4	4.4	7.3	7.6	6.8	5.7	17.3	8.6
Costa Rica	3.5	30.4	17.0	53.5	21.6	28.0	17.8	14.5	13.0	10.9	20.5	10.1
Total	11.5	100.0	31.8	100.0	76.9	100.0	96.3	100.0	119.2	100.0	201.7	100.0

Source: *Donald Castillo Rivas, Acumulacion de Capital y Empresas Transnacionales en Centroamerica, Siglo XXI, Mexico 1980.*

Haiti had assumed considerable strategic importance to the United States after the building of the Panama Canal; the sixty-mile stretch of water between Haiti and Cuba, known as the Windward Passage, was part of the only direct water link between the eastern coast of the United States and the Panama Canal. Political instability, economic bankruptcy and increasing French and German involvement in the country convinced the United States of the need to take direct action to defend its interests. In December 1914 a contingent of marines arrived to occupy the country, they took over the customs houses and established martial law. They were mostly from the deep south and they exacerbated racial and social divisions between the negroes and mulattos on the island and reinforced the rigid social structure. When they finally withdrew in 1934 their only contribuation to the country was a few roads and sewers and a pro-United States local militia; the American presence in these years has been described as 'socially and politically sterile'.

Laying Down the Law

'Our ministers accredited to the five little republics, stretching from the Mexican border to Panama . . . have been advisers whose advice has been accepted virtually as law in the capitals where they respectively reside . . . We do control the destinies of Central America and we do so for the simple reason that the national interest absolutely dictates such a course . . . Until now Central America has always understood that governments which we recognize and support stay in power, while those we do not recognize and support fail.'

Excerpt from a 1927 State Department memorandum by Under-Secretary of State Robert Olds.

United States marines occupied Nicaragua from 1912 until 1925 and returned again in 1926 after a civil war had broken out, provoked by the results of a United States supervised election. This second intervention was 'to protect American lives and property' and maintain United States supremacy in the region which the Secretary of State at the time claimed was threatened by 'Mexican fostered Bolshevik hegemony between the United States and the Panama Canal'. At the time the Mexican government was supporting the Liberals in Nicaragua while the United States backed the Conservatives. This time, however, the United States did face a serious challenge. Augusto Cesar Sandino refused to accept a United States imposed political solution to Nicaragua's civil war. He was a nationalist, opposed to foreign intervention and to the concentration of land in the hands of a tiny oligarchy, and he drew the Americans into the first anti-guerrilla war they had to face in Latin America. 4,000 United States marines were sent to the country and the techniques used against Sandino's forces included aerial bombing.

However, the involvement of United States troops in the struggle brought strong criticism at home and no outright victory in Nicaragua. In 1931 the United States began a gradual withdrawal but not before it had solved the problem of maintaining order in the country. The Americans created a local Nicaraguan military force — the National Guard — trained, equipped and advised by the United States, and when they finally withdrew in 1933 they crowned their legacy to the country by selecting the National Guard's commander: Anastasio Somoza. Somoza, who subsequently became President, as did his two sons after him, gave the first indication of the perfidy which characterized his dynasty's forty-three year rule in Nicaragua. Sandino had been persuaded to accept a gradual disarmament and in 1934, in good faith, he came to Managua to negotiate with the government where he was murdered on Somoza's orders.

General Smedley D. Butler, who headed many of the American interventions in the region in the early part of the twentieth century, gives a frank account of his achievements in his writings in 1935:

I spent thirty-three years and four months in active service as a member of our country's most agile military force — the Marine corps. I served in all commissioned ranks from a second lieutenant to major-general. And during that period I spent most of my time being a high-class muscle man for Big Business, for Wall Street and, for the bankers. In short, I was a racketeer for capitalism . . . Thus I helped make Mexico and especially Tampico safe for American oil interests in 1914. I helped make Haiti and Cuba a decent place for the National City Bank to collect revenues in . . . I helped purify Nicaragua for the international banking house of Brown Brothers in 1909-1912. I brought light to the Dominican Republic for American sugar interests in 1916. I helped make Honduras 'right' for American fruit companies in 1903.

The Dictators

As the 1920s progressed there was a growing feeling in United States government circles that the frequent use of the services of General Smedley D. Butler and Co. were becoming too costly. The Nicaraguan experience reinforced this doubt; over one hundred marines were killed in that escapade. The United States sought means of avoiding direct intervention while safeguarding their interests.

Banana Napoleons

'(Somoza) ruled Nicaragua for a quarter of a century and then be-
queathed the job to his sons. Before wrapping the presidential sash
across his breast, Somoza had conferred upon himself the Cross of
Valor, the Medal of Distinction, and the Presidential Medal of
Merit. Once in power he organized various massacres and grand
celebrations for which he dressed up his soldiers in sandals and
helmets like Romans. He became the country's biggest coffee producer, with forty-six plantations, and raised cattle on fifty-one additional haciendas. But he was never too busy to spread terror. During
his long reign he lacked for nothing and even recalled with some
wistfulness his youthful years when he had to forge gold coins to pay
for his amusements.

Hernández, a vegetarian crank and theosophist, maintained that
"killing an ant is a greater crime than killing a man, because a man is
reincarnated after death while an ant dies once and for all", He said
he was protected by "invisible legions" who reported all plots and
were in direct telepathic communication with the president of the
United States. A pendulum clock showed him if food on a dish placed beneath it was poisoned, or showed places on a map where pirate
treasure or political enemies were hidden. He used to send con-
dolence notes to the parents of his victims, and deer pastured in the
patio of his palace. He ruled until 1944.

Like all the Caribbean tyrants, Ubico thought he was Napoleon.
He surrounded himself with busts and portraits of the Emperor who,
he said, had the same profile. He believed in military discipline: he
militarized post office employees, schoolchildren, and the symphony
orchestra. Dressed in uniforms, the orchestra members played
Ubico's selections, with techniques and instruments decided by him,
for $9 a month. He felt that hospitals were for sissies, and patients
who were poor as well as sick were put on the floors of corridors and
passageways.'

From Open Veins of Latin America, *Eduardo Galeano, 1973.*

The 'Somoza' solution seemed ideal and had already been successfully tried out in the Dominican Republic. Before their final
withdrawal from that country, the United States had created a National Guard and placed at its head a man called Rafael Trujillo. In
1930, backed by American companies, Trujillo ousted the incumbent
President and began a tyrannical rule which was to last 31 years. A
United States trained army and a friendly dictator became the
established and favoured means of maintaining order in the region
and protecting American interests. It was only a minor embarrassment

21

that these dictators shared basic characteristics of extreme cruelty, corruption and megalomania and that their rule reinforced the already grinding poverty in which the majority of the people lived.

Even when the United States was not directly responsible for the installation of dictatorial regimes the desire to protect American interests led to tacit support when such regimes appeared all over Central America in the early 1930s. These were the years of the Great Depression. The world economic crisis affected the vulnerable Central American economies with particular severity due to their dependence on external markets and United States investment, both of which contracted with the crisis.

Coffee and banana prices plummeted as demand slumped. Peasants, unable to pay their debts, were evicted from their land, while workers were thrown out of their jobs or had their wages slashed. The result was a wave of social unrest in city and countryside throughout the region. Strikes broke out on the American-owned plantations and, as in Costa Rica in 1934, were ruthlessly suppressed by the local armed forces. The oligarchies, alarmed by the course of events, looked to the military as the only way to suppress the social conflicts and maintain their domination. In this way the workers and peasants were forced to bear the brunt of the Depression.

A series of strongmen emerged to dominate the political scene throughout the Depression: Jorge Ubico in Guatemala (1931-44), Tiburcio Carias Andino in Honduras (1931-48) and Maximiliano Hernandez Martinez in El Salvador (1931-44). Although the latter did not enjoy immediate support from the United States — the banana companies had not established themselves in El Salvador and the country had not yet come as directly into the American orbit as the other countries — the United States sent a cruiser and two destroyers to stand by during the peasant rebellion of 1932 (two Canadian destroyers were also sent at the behest of the British). Though the revolt was eventually crushed without their help and with the massacre of some 30,000 peasants, the Americans had shown themselves to be 'good neighbours'.

Good Neighbour Policy

President Franklin D. Roosevelt decared in his inaugural address in March 1933 that United States foreign policy towards Latin America would henceforth follow the policies of the 'good neighbour' and that it was opposed to armed intervention.

In practice this policy meant the temporary abandonment of direct intervention at a time when the Depression preoccupied the government at home. United States investment in the region also declined in these years as there was little surplus capital. Investment did not begin to rise again until the 1940s by which time the relative importance of Central America to American business had declined as it turned increasingly to South American oil and to manufacturing industry.

The new policy did not mean that the United States entirely gave up interference in the affairs of its backyard, nor did it abandon the threat of force. In September 1933 United States warships were stationed in every harbour of Cuba as a hint that events there did not please Uncle Sam.

Between 1925 and 1933 United States interests in Cuba had been looked after by Gerardo Machado, nicknamed 'the Butcher'. By the 1930s increasing social unrest and fear of a left-wing revolution convinced the United States that he was more of a liability than an asset. A special ambassador, Sumner Welles, was sent to Cuba charged with preventing a left-wing government from replacing Machado. The 30 warships stationed round the island helped reinforce the message. The United States eventually put their trust in Fulgencio Batista, while Batista, according to Laurence Duggan of the State Department, '. . . saw it was hopeless for Cuba, whose life depended on a restored sugar market with the United States, to risk our disapproval'. Batista formed an alliance with the conservative pro-American elite and was rewarded with twenty-five years of power, notorious for the corruption and repression which characterized it.

The United States made a new sugar agreement with Cuba which, while it secured a stable market for Cuban sugar, reinforced Cuban dependence on the United States as Cuba had to agree to lift import duties on a large number of American goods inhibiting the development of local industry. The United States did abrogate the Platt Amendment but kept the right to its base at Guantanamo.

The War Years

The United States military presence in the Caribbean increased considerably during the Second World War when it expanded its installations in Panama, Puerto Rico and the Virgin Islands. In Puerto Rico, for instance, US$200 million were spent on military building projects. Roosevelt Roads, a huge naval complex, and Ramey air force base were built in these years.

But the United States now began to assert a claim to the Caribbean basin as a whole, much of which was still under British, Dutch and French colonial rule. The immediate aim was to defend the area from the German menace. In return for fifty obsolete destroyers Britain allowed the United States to set up bases in Trinidad, Barbados, St Lucia, and British Guiana. As Gordon Lewis, author of *The Growth of the Modern West Indies*, has written: 'The kaleidescope fortunes of the islands have been made and unmade by the treaty arrangements of European congresses or, more latterly as with the 1940 Anglo-American bases-destroyers deal, of British Prime Ministers and American Presidents'. The American presence was to have a profound impact on the countries concerned, particularly Trinidad. American culture penetrated the country through the occupying troops, and US dollars amassed by local operators servicing the Americans' needs helped create the financial basis for local politics.

Roosevelt also made clear to the British in these years that the Americans would no longer accept its colonial presence in the region. The Commonwealth Caribbean was not only strategically part of the American 'sphere of influence', it was also of growing economic importance. Large United States corporations had begun to penetrate the West Indies: United Fruit, W.R. Grace, Standard Oil and Texaco, the Chase Manhattan and First National City Banks, and, of particular importance, the bauxite companies. Alcoa and its sister company Alcan had secured an almost complete monopoly over bauxite deposits in the British and Dutch Guianas between 1912 and 1925, mostly through double dealing and trickery. The companies did not process the low-value ore in the Guianas, however, but shipped it back to North America to be smelted into aluminium, so that the Guianas never reaped the benefit of locally-produced, high-value aluminium. Aluminium is used in the aircraft and arms industry and Guianese bauxite made a substantial contribution to the Anglo-American victory in the Second World War. There was no reward for the impoverished Guianese people, however. When Arthur Vining Davis of Alcan Aluminium died in 1962 he left a fortune of US$400 million most of which he gave to a foundation on condition that its funds could not be used to benefit the citizens of the Caribbean bauxite-producing countries or any country other than the United States and its possessions.

During the war an Anglo-American Caribbean Commission was set up with headquarters in Trinidad. Its purpose was to maintain 'stability' in the region during the war but also to consolidate the growing United States influence in the area. The results of British and American collaboration in these years was the emergence of a joint strategy for the post-colonial Commonwealth Caribbean which rested on the establishment of a West Indian Federation. The Federation, which was set up in 1958, was virtually imposed by the British and took almost no account of the real needs and interests of the people of the region; it collapsed in 1961. Instead of the Federation becoming

24

independent as a unit as planned, the individual countries became independent on their own. The United States was forced to think again.

This increasing American involvement in the Commonwealth Caribbean reflected the gradual emergence throughout the war years of United States economic and political supremacy over Europe as a whole. In Central America the United States pressured governments to confiscate German investments and property and as European markets were closed the countries of the region came to depend on the single market of the United States. Between 1930 and 1934 Central America sold 20% of its total coffee harvest to the United States and 75% to Europe; between 1940 and 1944 the United States share increased to 87%. As coffee represented 70-80% of the region's total exports its dependence on the United States was consolidated still further.

The Post-War World

Throughout the war the United States was planning and preparing for its future role in the post-war world. The United States was in a unique position to impose its world view; it emerged from the war unrivalled economically and militarily. The new order it would help shape would centre around its need for large export markets and unrestricted access to key raw materials. United States planners identified three separate areas — the Western Hemisphere, the Far East and the British Empire — which had to be economically integrated and militarily defended in order to safeguard America's interests.

The United States therefore planned for a cooperative and stable world-wide economic system based on the elimination of trade restrictions, the creation of international financial bodies to stabilize currencies, the establishment of international banking institutions to aid investment, and the development of backward areas. In the words of Cordell Hull, Roosevelt's Secretary of State:

Through international investment, capital must be made available for the sound development of latent natural resources and productive capacity in relatively undeveloped areas . . . Leadership towards a new system of international relationships in trade and other economic affairs will devolve largely on the United States because of our great economic strength. We should assume this leadership and the responsibility which goes with it, primarily for reasons of pure national self-interest.

The institutional bases of the new order were elaborated by the Bretton Woods conference in 1944 which was followed by the establishment of the World Bank and the International Monetary

Fund. The overseas expansion of United States capital which took place subsequently was unprecedented and centred round the emergence on a grand scale of giant companies with interests in all parts of the globe. These multinational corporations came to dominate the United States economy and that of many regions of the world.

The United States was thus instrumental in establishing an integrated international economic system which for many years it was able to dominate and which it was committed to defending. The emergence of the socialist bloc and the Cold War provided the rationale for United States economic aggression. United States capital was in the vanguard of a crusade: to stem the tide of international communist subversion; 'manifest destiny' re-emerged in a new form and to meet new needs. American capital would bring development to backward regions and Latin American elites came to see it as the key to progress. The years following the Second World War saw a huge inflow of United States capital into Latin America. Direct investment grew from US$3 billion in 1946 to US$8 billion in 1961. In Central America direct investment increased from US$173 million in 1943 to US$389 million in 1959 (see Table). The economic importance of Central America to the United States was slight, but the region's dependence on virtually one source of foreign investment consolidated the United States' hold over its economic development.

US Direct Investment in Central America 1936-1959
(in millions of US dollars)

Country	1936	1940	1943	1950	1959
Costa Rica	13.0	24.0	30.0	60.0	73.2
El Salvador	17.0	11.0	15.0	17.0	43.9
Guatemala	50.0	68.0	87.0	106.0	137.6
Honduras	36.0	38.0	37.0	62.0	115.5
Nicaragua	5.0	8.0	4.0	9.0	18.9
Total	121.0	149.0	173.0	254.0	389.1

Source: *Donald Castillo Rivas,* Acumulacion de Capital y Empresas Transnacionales en Centroamerica, *Siglo XXI, Mexico 1980.*

The United States encouraged the belief that there was an identity of interests between the two regions, an inter-American system based on mutually compatible objectives. In 1948 the ninth Pan-American conference set up the Organization of American States (OAS); one of its aims was 'to provide facilities for United States investors wishing to exploit the resources of Latin America'. It was also to be used by the United States as a means of isolating regimes which tried to withdraw from the inter-American fraternity or to challenge its ideological basis. In 1954 a resolution was passed by the OAS 'updating' the Monroe Doctrine, it became known as the Caracas Declaration:

The domination or control of the political institutions of any American state by the international communist movement, extending to this Hemisphere the political system of an extracontinental power, would constitute a threat to the sovereignty and political independence of the American states, endangering the peace of America and would call for a meeting of consultation to consider the adoption of appropriate action in accordance with existing treaties.

The Cold War had reached Latin America.

The Cold War

In 1947 President Truman pledged the United States to 'support free peoples who are resisting attempted subjugation by armed minorities or by outside pressure'. The statement was made in the context of the United States' decision to prevent what it described as Soviet interference in Greece and Turkey. But it marked an important stage in United States foreign policy as the all-embracing nature of the statement suggests: America had decided to stop Soviet aggression wherever it occurred and in whatever form.

In the late 1940s institutions were set up suited to the politics of the Cold War era. In 1947 the National Security Act created the National Security Council, the Central Intelligence Agency and the Department of Defense, which brought together the previous Departments of War and the Navy. It was not long before Cold War politics, elaborated and implemented through these institutions and others, came to effect developments in Central America and the Caribbean.

Within Central America the years of dictatorship in the 1930s and 1940s had succeeded in suppressing popular discontent but not eliminating it. In the post-war years, sectors of the middle class — students, teachers, professionals, small traders, and others — began to channel this discontent into liberal demands for wider political participation, human rights and socio-economic reforms. The stagnation of the rural economy since 1930 encouraged them to question the model of development based on the export of coffee and bananas and the concentration of wealth and land in the hands of the oligarchy. Their demands were liberal rather than socialist, calling for the modernization of the economy and the elimination of traditional semi-feudal structures.

Nowhere did they succeed in substantially altering the structure of rural power which was the prerequisite for an alternative, nationalist model of development oriented towards the internal market. Only in Costa Rica, and following a civil war in 1948, did Jose Figueres successfully lead a liberal reform movement which brought political stability to the country in a form unique to the region. In El Salvador, on the other hand, the 1944 revolt in which a doctor, Arturo Romero, played a leading role, was short-lived. In most countries the oligarchy was able to survive the political crisis and reassert its dominance through the military. In Guatemala the outcome could have been somewhat different but here the United States resolved to apply Truman's Cold War doctrine.

Guatemala 1954

In 1944 President Ubico was overthrown and the liberal reformers under Juan Jose Arevalo succeeded in winning the election which followed. Arevalo was a very cautious reformer. While the new constitution of 1945 prohibited *latifundios* and stated that private property had to have a social function, Arevalo was unwilling to introduce a land reform of any significance. But for the first time legislation was passed to improve the conditions of the labour force, and workers on the foreign owned plantations and railways were allowed to organize to defend their rights.

Arevalo's successor, Jacobo Arbenz, went further and announced his intention of introducing a land reform. His aim was to transform Guatemala's semi-feudal form of production into a modern capitalist one and to create an internal market so that industry could develop.

In 1952 the agrarian reform law was introduced. It was a mild law aimed at large properties with unused lands and in no way challenged private property as such. The greatest danger to the landed oligarchy was that for the first time peasants would be allowed to organize in order to participate in the agrarian reform.

Expropriation began in 1953; 100,000 peasants received land and 1,002 plantations were affected, about 16% of the country's total idle cultivable lands in private hands. The landowners reacted violently against this relatively moderate redistribution and when the lands of the country's biggest landowner, United Fruit, were affected they found a useful ally in the American government.

United Fruit owned 555,000 acres, of which it used only 15% in a country where the majority of the people were landless or lived on tiny subsistence plots. The government expropriated 387,000 acres and offered over one million dollars in compensation based on the company's own tax declarations. The company claimed compensation of US$16 million. The new US ambassador to Guatemala reported to his government that 'Arbenz thought like a communist and talked like a communist and if not actually one would do until one came along'.

The State Department did not need much convincing that United States interests were threatened, the close ties between the government and United Fruit ensured that. John Foster Dulles, the Secretary of State, had represented United Fruit when a company lawyer in negotiating a contract with the Guatemalan government, and the brother of John M. Cabot, the Assistant Secretary of State for Inter-American Affairs, was a director and former president of United Fruit, to mention just two of the links.

In 1954 Colonel Castillo Armas crossed the border from Honduras into Guatemala and overthrew the Arbenz government. The coup was planned, organized and financed by the CIA. President Eisenhower subsequently clarified why: 'In 1950 military officer Jacobo Arbenz Guzman came to power and by his actions soon created the strong suspicion that he was merely a puppet manipulated by the communists. For example on February 24, 1953, the Arbenz government announced its intention, under an agrarian reform law, to seize unused United Fruit Company land'.

Castillo Armas immediately began to reverse all the progressive measures introduced by Arbenz. By January 1956 99.6% of all land expropriated under the agrarian reform law had been returned to its owners. The trade union movement and peasant organizations which had emerged under Arbenz and which were seen as a particular threat by the oligarchy were declared illegal and their members imprisoned, tortured and murdered. Peasants, who for the first time had been given some opportunity to defend their interests against the oligarchy, saw their lives return to the servitude of the pre-1944 years and rural organization was never to be permitted to recover.

Under United States guidance a new programme of modernization was introduced. Guatemala was intended to be a showcase for United States policy in the region, a country 'liberated' from communism. For the first time foreign aid was used as a weapon of United States foreign policy and it was poured into the country to rescue it from bankruptcy. The United States aid mission was increased from 28 people in 1954 to 165 in 1959. President Eisenhower virtually ordered the World Bank to provide a loan to build an Atlantic highway. Klein and Saks, a consultancy agency providing 'private enterprise prescriptions for sick national economies', became advisors to the Guatemalan government operating out of the presidential palace itself.

The US aid mission worked closely with a powerful new organization, CACIF (Coordinating Committee of Agricultural, Commercial,

Industrial and Financial Associations), which was founded in 1957 to defend free enterprise in Guatemala and which represents all sectors of the oligarchy.

Foreign investment became a cornerstone of the new strategy. All nationalist legislation restricting such investment, for instance taxes on profits remitted abroad, was repealed and new measures such as low tax rates and restrictive labour legislation introduced. In March 1955 Guatemala became the third Latin American country to sign an investment guarantee agreement with the United States, this insured American enterprises against losses from expropriations. In 1959 United States investment in Guatemala was US$138 million. In the next ten years it rose by a further US$149 million.

The source and direction of this investment also changed. United Fruit, which had helped organize the invasion of Guatemala, no longer saw the country as a main area for expansion. New economic interests in the United States began to look to Guatemala. These were mostly from the 'sunbelt' states of Florida, Texas and southern California. They were closely linked to Vice-President Nixon who visited Guatemala in 1955 and they played an important role in organizing a pro-Castillo Armas lobby in the United States which helped mobilize the substantial aid package for the country. These groups helped promote the industrialization strategy which developed in the 1960s. This would no longer be based on expanding the internal market through land reform as Arbenz had intended, but in creating a market of the middle and upper class consumers of Central America through an economic integration scheme for the region.

Hopes of an agrarian reform were now completely abandoned. Colonization schemes in the remote north eastern jungle region replaced land reform as the favoured solution to the pressures on the land. Some changes did take place in the rural areas but these did not benefit the peasants. The attempts of the Arevalo and Arbenz governments to modernize the economy had led to the emergence of a new business class with interests in banking and industry as well as the land. These groups helped stimulate the diversification of agricultural production to include cotton, sugar and cattle exports as well as coffee. They did not challenge the traditional coffee oligarchy, however, but were incorporated into it and they were just as tied to export markets and just as ruthless in their determination to prevent any form of radical social change. An alliance with foreign capital was more profitable to these groups than a model of development based on national interests which would inevitably mean a confrontation with the oligarchy and greater political participation by peasants and workers.

United States intervention in Guatemala led to the overthrow of the most progressive government in the country's history, and one which, despite its limitations, could have become a rallying point for change in the region. It also enabled the United States to shape the country's economic future to the changing requirements of American capital. It was a model of growth from which the mass of the Guatemalan people were excluded and it could only be imposed by force. In reinforcing the power of Guatemala's traditional ruling class the United States became directly involved in the maintenance of one of the most reactionary and repressive oligarchies in the world.

Caribbean Political Earthquake

In 1959 Fidel Castro overthrew the Batista regime in Cuba. The reasons for his success are not difficult to find. Cuban society and the Cuban economy were dominated by American big business and its Cuban henchmen. It was a centre of corruption of all kinds and had become known as the 'whorehouse of the Caribbean'. Fidel Castro summed it all up in his speech in 1953 before the court which was trying him for subversion:

Eighty-five percent of the small farmers in Cuba pay rent and live under the constant threat of being evicted from the land they till. More than half our most productive land is in the hands of foreigners. In Oriente, the largest province, the lands of the United Fruit Company and the West Indies Company link the northern and southern coasts. There are two hundred thousand peasant families who do not have a single acre of land to till to provide food for their starving children . . . Ninety percent of the children of the countryside are consumed by parasites which filter through their bare feet from the ground they walk on. Society is moved to compassion when it hears of the kidnapping or murder of one child, but it is criminally indifferent to the mass murder of so many thousands of children who die every year from lack of facilities . . .

At first the United States was uncertain how to react. Batista's dictatorship was utterly discredited, the revolution enjoyed overwhelming popular support and Castro himself was an unknown quantity. In January 1959 Castro had assured property owners that he did not oppose capitalist enterprises as such so long as they did not conflict with Cuban law. Moderate professionals predominated in the government and elections were planned for two years later. The Land Reform Act of May 1959 abolished only the very largest estates. 'Our revolution is neither capitalist nor communist', Castro declared in May 1959.

But land owned by US companies was affected by the land reform and the United States insisted on prompt compensation in cash rather than the twenty year bonds proposed by Castro. This demand would have seriously undermined the reform programme Castro now embarked on. He was already in a considerable dilemma about how to pay for the reforms which included wage rises, public works to cut unemployment, rent reductions, and cheaper medical services and public utility rates. An increase in purchasing power would increase demand for food and consumer goods which would have to be imported. Cuba was still almost totally dependent on sugar for its foreign exchange earnings: it represented 80% of its exports, and two-thirds of Cuba's sugar exports went to the United States. Castro was anxious to diversify the economy but he faced a severe shortage of capital.

He therefore turned to foreign aid. But United States aid was only forthcoming with stringent political conditions. According to the *New York Times* the United States decided 'to let the Castro government go through the wringer' of economic pressures in the hope that it would be forced to shelve the revolution in return for economic assistance.

In September 1959 Castro announced that henceforth the state would play a key role in economic development. In November new laws were introduced against foreign companies, empowering the state to take over firms which found themselves in difficulties or tried to cut their losses by reducing production. The subsequent nationalizations and the land reform measures which were considerably extended towards the end of 1960 eroded the social base of the old order. Batista's army had been destroyed by Castro and his rebel forces who now controlled the real power in the country. Many businessmen, professionals and landowners began to leave the island; at least half a million people left Cuba during Castro's first three years in power.

Relations with the United States deteriorated still further in 1960. The CIA was working closely with Cuban exiles in Florida who carried out acts of sabotage and even bomb attacks on Cuba from the air. The United States was also supplying arms to counter-revolutionaries within the country. In March 1960 President Eisenhower accepted a CIA recommendation to begin to train and arm Cuban exiles for an invasion, an action which had been urged by President Nixon a year earlier. The 1954 Guatemalan operation was a useful model; Guatemala's President Ydigoras even allowed his country to be used as a training base.

In May 1960 Castro resumed diplomatic relations with the Soviet Union and Russia agreed to supply oil in return for sugar. In June US oil companies in Cuba refused to refine the Soviet oil and Castro seized their installations. The US responded by carrying out a threat to cut off Cuba's sugar quota. Cuba moved to greater reliance on the Soviet Union as the United States imposed a trade embargo on the country and urged other Latin American countries to cut diplomatic and trade relations with Cuba.

Clearly the United States was not exclusively responsible for the radicalization of the revolution; there were many internal factors involved. But it certainly helped force Cuba into a closer relationship with the Soviet Union, and the Bay of Pigs invasion consolidated that trend still further.

The invasion was a disaster for the new US President, John Kennedy, and a triumph for Castro. The invasion force of 1,400 ex-Batista supporters and mercenaries was to be coordinated with action by the right-wing underground within Cuba, while the United States would provide air cover. It failed completely: local militias easily defeated the invasion force and the local uprisings were just as quickly suppressed. Castro's prestige and support within Cuba was greatly strengthened by the abortive invasion. From now on the United States had to adjust to communism in its 'backyard', something which it has never really come to terms with. In fact it never abandoned its objective to destroy the Cuban revolution and throughout the 1960s the CIA was particularly active in its attempts to assassinate Castro and sabotage the Cuban economy (see box, page 34). The revolution also made the United States resolutely determined to prevent 'another Cuba'.

Dirty Tricks

In November 1975 a Senate Committee held hearings on the CIA's alleged involvement in assassination plots against foreign leaders. The hearings provide ample evidence of CIA plots to get rid of the Castro government. CIA Director Richard Helms testified that although he had never discussed assassination with his superiors, he believed:

> '. . . that in these actions we were taking against Cuba and against Fidel Castro's government in Cuba, that they were what we had been asked to do . . . In other words we had been asked to get rid of Castro and . . . there were no limitations put on the means, and we felt we were acting well within the guidelines that we understood to be in play at this particular time.'

CIA Director John McCone, in a memorandum dated April 14 1967, stated:

> 'Through the years the Cuban problem was discussed in terms such as "dispose of Castro", "remove Castro", "knock off Castro", etc. and this meant the overthrow of the Communist government in Cuba and the replacing of it with a democratic regime. Terms such as the above appear in many working papers, memoranda for the record, etc., and, as stated, all refer to a change in the Cuban government.'

The Senate report also contains a chronology of CIA dirty tricks in Cuba:

1959

December 11 — Dulles approves 'thorough consideration be given to the elimination of Fidel Castro'.

1960

January 13 — Special Group meeting considers Castro's overthrow.
Spring 1960 — Meetings on covert action against Cuba at levels of CIA, Special Group, and NSC.
Event involving CIA request that a Cuban arrange an 'accident' involving Raul Castro.
August 1960 — Bissell and Edwards have discussion concerning use of underworld figures to aid in assassination of Castro.
Late September — Bissell and Edwards brief Dulles and Cabell about operation against Castro.

October 18 — Memo from Hoover to intelligence agencies detailing Giancana's statements about an imminent Castro assassination but not mentioning CIA.

November 3 — Special Group discusses covert action against Castro regime. **Sometime after November 8** — Dulles and Bissell jointly brief President-elect Kennedy on details of planned invasion of Cuba.

1961

January — Rosselli passes pills to a Cuban in Miami.

April 15-17 — Bay of Pigs invasion fails.

April 19-20 — The Cuban involved in the underworld assassination plot and the Bay of Pigs invasion attends meeting at which the President, other Cubans, and high Administration officials not witting of the plot are present.

April 22-June 19 — Taylor/Kennedy Board of Inquiry into Bay of Pigs invasion.

May 22 — Hoover memo to Attorney General Kennedy noting CIA had used Giancana in 'clandestine efforts' against Castro.

October 5 — National Security Action Memorandum 100 directs assessment of potential courses of action if Castro were removed from the Cuban scene. CIA makes intelligence estimate.

November 9 — President tells Tad Szulc that he is under pressure from advisors to order Castro's assassination, but does not name advisors.

1962

January 18 — Lansdale assigns 32 planning tasks against Castro regime.

January 19 — MONGOOSE meeting at which Attorney General says solution to Cuban problem carrries top priority.

January 29 — Richard Helms succeeds Richard Bissell as Deputy Director, Plans, CIA.

Early April — Harvey establishes contact with Rosselli.

Late April — Harvey passes poison pills to Rosselli in Miami.

May 7 — Houston and Edwards brief Attorney General on pre-Bay of Pigs underworld assassination plot. Thereafter decision made not to prosecute.

August 8 — Special Group (Augmented) adopts a stepped-up plan designed to inspire internal revolt of Cuba.

August 10 — The subject of assassination is raised at a meeting of the Special Group (Augmented).

September 7 — Rosselli tells Harvey the pills are still in Cuba.

October 4 — Attorney General advises Special Group (Augmented) that President wants more priority given to operations against Castro regime.
October 22-28 — Cuban Missile Crisis.
November — Operation MONGOOSE ends.

1963

Early 1963 — CIA Technical Services Division explores exploding seashell and contaminated diving-suit schemes.
June 19 — Special Group authorizes sabotage program against Cuba.
August 16 — McCone is given memorandum detailing pre-Bay of Pigs assassination plot against Castro.
Fall 1963 — Atwood explores possible accommodation with Castro.
November 22 — AM/LASH given poison pen device for assassinating Castro.

1964

March-May — Caches of arms delivered to AM/LASH in Cuba.
April 7 — Special Group discontinues CIA-controlled sabotage raids against Cuba.

1965

Early 1965 — AM/LASH put in contact with leader of anti-Castro group and receives weapon with silencer from him.

1966

1966 — Helms reports to Rusk that CIA not involved with AM/LASH in Castro assassination plot.

'Alleged Assassination Plots Involving Foreign Leaders': Report of US Senate Select Committee, 20 November 1975, US Government Printing Office, Washington 1975.

The Flexible Response

In October 1962 the United States forced the USSR to withdraw the missiles it intended to place on Cuba, in return it pledged not to invade the country. The United States success in this confrontation encouraged it to be firm in its actions in the region; but it was firmness coupled with flexibility. Indeed this was the new doctrine for the 1960s: the flexible response.

One of Those Things That Governments Do

'Suppose that Fidel Castro had organized or participated in at least eight assassination attempts against the various presidents of the United States since 1959. It is safe to conclude that the *New York Times*, CBS News and the mass media in general would have portrayed him as an international gangster and assassin, who must be excluded from the community of civilized nations. But when it is revealed that the United States has made or participated in that many attempts on Castro's life, it's just "one of those things that governments do". The press will hardly suggest on the basis of such information that the world's "nations have to evaluated the US potentiality as a responsible world citizen", to paraphrase a recent *Christian Science Monitor* editorial that had the gall to assert that the United States, after the record of the past 30 years, is entitled to stand in judgment over Vietnam for its alleged violations of human rights!

Suppose further that Fidel Castro had arranged for his agents in the United States to disperse various disease carriers in agricultural regions in an attempt to poison and destroy livestock and crops. Can one imagine the hysteria of the *Wall Street Journal* and the *Times* on the depths to which barbarian evil can sink under communism? The United States actually did carry out such an act against Cuba, reported in the press in early 1977 as a minor news item on the back pages — 500,000 pigs had to be destroyed in Cuba as a result of a deliberately spread viral disease. And according to a recent statement of a Canadian adviser to the Cuban government, as early as 1962 he was paid $5,000 by a Defense Intelligence Agency representative to infect Cuban poultry with a viral disease. Editorial outrage over these claims has been modest, to say the least.'

Noam Chomsky & Edward S. Herman, 'The United States versus human rights in the Third World', Monthly Review, *New York, July-August 1977.*

The doctrine was based on ideas developed by Henry Kissinger who had headed a Council on Foreign Relations study group on nuclear weapons and foreign policy. It was a strategy for the nuclear age when the 'massive retaliation' approach of the 1950s could have disastrous consequences. It was also based on the realization, which the Cuban missile crisis reinforced, that most of the armed conflicts in the world were now taking place in the Third World, in areas where the United States and the former colonial powers no longer had direct control but still had vital interests. President Kennedy summed up the problem: 'The periphery of the Free World will slowly be nibbled away. The balance of power will gradually shift against us. The key areas vital to our security will gradually undergo Soviet infiltration and domination. Each such Soviet move will weaken the West, but none will seem sufficiently significant by itself to justify a nuclear war which might destroy us'.

So the United States prepared for a new type of war: the non-conventional 'limited war' based on anti-guerrilla tactics. In 1961 President Kennedy ordered a fivefold increase in the army special forces whose main role was counter-insurgency. At the same time the United States capacity for intervention — the 'rapid deployment' category — was increased. Giant C-5A transport aircraft, capable of transporting 700 troops, and huge military transport ships were procured, and instant air bases were designed which could turn a disused airstrip into an operational airfield for F-4 fighter bombers within seventy-two hours. In addition, a vast new programme of counter-insurgency research was launched.

Research was also carried out into the causes of revolution. Cuba was an unprecedented threat to the United States on the ideological front: it offered an alternative model of development. The American mission to spread its superior 'way of life' throughout the Western Hemisphere and beyond had hitherto rested on the claim that this would bring progress to 'backward' regions. Not only had these regions not seen progress, except for a small minority of their populations, but there was in Cuba a country which, however much it could be criticized politically, brought housing, education, medicine and nutrition to the majority of its population.

The lessons the Americans drew were to emerge in a two-pronged strategy. On the one hand there was counter-insurgency and the repression which invariably accompanied it and, on the other, attempts to pre-empt those who put forward socialist solutions by promoting moderate reforms, sufficient to broaden the social base of pro-American regimes but not to challenge them. It included projects for the modernization of the economies concerned: economic development through injections of foreign capital. In Latin America this strategy was as usual given a grand and mystifying title: the Alliance for Progress.

PART 2
The Eagle Rampant

Contents

1960	Central American Common Market is established
1961	USAID and AIFLD set up; Alliance for Progress signed
1962	Jamaica and Trinidad become independent
1964	CONDECA is established
	Burnham defeats Jagan in Guyanese elections following CIA-AIFLD-fomented destablization campaign
1965	US marines invade the Dominican Republic
1966	The first death squads appear in Guatemala with US complicity — they are responsible for 20,000 deaths from 1966-76
	Guyana and Barbados become independent
1972	UPEB is founded and challenges banana companies
1974-76	Jamaica takes on the bauxite companies

The Alliance for Progress

The formal charter of the Alliance for Progress was signed in Punta del Este, Uruguay on 17 August 1961. Its stated aims were impressive, with an emphasis on economic and social development, comprehensive agrarian reform 'leading to the effective transformation where required of unjust structures and systems of land tenure and use', and representative democracy.

It was reform 'from above' to prevent revolution 'from below' as President Kennedy spelt out on the first anniversary of the Alliance: 'Those who possess wealth and power in poor nations must accept their own responsibilities. They must lead the fight for those basic reforms which alone can preserve the fabric of their own societies. Those who make peaceful revolution impossible will make violent revolution inevitable'. While Teodoro Moscoso, the first coordinator of the programme, made it even clearer: 'In supporting the Alliance, members of the traditional ruling class will have nothing to fear'.

The basic premise of the Alliance was that ruling elites in Central and South America would voluntarily accept certain land and tax reforms in order to pre-empt demands for real socio-economic change. The assumption proved untenable. The oligarchies would not relinquish one iota of their economic power.

The response of the United States was to abandon the reforms or to accommodate them to the intransigence of the oligarchy. This is particularly evident in the fate of agrarian reform, considered a key element in the Alliance. Agrarian reform can mean many things. As originally stated in the Alliance charter it meant 'effective transformation'. Gradually a shift in emphasis became apparent from the speeches of the officials in charge of the Alliance, a move away from 'redistribution' and towards 'modernization'. Moscoso expressed the shift in this way:

Agrarian reform . . . (as a big chapter in the Charter of the Alliance) gave rise very quickly to the misconception that all that was wanted or needed was the splitting up of the large landed estates which were owned by a few wealthy men who also played a decisive role in controlling the political destiny of their countries. But it is not this simple . . . I prefer to speak rather in terms of modernizing agriculture. By that we do not necessarily mean taking land away, dividing it up and redistributing it, but orderly reorganization, including possible changes in land tenure, supervised credit and extension service and farm to market roads . . . this is the rational way in which the Alliance is tackling the problems of agriculture. It is the right way . . .

It was also the way least likely to upset the balance of power within Central America. The objective of the Alliance was now to increase productivity, with production geared to the world market. This would be achieved through subsidies and credits to improve the efficiency of large landowners and to encourage shifts to cash crops and modern farming methods. Colonization schemes on previously unused and frequently remote and infertile lands were introduced to deal with the problem of landless peasants.

The United States promoted these policies through its aid programme. Lincoln Gordon, at the time a consultant to the President's task force on Latin America, explained this in 1961: 'We obviously can't say we are going to dictate the land reform legislation of another country, but we are going to help when the right kind of legislation is forthcoming and refrain from providing help where it doesn't'.

Despite the emphasis on productivity, however, per capita agricultural production in Central America grew by only 2.2% from 1960 to 1965 and only 1.6% from 1965 to 1970. At the same time food production was increasingly geared to the export market, providing those who controlled the land and governments in the region with valuable foreign exchange while the countries concerned became less and less able to feed their own populations. In Guatemala, for instance, 87% of all government credits between 1964 and 1973 went to finance export production, while rice, corn and beans, which were mostly produced on small plots for local consumption, received only 3%. In El Salvador export-oriented agriculture received 80-90% of all government credits between 1961 and 1975.

Until the 1960s ranching in Central America was geared entirely to local demand. Between 1962 and 1972 beef production increased only 5% a year while beef exports rose at least 18% a year. For example, in Costa Rica in 1954-55 93% of beef production was consumed in the country, this was reduced to 44% from 1974-75; exports in this period increased from 7% to 56%. In Central America as a whole beef exports rose from 13,700 tons in 1960 to an average of 79,200 tons a year from 1971 to 1974; this implied a considerable decline in local consumption.

These developments coincided with the expansion of food processing multinational corporations in Central America. The region was one of the most important growth areas for these companies in the 1960s, largely as a result of the creation of the Central American Common Market. Enormous profits were made from producing highly processed, expensive 'junk' foods of low nutritional value for the local population.

In 1972 the Permanent Secretariat for Central American Economic Integration (SIECA) estimated that 57% of the population suffered a calorie and protein deficiency of up to 53%; 14% consumed sufficient calories and protein; and 29% consumed more than their necessary requirements. The situation was particularly serious in Guatemala, El Salvador and Honduras.

The Alliance thus silently abandoned the issue it had cited as being one of its most crucial elements: agrarian reform. But more than this, the policies which were pursued in the 1960s actually aggravated the problem of landlessness and rural unemployment. The mechanization introduced to increase landowners' efficiency resulted in fewer jobs on plantations. In Nicaragua some 15,000 jobs were lost in the agricultural sector from 1963 to 1973. The encouragement given to the growth of cash crops for export led to further expulsions of peasants from their small plots. In El Salvador in the early 1960s the boom in cotton production as world prices soared led to a massive expulsion of *colonos* (farm labourers who receive a small subsistence plot in return for their labour) from their land. Between 1961 and 1971 the number of *colono* plots declined by 70% to make way for cotton plantations. The proportion of the rural population without land in that country rose from 12% in 1961 to 29% in 1971 and 41% in 1975. As both coffee and cotton require only seasonal labour employment opportunities for the landless are few. Between February and October in El Salvador unemployment and underemployment can affect 50%, and sometimes 80%, of the rural workforce, while the number of permanently unemployed was over 45% by 1975.

In 1963 John Moors Cabot, a former Assistant Secretary of State for Inter-American Affairs, cautiously acknowledged the constraints on American policy: 'Whereas our policy seeks to promote reform and social justice in Latin America, the need to protect our large economic stake injects a conservative note into our policies.'

The Alliance for the Progress of Big Business

A notable feature of the Alliance was the way it restored United States business confidence in Latin America, which had been severely shaken by the Cuban revolution. In fact the Alliance had always been conceived with American business interests in mind and the influence of these interests over the Alliance grew in the early 1960s.

Kennedy set up the Commerce Committee for the Alliance for Progress (COMAP), made up of twenty-five business leaders and headed by J. Peter Grace, president of W.R. Grace and Co., a multinational with vast interests throughout Central America and the Caribbean. Its report in early 1963 called for United States aid to be used to encourage Latin nations to pass legislation favourable to foreign investment. In 1964 David Rockefeller, the powerful banker and member of COMAP, expressed his satisfaction with the way the Alliance was go-

Progress for Whom?

The following is a statement by Frank M. Coffin, Deputy Administrator, Agency for International Development (AID):

'Our basic, broadest goal is a long-range political one. It is not development for the sake of sheer development . . . An important objective is to open up the maximum opportunity for domestic private initiative and enterprise and to insure that foreign private investment, particularly from the United States, is welcomed and well treated . . . The fostering of a vigorous and expanding private sector in the less developed countries is one of our most important responsibilities. Both domestic private initiative and management and outside investment are important . . . Politically, a strong and progressive private business community provides a powerful force for stable responsible Government and a built-in check against Communist dogma.'

Human Rights and American Foreign Policy, *Noam Chomsky, Spokesman Books 1978.*

ing, especially as the State Department now recognized that the Alliance had laid too much emphasis on social reform.

A key role in the revival of American business confidence in Central and South America was played by such international agencies as the IMF, the World Bank and the Inter-American Development Bank, and by American government foreign assistance programmes. These became increasingly important in shaping the economic policies of governments in the region to the needs of big business through the loans and grants they offered and the recipes for development or panaceas for economic ills they tried to impose. The IMF's function, for example, was to provide temporary relief for countries with balance of payments difficulties, but in order to receive IMF funds the borrowing government has to comply with a 'stabilization' plan worked out in advance with the IMF. This plan usually involves measures which fall heavily upon the poorest sectors of the population, such as cuts in public expenditure, a wage freeze and devaluation. Other American and international agencies frequently wait for the IMF 'stamp of approval' before they offer loans. American bilateral assistance became a direct instrument of US foreign policy, a reward for friendly regimes and a means of blackmailing or punishing unfriendly ones by withholding or threatening to withdraw aid.

United States aid programmes were reorganized at the time of the

Alliance. The 1961 Foreign Assistance Act stipulated that United States aid must be used to favour the United States economy so that most of US 'aid' is in fact in the form of loans tied to the purchase of American goods and services. Of the US$1,500 million aid disbursed in the first two years of the Alliance, US$600 million was in the form of loans from the Export-Import Bank.

Section 620(e) of the Foreign Assistance Act instructs the President to cut off foreign aid to any country which nationalizes or places excessive tax burdens upon United States corporations and it can only be resumed if speedy compensation is given. An amendment in 1963 made any country terminating contracts with United States companies ineligible for foreign aid.

The US Agency for International Development (AID), which was set up in 1961, has played a notorious role in furthering US business interests under the guise of 'aid programmes'. AID became the main vehicle for channelling Alliance funds and these were used to finance programmes aimed at reinforcing the private sector in the recipient countries and promoting the interests of United States corporations. AID, for instance, would often finance infrastructural projects, such as roads and ports, which opened up areas for the penetration of foreign capital but did little to improve the living standards of the local population.

AID has also played an important role in subverting popular organizations in order to moderate their demands and effectiveness. This has mostly been carried out in close collaboration with the American Institute for Free Labour Development (AIFLD), another institution set up in 1961 by the American trade union confederation the AFL-CIO, made up of business, labour and government representatives and chaired by that ubiquitous committee figure, J. Peter Grace.

AID and AIFLD, both closely linked to the CIA and often used as vehicles for its clandestine operations, are two more instruments of US foreign policy. AIFLD has been very active in Central America and the Caribbean, attempting to subvert and coopt the labour movement in the region. In 1962, for example, AID signed a contract with the Ministry of Labour of El Salvador which allowed AIFLD to train peasant leaders as part of the Alliance for Progress programme. The result was the establishment in 1968 of the Salvadorean Communal Union (UCS), a peasant union whose role has been more to control peasant social unrest than to represent peasants' demands. In Guyana in the early 1960s, while it was still a British colony, AIFLD participated in a CIA campaign to overthrow the government of Cheddi Jagan.

The Politics of Aid

The following is an extract from a statement by Professor Miles Wolpin before US congressional subcommittee hearings on human rights in Nicaragua, Guatemala and El Salvador

'Economic aid to right-wing military regimes tends for the most part to be either absorbed by the regime and allied oligarchic groups or to reinforce the internal hold of such regimes. One argument in support of military dictatorships has been that they promote economic development. However, the rate of increase in per capita Gross Domestic Product for these three countries is not only behind that of neighbouring democratic Costa Rica but also behind the average for Latin America . . . The military regimes of El Salvador, Guatemala and Nicaragua have not responded to desperate needs for substantial improvements in mass living standards. Malnutrition, illiteracy, infant and child mortality are scandalously high.

Although the need for material improvement cannot be exaggerated, the efficacy of aid is problematic at best. An administrator in El Salvador pointed out that US aid cannot be expected to produce any substantial, lasting change in the welfare of the people in countries whose governments are not committed to programs of improvement of living conditions for the majority of the population. Furthermore . . . much of our aid has not been directed to the improvements that benefit the majority of the population, but rather to improvements that benefit the small middle and upper sectors.

According to an analysis of US aid to El Salvador, we spent 20 percent of our aid on improvements of infrastructure which reduces costs to industry (such as ports, roads, international airport), 17 percent directly went into industrial investment, 7 percent for telecommunications, 4 percent for a new market complex, 12 percent for housing for urban middle class, 11 percent for agriculture (these funds tended to concentrate in the hands of large landholders, for whom they were not intended) and 5 percent for electricity and piped water. Even aspects of aid programs which appear directed to improvements of the lot of the majority are frequently not what they seem. Projects such as the Institute for Peasant Welfare ($14 million US loan) in Nicaragua are using as 'target' areas those zones of major guerilla activities . . . The AID Director for Nicaragua supervised similar projects in Vietnam from 1966-68. Many people fear that (this) operation will, at best, waste taxpayers' funds . . . At worst, it will be used for covert counter-insurgency activities.'

House Subcommittee on Human Rights in Nicaragua, Guatemala and El Salvador, *June 1976.*

The Central American Common Market

The Alliance for Progress was established at a time when changes were taking place in United States investment strategy which involved a shift away from cash crop production and mineral extraction towards manufacturing industry. This trend began in the 1950s but expanded considerably in the 1960s as United States multinational corporations came to control the most dynamic sectors of Latin American industry, particularly in Mexico, Brazil and Argentina.

Many Latin American countries had taken advantage of the disruptions in the world economy since 1929 to launch a programme of industrialization based on the manufacture of goods previously imported. This had not taken place in Central America where the only market for manufactured goods was a small elite which imported luxury consumer items. In the absence of major socio-economic change, industrialization had to be linked to a process of regional integration which could forge a market out of the elites of all the countries.

Unlike in most South American countries, industrialization did not take place as a result of a crisis in the export sector; despite fluctuations in prices, coffee production increased threefold in the post-war period, bananas twofold and other products such as cotton, sugar and meat expanded considerably in the 1950s. Industrialization did not therefore involve any rupture in the power of the oligarchy which controlled these exports, but rather an extension of their economic interests and those of foreign capital with which they remained close allies.

The idea of a Central American Common Market was first suggested by the United Nations Economic Commission for Latin America (ECLA) as a way of bringing development to Central America without challenging existing elites. The ECLA project saw the process as a gradual one with mechanisms for regional planning to protect the less developed economies in the region.

The United States watched the initiative with interest; a Central American free trade area would create new opportunities for United States investment and would fit in well with the Alliance for Progress objective of promoting economic growth as a means of reducing social tensions.

With an offer of US$100 million in aid, the United States was able to exclude ECLA from influencing the final agreement which set up the Central American Common Market (CACM) in December 1960. This agreement eliminated mechanisms for regional planning and emphasized unrestricted free trade rather than balanced growth.

The CACM became very important to United States strategy towards the region. In 1962 a regional AID office for Central America and Panama (ROCAP) was set up in Guatemala to coordinate United States policy and enable it to influence directly the process of integration. In 1965-66 the contribution of the United States towards the institutions of the CACM was US$3.8 million while that of Central American governments totalled only US$915,000. Foreign investment in the region grew from US$30 million in 1960 to US$297 million in 1970, and of this increase 60% went into manufacturing industry mostly substituting goods previously imported. In 1967 the United States accounted for 83% of all foreign investment in the area.

The 1960s witnessed a considerable increase in regional trade and industrial growth. Between 1960 and 1970 the contribution of industry to Gross Domestic Product for the region as a whole grew from some 13% to nearly 18%. Although the industrial structures of Nicaragua and Costa Rica grew more rapidly it was Guatemala and El Salvador which dominated regional trade. In addition to the traditional industries such as tobacco, textiles and clothing there was an expansion of new intermediate industries such as pulp and paper chemicals, fertilizers, cosmetics, plastics, oil refining and pharmaceuticals. But by the end of the decade the process was already slowing down and United States investment dwindling; there were limits to the expansion of a market based on the consumption of a small elite even from five countries. By then the industrialization process manifested clear characteristics: dependence on and in many sectors monopolization by the United States. Oil refining, pulp and paper, steel tubing, tyres and chemicals and a part of the food processing industry were almost totally controlled by a handful of American companies. In Guatemala the combined assets of US firms in pharmaceuticals, food processing and the oil industry accounted for one third of all US investment in the country.

Another way in which American multinationals penetrated the industrial sector of Central America was through joint ventures with local firms in which they maintained the majority ownership. This has led to very close ties between United States businessmen and local entrepreneurs, with the latter the junior and dependent partner. This alliance has helped consolidate United States control over the region, particularly in the case of Guatemala, one of the most favoured countries for US investment. Although the traditional landowning oligarchy never wavered in its warmth towards the United States, it was that new business class which had emerged in the 1950s, together with the bureaucrats, technocrats and senior officers of the army who ran the country who responded most vigorously to the opportunities opened up by the United States. As these groups entered industry, finance, commerce and an increasingly modernized agricultural export sector, their dependence on the United States which provided their market, often the investment capital and hence their incomes — became complete.

However, the process of industrialization which followed the creation of the CACM brought few benefits to the people of Central America, the majority of whose incomes were too low to take advantage of the new range of manufactured goods available. Nor did industrialization bring new job opportunities. The United States multinationals who controlled the process used capital-intensive, labour-saving technology inappropriate to the needs of the region with its rising levels of rural unemployment and landlessness.

There are many ways in which the CACM adversely affected the economies of the region. The region's balance of payments deficit with the rest of the world, for instance, more than doubled between 1963 and 1968 due to the increased imports of machinery, raw materials, technology and parts for the many assembly industries established during these years.

The CACM also aggravated the regional disparities in Central America so that the least developed countries, Nicaragua and Honduras, found that by the late 1960s they were accumulating large trade deficits with their partners. Honduras in particular ended up with a deficit of US$5 million with El Salvador alone and this was one of the principal factors behind the 'football war' between the two countries in 1969 which resulted in Honduras' withdrawal from the CACM. This provoked a crisis from which the CACM never properly recovered. However, United States interests in the region were well established and ready to adapt to changing regional and international conditions.

A Caribbean Investors Paradise

'Operation Bootstrap' in Puerto Rico in the late 1940s is said by some to have inspired the Alliance for Progress and the pattern of dependent industrialization which accompanied it. It is certainly another prime example of the disastrous impact of the American path to progress upon the majority of people in its backyard.

In 1951, in order to obscure the island's colonial status at a time when colonialism was becoming so out of fashion that even the Europeans were beginning to shed their dependencies, the United States had conferred upon Puerto Rico the status of 'Commonwealth' or 'Associated Free State'. Dutifully the United Nations confirmed in 1953 that Puerto Rico was no longer a colony. Adolf A. Berle, Assistant Secretary of State for Inter-American Affairs, proudly declared that now 'Puerto Rico has independence in everything except economics, defence and foreign relations'.

With Operation Bootstrap Puerto Rico became an island fiefdom for American big business. This quaintly named economic strategy was designed to drag Puerto Rico out of its dependence on sugar and tobacco exports by attracting United States industrial investment through generous tax incentives, cheap labour and political stability. It was the brainchild of Luis Munoz Marin, the country's first elected governor, who, unlike the nationalists in the country, was less concerned with Puerto Rico's political status than with the economic advantages of rapid industrial growth, at whatever price.

Teodoro Moscoso, later to play an important role in the Alliance for Progress, also made a substantial contribution to Operation Bootstrap. From his post as administrator of Puerto Rico's Economic Development Administration he financed many of the infrastructural projects which would encourage the massive flow of United States investment into the country during the 1950s and 1960s. Moscoso knew how to attract investors as is shown by the statement he makes in an advertisement which appeared in the 1970s:

There is no mystery about the steady influx of US manufacturers to Puerto Rico over the last twenty-five years. Operation Bootstrap, our economic self-help program, has always operated on the principle that business will go where the profits are . . . How about repatriation of profits to the US mainland? If you set up your Puerto Rican operation under Section 931 of the Internal Revenue Code, you may repatriate all of your profits completely free of US or Commonwealth taxes.

Between 1948 and 1968 foreign control of manufacturing increased from 22% to 77%. In 1947 there were thirteen American-owned factories on the island, by 1970 there were 2,000. At first, investment was concentrated in light industry, particularly textiles, which had been given a ten to twelve year tax free period. As this expired in the mid-1960s highly mechanized, energy-intensive and highly polluting industries such as petrochemicals, oil refineries and pharmaceuticals moved to the island.

These industries created few jobs. Unemployment was estimated to be as high as 30% in the 1960s, while between 1950 and 1970 615,000 people emigrated to the United States in search of work. In 1970 88% of all workers received less than the minimum income set by the Department of Health as necessary for a family to live on. A study in 1966 showed that in a population of two and a half million, 910,000 depended upon federal food hand-outs. In 1965 the poorest 20% of the population received only 5% of all personal income, the wealthiest 20% received 51%.

This is the country which the United States describes as its 'showcase' in the Caribbean, a success story. It is successful for the United States. Despite its small size Puerto Rico came to attract more United States investment than any other Latin American country, while it depends for 98% of its food, raw materials and manufactured goods on United States imports. Dependency is complete, a classic case of an economy which 'consumes what it does not produce and produces what it does not consume'.

The Military Alliance

There are those in the United States who consider that the Alliance for Progress somehow 'lost its way' as a result of such factors as the death of Kennedy or indifferent officials. Such a view does not see any fundamental incompatibility between the interests of United States capital and a process of development based on socio-economic justice.

What it ignores is that the Alliance was more than simply an economic strategy; from its inception it had a military dimension. According to Alliance planners, economic development based on the encouragement of foreign capital required a climate of law and order, of political stability. An essential feature of the Alliance strategy was the promotion of internal security through the strengthening of local military and police forces. As the 1960s wore on and the reformist objectives of the Alliance were abandoned, it was this military aspect of United States policy which provided its most lasting legacy.

The United States first began supplying Latin American armies with arms and equipment during the Second World War under the Lendlease Act. Afterwards the Rio Pact in 1947 between the United States and Latin American nations stressed cooperation between the regions against external attack and the Mutual Security Act of 1951 made funds available to strengthen Latin American armies in the interests of hemispheric defence. In the view of acting Assistant Secretary of State Charles H. Shuff, 'the most positive threat to hemisphere security is submarine action in the Caribbean and along the coast of Latin America'.

So until the Kennedy administration the emphasis of United States defence strategy was on the external threat. Following the Cuban revolution this shifted. The main danger to United States interests was identified as social unrest within Latin America which translated into the language of the Cold War became 'communist subversion' fomented as much by indigenous radicals as by the Soviet Union.

The Americans can hardly have been surprised that the extreme poverty and inequality in the hemisphere to which US policies had made a substantial contribution, should eventually explode into political action. The conditions which led to the Cuban revolution persisted throughout the region; however, there were no democratic means of expressing discontent or debating alternative models of development. It was almost inevitable that the Cuban road to change through armed struggle should be used as a model, even though it was often slavishly and mistakenly imitated, frequently with disastrous results.

The Americans perceived the emergence of a new kind of war: 'subversive insurgency', which President Kennedy said in a speech in 1962 required 'a whole new kind of strategy, a wholly different kind of force, and therefore a new and wholly different kind of training'.

In 1963 the United States Military Assistance Program (MAP) was greatly expanded to include training and assistance to help local armies deal with guerrilla movements. In the 1950s average annual US military assistance to Latin America was US$35 million while from 1960 to 1965 it was US$70 million. Between 1964 and 1968 22,058 Latin American military personnel were trained under MAP at the United States Army School of the Americas in the Panama Canal Zone, the Inter-American Defense College in Washington, and various other schools operated by the United States army, navy and air force.

In addition to grants of weapons and equipment, credit was made available for the purchase of arms through the Foreign Military Sales programme (FMS). But the Latin Americans were discouraged from buying major weapons systems and by 1968 87% of all such arms purchased by Latin American governments came from outside the United States, particularly Europe.

The United States was now only interested in supplying arms for internal security purposes as Defense Secretary Robert McNamara explained: 'The grant programme will provide no tanks, artillery fighter aircraft or combat ships. The emphasis is on vehicles and helicopters for internal mobility, communications equipment for better coordination of in-country security efforts, and spare parts for maintenance of existing inventories'.

The new approach was known as counter-insurgency, defined by the Pentagon as 'a combination of military, paramilitary, political, economic, psychological and civic action carried on by a government in order to destroy any movement of subversive insurgency'.

As well as military training and assistance it included increasing the capabilities of local police forces. This was carried out through the reorganization of the Office of Public Safety (OPS) of the Agency for International Development. David Bell, a former AID administrator, explained the importance of the programme to the Foreign Assistance Appropriations Committee in 1965:

. . . the police are a most sensitive point of contact between government and people, close to the focal points of unrest, and more acceptable than the army as keepers of order over long periods of time. The police are frequently better trained and equipped than the military to deal with minor forms of violence, conspiracy and subversion.

Between 1961 and 1969 the United States spent US$8.2 million on police assistance to Central America (see Table top of page 55).

Counter-insurgency techniques also included civic action programmes, such as public works and food handouts to the local peasantry, designed to improve the standing of the military amongst the population and to prevent radical ideas taking root. These were first tried out in Guatemala, a popular testing ground for many of the United States' policies. A United States civic action advisory team visited the country in late 1960. The visit coincided with growing social unrest and widespread repudiation of the corruption and incompetence of the Ydigoras government. Following the failure of an uprising led by young army officers in November 1960 the first guerrilla movements appeared in the country. Civic action was immediately supplemented by other techniques of counter-insurgency. In May 1962 a secret United States base was established in the province of Izabal, its aim was to turn the Guatemalan army into an efficient fighting force capable of crushing the guerrillas. It was directed by five members of the United States Special Forces who had gained their knowledge of counter-insurgency while serving in Laos.

The American policy of strengthening the military establishment of Central and South America was rationalized at the time by various academic reassessments of the role of the military in Third World countries. In 1961 a study mission sent to Latin America by the United States Senate concluded that the government 'should take a more favourable attitude toward the military groups in most Latin American countries . . . We are convinced that the military are not only the sole force of stabilization but they also promote democratic institutions and progressive changes of a socio-economic nature'. John J. Johnson of Stanford University wrote a book in 1964 which asserted that by forestalling violent revolution the military allows the achievement of reforms through democratic processes.

The inherent contradiction of a policy of arming and training the military in order to promote democracy became rapidly apparent in Central America. Although the wave of coups which took place in the region in the early 1960s (El Salvador in 1961; Guatemala, the Dominican Republic and Honduras in 1963) cannot be explained exclusively in terms of the United States' role, the American counter-insurgency programme was bound to have a profound effect on the

US Military Assistance Programs, 1946-76
(By fiscal years in millions of US dollars)

MAP Grants: Grants of arms, equipment and services under the Military Assistance Program.
FMS Credit: Credits awarded under the Foreign Military Sales programme for the purchase of US arms.
Excess Items: Deliveries of "surplus" US arms.
IMETP: Training provided under the International Military Education and Training Program.
Sec. Supp. Assist.: Subsidies awarded under the Foreign Assistance Act to threatened pro-US regimes.

Country	MAP Grants 1950-76	FMS Credits 1950-76	Excess Items 1950-76	IMETP Grants 1950-76	Sec. Supp. Assist. 1946-76	Total 1946-76
Costa Rica	0.9	—	0.1	0.9	—	1.9
Cuba	8.6	—	5.5	2.0	—	16.1
Dominican Republic	21.7	1.5	3.9	9.1	209.2	245.4
El Salvador	4.9	3.5	2.5	5.4	—	16.3
Guatemala	16.4	10.9	6.7	7.1	33.5	74.6
Haiti	2.4	—	0.2	0.9	47.7	51.2
Honduras	5.6	5.5	1.9	7.0	1.6	21.6
Jamaica	1.1	—	—	—	—	1.1
Nicaragua	7.6	5.5	5.3	10.7	—	29.1
Panama	4.3	0.5	1.8	3.5	27.0	37.1
Trinidad and Tobago	—	—	—	—	29.7	29.7

Source: *Michael T. Klare,* Supplying Repression: US Support for Authoritarian Regimes Abroad, *Institute for Policy Studies, 1977.*

military institutions in the region.

Armies acquired skills and training which involved them in questions of fundamental political and economic importance. Their perceptions of society and their role within it were geared to the need to preserve a particular socio-economic order and their mental reflexes were trained to interpret any challenge to that order as 'communism'.

Within Central America the military came to act with much greater institutional unity. It no longer acted as a mere arbiter between different factions of the elite struggling for state power. Increasingly it

US Assistance to Foreign Police Forces Under the Public Safety Program, Fiscal Years 1961-73
(in thousands of US dollars)

Country	Students trained in the US	US Public Safety Advisers	Total Expenditures
Costa Rica	160	4	1,921
Dominican Republic	204	3	4,193
El Salvador	168	1	2,092
Guatemala	377	7	4,855
Guyana	53	—	1,299
Honduras	105	3	1,741
Jamaica	92	1	780
Nicaragua	81	2	315
Panama	202	3	2,148

Source: *Michael T. Klare,* Supplying Repression: US Support for Authoritarian Regimes Abroad, *Institute for Policy Studies 1977.*

Training of Foreign Military Personnel by the United States, Fiscal Years 1950-76
(Students trained under the Military Assistance Program and International Military Education and Training Program in the United States and in the Panama Canal Zone)

Costa Rica	696
Cuba (1950-60)	523
Dominican Republic	3,945
El Salvador	1,925
Guatemala	3,213
Haiti (1950-63)	593
Honduras	2,888
Jamaica	11
Nicaragua	5,167
Panama	4,389

Source: *Ibid.*

came to take over the State, in close alliance with the oligarchy, but with institutional interests of its own. Now its principal concern was the new challenge posed by the increasing unemployment, poverty and landlessness in the rural areas and the emergence of new urban social classes and political movements which accompanied the process of industrialization. Counter-insurgency came to involve the repression not only of guerrilla movements but also of civilian opposition groups and organizations such as trade unions and peasant bodies whose purpose was to defend the interests of those excluded from economic and political power. It became less a question of how peasants and workers might be persuaded to support their governments but how they could be prevented from helping the guerrillas.

In 1967 the American political scientist Professor Lieuwen reported to a subcommittee of the Senate Foreign Relations Committee:

The wave of military interventions suggests that the US training programs, the work of the missions, and the contact between United States and Latin American military men did little to improve military respect for civilian authority and constitutional processes. Most of the Latin American military leaders who conducted the nine coups between 1962 and 1966 had been recipients of US training.

If the Americans increased the propensity of the military to intervene in politics they also provided them with the means to do so. The political scientist John D. Powell has pointed out that military aid to Nicaragua in the early 1960s gave every member of Somoza's National Guard an average of US$930 of equipment and training in order to take violent action against a population whose annual per capita income was US$205; in Guatemala the figure was US$538 per soldier to use against a population whose annual income was US$185 a head.

The US government was unconcerned about the consequences of its policies. In 1964 Secretary of Defense Robert McNamara stated that 'the essential role of the Latin American military as a stabilizing force outweighs any risks involved in providing military assistance for internal security purposes'.

By President Johnson's time, the ultra-conservative Assistant Secretary of State for Inter-American Affairs, Thomas Mann, could state quite candidly that the Alliance for Progress preference for democratic regimes no longer applied.

The United States Defensive Triangle

During the 1960s the importance of the Panama Central Zone and Puerto Rico as two points of the United States defensive triangle in the

Caribbean (the third is the Guantanamo naval base on Cuba) grew considerably. At the same time the Canal Zone became one of the key centres for training in counter-insurgency techniques.

By 1971 military investment in the Canal Zone was estimated to be US$4,800 million. The Canal Zone is the headquarters of the United States Southern Command (Southcom); one journalist has called it a 'miniature Pentagon'. Southcom coordinates all United States military and intelligence activities in Latin America, supervises the military assistance programmes, and the military advisory missions resident in each country. It also controls the vast military complex in the Canal Zone consisting of 14 military bases and about 14,000 American soldiers. It includes the headquarters of the 8th United States Special Forces, the Green Berets. In the 1960s the Latin American contingent of this body consisted of 1,109 officers and men who made up twenty-four mobile training teams. These have travelled to every Latin American country except Cuba, Haiti and Mexico providing intensive training in counter-insurgency.

In addition, Southcom supervises the training of Latin American army personnel. This mostly takes place at the School of the Americas at Fort Gulick in the Canal Zone. Between 1961 and 1964 out of a total of 16,343 Latin American students trained at the school, 8,154 were Central American. As of 1978 a total of 43,374 officers from all over Latin America had been trained there, many of them have subsequently become leading political figures in their own countries. In October 1973 over 170 graduates of the School of the Americas were heads of government, cabinet ministers, commanding generals or heads of intelligence in their own countries.

According to the United States Defense Department, 'the emphasis of the training has been given to counter-insurgency . . . The courses and operations of counter-insurgency were started in July 1961 and they take place four times a year'. There is a strong ideological element in the courses. One study noted that 15-20% of officers' course time was devoted to anti-communist and pro-United States propaganda (see box, page 58).

These and other United States military training programmes were considered an essential part of United States strategy towards Central America in the 1960s. Robert McNamara told the House of Representatives Appropriations Committee in 1963:

Probably the greatest return on our military assistance investment comes from the training of selected officers and key specialists at our military schools and training centres in the United States and overseas. These students are hand-picked by their countries to become instructors when they return home. They are coming leaders, the men who will have the know-how and impart it to their

School of Coups

'Besides merely improving the military capabilities of the Latin American officers there are certainly other consequences that result from soldiers of Central and South America receiving training in the Canal Zone . . . a substantial number of Central American soldiers have been trained in the Canal Zone (and) the various facets of the Southern Command's military training programs are significant in regard to the type of political indoctrination that Latin American soldiers are exposed to under the programs.

Of the Southern Command training schools the School of the Americas at Fort Gulick is the best known; throughout Latin America it is commonly referred to as the "escuela de golpes" (school of coups). The school of the Americas has trained more Latin American soldiers than any of the other schools and it therefore has the most apparent and noteworthy influence on the soldiers.

During the 1960s the School of the Americas was divided into two departments: one to teach soldiers techniques of counterinsurgency and the other to train military students to apply technical operations to civil action programs. The course at the School of the Americas lasted from two weeks to forty weeks depending upon the program of study and the rank of the Latin American soldiers. Professor Miles Wolpin has noted that 70 percent of the course hours offered in the 1969 curriculum at the School of the Americas concerned counter-insurgency training while the remainder related to technical instruction. In reference to the school's program for teaching internal security, Ronning and Barber have stated that it "provides instruction in every aspect of counter-insurgency: military, paramilitary, political, sociological, and psychological." Wolpin reported that in the 1969 curriculum between 2 and 4 percent of the enlisted trainee's course time and between 15 and 20 percent of the officers' course time was devoted to anti-communist and pro-United States ideological indoctrination. Examples of some of the courses listed in the Fort Gulick Catalog (1969) are as follows:

For military police officers a class dealt with the "Communist threat". "Communism" and "the threat it poses" was the subject for a military intelligence officer course. A forty week course for command officers, which included a tour of the United States examined Communism and the US response to it.

In addition to the political propaganda that is included in the training courses at the School of the Americas, Fort Gulick distributes a plethora of pamphlets that attempt to influence the political thinking of the Latin American soldiers. Wolpin has noted that the political themes conveyed in such pamphlets are often presented in "grotesque stereotypes" that are "crude and over-simplified" with much reliance on cartoon and cinematic media.

Such an effort by the Southern Command to politically indoctrinate Central and South American soldiers about the "evils" of communism has probably helped increase their fear of political groups that advocate reforms. The emphasis on anti-Communist propaganda in the Canal Zone training courses during the 1960s served only to reinforce and to promote conservatism while instilling a vehement mistrust of reformism and liberalism. The propaganda aspect of the Southern Command's training of Central American soldiers also seems to have augmented the tendency of the Central American military officers to justify the use of military repression under the pretext of retarding communism.

Historical evidence validates the proposition that the Central American armed forces have justified coups and repression as attempts to retard communism. Moreover in recent years coups and military repression have been utilized by the armed forces of every Central American nation except Costa Rica to thwart liberalism, unionism, and reformism because these are seen to be the same as communism. In fact the armed forces of the five militarized isthmian states have often construed all social protest and criticism to the work of Communist subversives. The militaries' hypersensitive attitude to protest and criticism has resulted in the oppression of civilian political parties, popular politicians, newspapers, radio stations, universities, and of any citizen who enthusiastically advocates radical change. Finally the armed forces of Central America have used repression to retard the growth of labour unions and peasant cooperatives because military officers believe these groups must be communist inspired.'

Statement by Don Etchison before House Subcommittee on Human Rights in Nicaragua, Guatemala and El Salvador, June 1976.

forces. I need not dwell upon the value of having in positions of leadership men who have firsthand knowledge of how Americans do things and how they think. It is beyond price to us to make friends of such men.

The United States understood that, whereas governments are short-lived, the armed forces are a permanent institution and a more reliable vehicle for its influence.

While Panama became a strategic centre for the United States army, Puerto Rico came to play a similar role for the navy. It is seen as the 'gateway to the Caribbean' and has been used as a base for training, surveillance and interventions throughout Latin America and the Caribbean.

United States military operations in Puerto Rico come under the direction of the Atlantic Command (Lantcom) which is responsible for all military forces in the Atlantic Ocean, the Caribbean sea and the waters round Central and South America and Africa. The Commander, South Atlantic Force (Comsolant) is subordinate to Lantcom and controls all naval activity in the Caribbean and the Atlantic Ocean south of the Tropic of Cancer. It commanded the naval blockade of Cuba in 1962 and directed the naval support operations when the United States invaded the Dominican Republic in 1965.

Roosevelt Roads is an all purpose naval base on the east coast of Puerto Rico which is large enough to berth any warship in the world. Vieques, an island off the east coast is used for United States naval training and Culebra a nearby island is used for combing and shelling exercises. Ramey air force base houses a number of heavy transport aircraft able to airlift military equipment and large numbers of troops to anywhere in the Caribbean and Latin America. In 1965 Ramey was used to ship United States troops involved in the invasion of the Dominican Republic.

CONDECA

As well as encouraging the economic integration of Central America, the United States was anxious to promote collaboration and cooperation between the armed forces of the region.

The Guatemalan and Nicaraguan governments were the most enthusiastic about the idea. In 1962 two guerrilla movements had appeared in Guatemala, the 13 November Revolutionary Movement (MR 13 de Noviembre) and the Rebel Armed Forces (FAR). In Nicaragua the Sandinista National Liberation Forces (FSLN) was formally founded in 1961.

In September 1962, in order to promote coordination, the United States sponsored a series of military exercises which were given the name 'Operation Brotherhood'. They involved armed units from Honduras, Guatemala, El Salvador, Nicaragua, Colombia and the Canal Zone and they centred around a hypothetical guerrilla attack on Honduras' national airport. In 1964 with strong United States backing the defence ministers of Guatemala, Honduras, El Salvador and Nicaragua signed an agreement establishing the Central American Defense Council (CONDECA). Costa Rica, whose army had been abolished in 1948, and Panama were given observer status with an option to join.

The objectives of CONDECA were to coordinate action against internal subversion, and to facilitate United States control over such action. The CIA and the Central American representatives of the United States armed forces acted as advisors to CONDECA. It was also seen as a convenient way of standardizing the training and equipping of the region's armies and reducing regional military rivalries. In addition, the United States tried to use the organization to promote the militarization of Costa Rica and in 1966 Costa Rica secretly took part in one of CONDECA joint manoeuvres known as 'Operation Nicarao'.

Altogether some ten anti-guerrilla manoeuvres were conducted under the auspices of CONDECA, the last one, 'Operation Aguila VI', took place in Nicaragua in 1976. In 1972 there were strong suggestions that the Nicaragua and Guatemalan air forces helped a right-wing government in El Salvador crush an attempted coup.

However the organization never achieved the regional military coordination the United States had hoped for. Honduras withdrew after the war with El Salvador in 1969, and in 1979 the fall of Somoza, whose National Guard had been the backbone of the alliance, further contributed to its decline. By then the United States had in any case reached the conclusion that regional rivalries and differences prevented the organization becoming an effective instrument of coordinated counter-insurgency and had ceased to have a formal advisory role in it. Nevertheless, CONDECA has left a legacy of friendship and personal ties between the most right-wing army officers of the region and the idea of mutual assistance has not been abandoned.

The Dominican Republic 1965

The establishment of CONDECA reflected the American preference for using national, and secondly, neighbouring armies to defend their interests rather than sending in their own troops. In 1967 McNamara pointed out:

The United States cannot be everywhere simultaneously . . . The balance of forces and the variable alternatives which challenge us in the changing contemporary world can only be conquered with faithful friends, well-equipped and ready to carry on the duty assigned to them . . . The Military Aid programme has been devised to conquer such forces and alternatives, since it helps maintaining military forces which complement our own armed forces.

Although direct involvement was to be avoided if possible, local armed forces were only seen as a 'complement' to the might of the American marines at this stage in American thinking, and in the last resort the marines were ready and waiting. The years from 1964 to 1967 saw the most intense escalation of United States involvement in Vietnam; less publicity was given to the invasion of the Dominican Republic which took place at the same time.

By 1961 President Trujillo and a handful of United States companies owned the Dominican Republic. But Trujillo's share, an estimated 65-85% of the country's economy, was rather larger than that of his allies who had to content themselves with a percentage of the sugar industry. This restriction on investment opportunities together with the United States' need to secure its sugar supplies following the 'loss' of its Cuban sugar mills in 1960 contributed to a rift in the traditional friendship. This found a local echo in the growing resentment of the traditional agricultural oligarchy at the concentration of economic power in the hands of Trujillo and his supporters. It was these factors rather than Trujillo's brutally repressive record (in 1937 for example, Trujillo was reputed to have ordered the massacre of thousands of Dominican and Haitian workers) which led to his assassination in 1961. A Senate investigation in 1975 revealed the deep involvement of the CIA in the plot.

Trujillo's wealth came under state control following his death, giving Juan Bosch who was elected President in 1962 a unique opportunity to plan the nation's economic future. At the time average per capita income was less than US$200 (under US$100 for the majority of workers) and there was a 60% illiteracy rate.

Bosch was a moderate nationalist reformer as even the Kennedy administration had recognized when it backed his candidacy in the 1962 elections. His victory had also been facilitated by the divisions within the local ruling elite. In 1963 Bosch encouraged the two warring local groups to join forces with the United States by challenging the interests of all three. He refused to denationalize Trujillo's property and sought to limit the power of foreign capital and local landowners while defending the rights of the peasantry. Kennedy conditionally supported the coup led by General Wessin y Wessin which overthrew him in October 1963. The new head of government was Donald Reid Cabral, a local CIA agent nicknamed *'el americanito'* (the little American). Cabral lived up to his name and began to transfer Trujillo's wealth to the private sector while USAID started to fund infrastructural projects in the country.

With the support of anti-Trujillo sections of the army, Bosch organized an alliance to bring down the government and to restore the 1963 constitution. The constitutionalists took power in a coup on 25 April 1965 with strong support from the urban working class and professional middle class.

The CIA immediately tried to set up an alternative junta under Colonel Benoit, although it had to be confined to the San Isidro air base. Hearings before the Senate Foreign Relations Committee later in the year revealed the extraordinary series of events which began on 28 April with a cabled request from Benoit to US Ambassador Bennett for American troops 'because a Communist takeover threatens'. But US intelligence reports had stated that same day that no more than two of the 'prime leaders of the rebel forces (were men) with a long history of Communist association'. Ambassador Bennett then informed Benoit that American troops could only be brought in if the justification became the need to protect American lives. Benoit's second cable read: 'Regarding my earlier request, I wish to add that American lives are in danger . . .'

The United States dispatched 400 marines from bases round the Caribbean that very day and they were followed by a further 20,000. An estimated 2,500 civilians were killed in the fighting which followed.

A provisional government was set up and elections held in 1966. The United States and their favoured candidate, Trujillo's former Vice-President Joaquin Balaguer, spent an estimated US$13 million on the election which Balaguer naturally won. The United States made sure he would enjoy the security of a strong military and police force. The Dominican Republic received US$10.3 million in military assistance from 1963 to 1968 and US police assistance rose from US$97,000 in 1965 to US$769,000 in 1967

The invasion by the marines was followed by an invasion of American capital. AID spent US$500 million in the country between 1962 and 1967, the highest per capita AID programme in Latin America at the time. It funded every single public project in 1966 and 1967: roads, lighting, water and housing, the essential infrastructure required by the foreign investors who now flocked to the country. In 1961 US investment was US$150 million, by 1975 it had risen to US$411 million. It was encouraged by a series of laws beginning with the Investment Incentives Law of 1968 which granted generous tax benefits to new investments particularly those geared to export markets. In 1970 the Free Zones Law allowed foreign companies to set up assembly plants in zones exempt from taxes for ten to twenty years. In 1971 the Tourist Promotion Law and a Mining Code gave tax exemptions and profit repatriation guarantees to investors in those sectors.

Under Balaguer, the Dominican Republic lost all control of its natural resources. In accordance with an increasingly familiar pattern in the region its economy now meets the needs of American business rather than those of its own people. The country's gold deposits are controlled by Rosario Resources, Alcoa dominates the bauxite in-

> **'A government freely chosen by the will of all the people . . .'**
>
> The following is an extract from an address by President Lyndon B. Johnson broadcast over nationwide radio and television on 2 May 1965:
>
> 'There are times in the affairs of nations when great principles are tested in an ordeal of conflict and danger. This is such a time for the American nations . . .
> I want you to know that it is not a light or an easy matter to send our American boys to another country, but I do not think that the American people expect their President to hesitate or to vacillate in the face of danger, just because the decision is hard when life is in peril . . .
> The American nations cannot, must not, and will not permit the establishment of another Communist government in the Western Hemisphere . . .
> Our goal is a simple one. We are there to save the lives of our citizens and to save the lives of all people. Our goal, in keeping with the great principles of the inter-American system, is to help prevent another Communist state in this hemisphere. And we would like to do this without bloodshed or without large-scale fighting.
> The form and the nature of the free Dominican government, I assure you, is solely a matter for the Dominican people, but we do know what kind of government we hope to see in the Dominican Republic . . .
> We hope to see a government freely chosen by the will of all the people.'

dustry, Gulf and Western, considered the largest single beneficiary of the US invasion, controls at least one third of the country's sugar production and Falconbridge mines the country's nickel, considered one of the thirteen basic raw materials required by an industrial society and an important metal in the arms industry.

Falconbridge, a nominally Canadian company in which the Superior Oil Company of Houston, Texas, gained a controlling interest in 1967, gained free access to the Dominican Republic's nickel at a timely moment for the United States. The loss of the Cuban nickel mines after the revolution and the gradual depletion of Canadian sources have considerably enhanced the importance to the United States of the Falcondo mine. The financial interests behind it have close ties with the political establishment in the United States as well as the Dominican Republic itself. Falconbridge's total capital investment in the country between 1962 and 1970 was US$195 million, in that time they provided Dominicans with a mere 1,828 jobs.

But it is Gulf and Western which exercises a real stranglehold over the economy. It has been called a 'state within a state'; the annual sales of this gigantic transnational exceed the gross national product of the Dominican Republic. The company first gained a foothold in the country when it purchased the sugar plantations and refinery of the South Puerto Rico Sugar Company in 1966. Almost its first action was to destroy the independent sugar cane workers union, the *Sindicato Unido* (SU). Eighty-three labour leaders were arrested and Damilo Brito Braez, at one time a leader of the CIA-funded union CONATRAL, was put in charge of creating a company controlled union at the corporation's Central Romana sugar refinery. A study in the mid-1970s found that cane cutters employed by Gulf and Western earned an average of US$1.50 for dawn to dusk back-breaking labour.

The company owns over 2% of the national territory of the Dominican Republic in a country where only 14% of the land surface is suitable for cultivation, 9% of landowners own two-thirds of the land, and where 75% of the peasantry is landless or lives on tiny subsistence plots. The steady expansion of land for sugar production has exacerbated the problem of landlessness and malnutrition as there is insufficient land to grow food for the local population. A nutritional survey in 1970 found that the average protein intake was 62% of the recommended minimum amount required and as low as 34% in some of the poorest communities.

Only 44% of Gulf and Western's land is used for sugar cultivation, 47% is dedicated to ranching and the rest to other export crops. The company now exports beef, winter vegetables, citrus fruits and tobacco, mostly to markets on the east coast of the United States and Puerto Rico. As part of its programme to diversify its interests, the company has also invested heavily in tourism and owns a multimillion dollar resort complex at La Romana as well as luxury hotels in the capital, Santo Domingo.

The company's expansion has been facilitated by its close relationship with the Balaguer government. The advantages it enjoys in the country go beyond those provided by the foreign investment laws and have often been achieved through special contracts between the company and the government. Suspicions have been aroused by the many loopholes which appeared in a 1972 law to restrict further land being used for sugar cultivation and which have rendered it meaningless. In 1976 there were revelations in the United States that foreign subsidiaries of Gulf and Western had made 'questionable' payments totalling US$416,000.

Gulf and Western was the first American company to set up an industrial free zone in the country in 1969; it has since been followed by a number of others. Labour is so cheap in these zones, where unions are not permitted, that many companies have closed their plants in Puerto Rico, where by the late 1960s labour costs had risen, and set them up in the Dominican Republic. The *New York Times* informed its readers in April 1973: 'Hourly wages in the Dominican Republic average about one-third to one-fourth of those in nearby Puerto Rico. Dominican labour is well-known for its willingness, cooperation and the innate capacity of its people quickly to learn intricate manufacturing processes'.

The 'willingness' of Dominican labour to sell itself for near starvation wages has been encouraged by CIA infiltration of the labour movement mostly through AIFLD — which spent US$1.6 million in the country from 1962 to 1969 — by massive unemployment, estimated in 1978 to be as much as 30% of the population and by the repression of militant, independent trade unionists. A right-wing terrorist organization known as *La Banda* helped organize this repression on behalf of the government. In 1971 a member of the organization admitted that police officials had ordered him to assassinate the head of the independent drivers' union. In the early 1970s *La Banda* is estimated to have murdered over 2,000 people.

The Dominican Republic is now second only to Puerto Rico as a market for US goods in the Caribbean, while the United States takes two-thirds of the country's exports. Half a million Dominicans now live in New York; about half entered the United States illegally, searching for a future their own country cannot offer.

The Organization of Violence

While American capital was invading the Dominican Republic, sophisticated techniques for suppressing social unrest were being developed in that laboratory of counter-insurgency, Vietnam. Guatemala was a favourite testing ground for these techniques in the Western Hemisphere.

In the mid-1960s the war against the guerrillas in Guatemala was not going to the Americans' liking. President Peralta Azurdia, for reasons of national and military pride, was ignoring the advice of the United States military mission in the country (by 1965 this consisted of thirty-four military advisors compared with fifteen in 1959) and was refusing AID projects and offers of loans. Worse still he was unwilling to allow an expansion of the military assistance programme and restricted the number of Guatemalan officers allowed to participate in US training schemes. When US Senator Wayne Morse publicly declared that the United States would intervene if things did not improve, Peralta responded angrily: 'We are not the Dominican Republic. The Guatemalan government can handle by itself any subversives.'

It was with relief therefore that the United States welcomed the victory of the civilian, Julio Cesar Mendez Montenegro in the 1966 presidential elections. In exchange for US support and increased aid (74% of all foreign loans between 1960 and 1970 were signed under Mendez), Mendez was reported to have promised the military and American counter-insurgency experts a free hand to crush the guerrilla movement.

The Americans' satisfaction was expressed publicly by US ambassador John Gordon Mein when in November 1967 he presented the Guatemalan armed forces with new armoured vehicles, grenade launchers, training and radio equipment and several HU-1B jet powered helicopters: 'These articles, especially the helicopters, are not easy to obtain at this time since they are being utilized by our forces in defense of the cause of liberty in other parts of the world. But liberty must be defended wherever it is threatened and that liberty is now being threatened in Guatemala.'

Colonel Carlos Arana Osorio, previously the Guatemalan military attache in Washington, was appointed as head of the military command in Zacapa, where guerrilla activity was most intense. Arana found his troops in poor condition and between July and October 1966 carried out an intensive training programme. He was assisted by a contingent of Green Berets. The extent of US involvement in the actual fighting is not known because the Americans try to make a distinction between their advisory and combat roles and they consistently deny the latter. However, at least one journalist reported in 1967 that, in addition to training local personnel in anti-guerrilla warfare and the interrogation of prisoners and cooperating in civic action programmes such as the distribution of dried milk and medicines, the US advisors accompanied the Guatemalan patrols on their missions.

The United States also stepped up its police programme in Guatemala. From 1957 to 1965 US police aid to the country was only US$759,000; between 1966 and 1970 it rose to over US$2.6 million. According to USAID, over 30,000 Guatemalan police personnel had received OPS training in Guatemala by 1970, one of the largest OPS programmes in Latin America. This was the period in which the Mobile Military Police were formed 'to combat rural insurgency and banditry where civilian police protection was lacking', while the Border Patrol (*Guardia de Hacienda*) was brought into counter-insurgency operations. These two police units have been the most frequently associated with the thousands of kidnappings and murders which have occurred in Guatemala since the mid-1960s.

There was a new element in Arana's campaign: organized violence, in the form of right-wing terror squads charged with eliminating 'subversives'. Arana used these anti-communist paramilitary groups to terrorize the local population and prevent them assisting the guerrillas.

The first death squad appeared in July 1966, one month before Mendez took office. A series of leaflets were distributed in Guatemala City announcing the formation of the 'White Hand' (*Mano Blanca*) 'that will eradicate national renegades as traitors to the country'. The following year other such organizations appeared. There is substantial evidence that these organizations include members of the army, police force and government officials. An extreme right-wing party, the National Liberation Movement (MLN) is also directly involved in the organizations. In 1966 it publicly called for the organization of armed groups of civilians to fight subversion. In December 1966 legislation was passed approving the commissioning of large landowners and their administrators as law enforcement agents authorized to bear arms.

Organized Violence

'I admit that the MLN is the party of organized violence. Organized violence is vigour, just as organized colour is scenery and organized sound is harmony. There is nothing wrong with organized violence; it is vigour, and the MLN is a vigorous movement.'

Official spokesman of the MLN in radio broadcast in Guatemala. Quoted in the Washington Post *22 February 1981.*

But reliable reports place the primary responsibility for the formation of these organizations with the US military attache in Guatemala City, Colonel John Webber. According to *Time* magazine in 1968 he had 'made no secret of the fact that it was his idea and at his instigation that the technique of counter-terror had been implemented by the Guatemalan army in the Zacapa and Izabal areas'. It is known that in 1968 the United States helped set up ORDEN, a similar paramilitary rural vigilante organization in El Salvador (see Part V).

Indeed, the promotion of such organizations by the US was not limited to these two countries. It was part of existing US military doctrine then practised and promoted wherever US mobile training teams were actively advising 'friendly' countries in counter-insurgency. This doctrine went by several names but most commonly was termed 'counter-terror' — i.e. the use of terrorism to fight 'terrorism'.

It was not long before the tortured, mutilated bodies of the victims of these organizations began to appear daily. Amnesty International estimates that up to 8,000 people died during Arana's campaign between 1966 and 1968. It was not without reason that he became known as 'the Butcher of Zacapa'.

The similarities between this campaign and United States operations in Vietnam are striking. The United States made no secret of the fact it was using Vietnam to develop and refine its techniques of counter-insurgency. General Maxwell Taylor told a Congressional Committee in 1963:

Here we have a going laboratory where we see subversive insurgency, the Ho Chi Minh doctrine, being applied in all its forms . . . On the military side . . . we have recognized the importance of the area as a laboratory. We have teams out there looking at the equipment requirements of this kind of guerrilla warfare . . . so even though not regularly assigned to Vietnam, they are carrying their experience back to their own organizations.

Some twenty-five American foreign service officials who previously served in Vietnam were assigned to the US embassy in Guatemala from 1964 to 1974. The campaign of rural terror has many parallels with 'Operation Phoenix', the rural pacification programme mounted in Vietnam in 1967 (see box, page 70).

As in that country, the Guatemalan army would frequently enter villages in search of arms, round up those peasants suspected of guerrilla sympathies and take them away to interrogation centres where the use of torture became a common practice.

Major Frederick Woerner, a combat veteran from Vietnam, headed the US civic action advisory staff in Guatemala from 1966 to 1968. Civic action he stated frankly: 'is a military weapon in counter-insurgency. I wish I could say that our main concern is in improving nutrition or in getting a better water system to the people. These are only by-products. The security of the country is our mission.'

The United States also introduced air power into the counter-insurgency operations in Guatemala, again a feature of its involvement in Vietnam. According to a leading Guatemalan newspaper editorial, B-26 bombers dropped napalm on areas, known as 'free zones', where guerrillas were active. The man in charge of training the Guatemalan air force for this purpose was Major Bernie Westfall who died in an air crash in September 1967 in the pilot's seat of a T-33 jet trainer, used for bombing guerrilla hideouts. The US government claimed he had been 'testing' the aircraft.

Countless civilians with little or no involvement in political activity

Operation Phoenix

Operation Phoenix was launched by the CIA in Vietnam in 1967. It was a campaign of terror and assassination aimed at 'neutralizing' leaders of the National Liberation Front (NLF) and terrorizing all those suspected of supporting its objectives. According to Wayne Cooper, a former Phoenix advisor, it was a 'unilateral American program', CIA operatives 'recruited, organized and supplied, and directly paid CT (counter-terror) teams . . . to use Viet Cong techniques of terror — assassination, kidnappings, and intimidations — against the VC leadership'. Between 1968 and 1972 a total of 26,369 South Vietnamese civilians were assassinated under the Phoenix programme, another 33,350 were imprisoned in US built 'Provincial Interrogation Centers' where most were tortured. Cooper claims that the majority of these people were non-communist nationalists not involved in the NLF. On 13 September 1974, William Colby, Director of the CIA, appeared at a conference on the CIA and covert activities on Capitol Hill.

Colby had supervised Operation Phoenix and he spoke of it at the conference: 'The Phoenix program was one part of the total pacification program of the government of Vietnam. There were several other parts: the development of local security forces in the neighbourhood to protect the villages; the distribution of a half a million weapons to the people of South Vietnam to use in unpaid self-defense groups . . . The Phoenix program was designed to bring some degree of order and regularity to a very unpleasant, nasty war that had preceded it. It did a variety of things to improve the procedures by which that was run. It provided procedures by which the identification of the leaders, rather than the followers, became the objective of the operation . . . over two and a half years of the Phoenix program there were 29,000 captured; there were 17,000 defected; and there were 20,500 killed, of which 87% of those killed were killed by regular and paramilitary forces and 12% by police and similar elements.'

died in these and other US-inspired anti-guerrilla operations, another parallel with South-East Asia.

In July 1970 Colonel Arana, the candidate of the MLN, became President of Guatemala. Other figures linked to right-wing terrorism, such as Mario Sandoval Alarcon of the MLN, rose to prominence with him. A 'state of siege' was declared in November 1970 and in the next six months at least 2,000 Guatemalans were murdered. According to Amnesty International over 15,000 people were listed as disappeared or dead between 1970 and 1973. The total number of deaths attributable to official and semi-official forces between 1966 and 1976 is

20,000. Most of the victims were trade unionists, students, journalists, social democrat politicians and especially peasants. The presidency of Arana marked a new stage in the violence: rather than a specific campaign to eliminate the guerrilla movement it was now an assault on the broad movement of democratic opposition to the government and the powerful economic interests behind it.

The Arana government received considerable support from the United States, and AID technicians even helped prepare an economic plan for the government prior to its election. The plan, financed by large inflows of foreign aid, abandoned all pretence at encouraging tax reforms and minor concessions to the poor and was based on economic expansion and growth within existing social structures.

Foreign investors were apparently unperturbed by the escalating brutality. Indeed, it could be said that at least one major foreign company benefited from it. Exploraciones y Explotaciones Mineras Izabal (EXMIBAL) is a company 80% owned by the International Nickel Company (INCO), another nominally Canadian corporation, and 20% by the Hanna Mining Company, based in Cleveland. In the 1960's EXMIBAL planned a considerable investment in Guatemala to develop the nickel deposits in the Izabal region, one of the centres of Arana's counter-insurgency campaign.

The company managed to gain extremely favourable concessions from the Guatemalan government, including a ten-year exemption from income tax and import duties. Its attempt to gain total exemption from foreign exchange controls sparked off such a movement of popular protest that the Arana government announced a review of the entire concession. While the review was taking place, leading critics of the EXMIBAL project were mysteriously assassinated, such as the lawyers Julio Camey-Herrera, who was shot in November 1970, and Adolfo Mijangos, who was gunned down in January 1971.

In February 1971 the Arana government completed an agreement with the company which ignored the recommendations of the academics, lawyers, labour and political leaders who wished Guatemala's nickel to be used for the benefit of the country. It is not surprising that a top executive in INCO's Wall Street office told a member of the North American Congress on Latin America (NACLA) in an interview in 1973: 'The military will continue to rule Guatemala for the foreseeable future . . . It is the only base of stability, really. It will rule even with a civilian government in power . . . the political prospects are good . . . one of the best prospects in terms of realism and pragmatism regarding foreign investment.'

Despite the intensity of the terror launched by Arana and his successors they did not succeed in suppressing the movement for change in Guatemala. The 1970s have, on the contrary, witnessed the growth, against enormous odds, of trade union and peasant organizations and the emergence of a more powerful and broadly-based guerrilla movement, a response to the closure of all peaceful channels for expressing discontent. The government, under the control of the military, and the oligarchy, whose interests it protects, have remained as ruthless as ever in their determination not to grant any concessions.

Thomas Melville, ex-Maryknoll priest and co-author of *Guatemala — Another Vietnam*, who was forced to flee Guatemala in 1968 because of his identification with the cause of revolutionary land reform, wrote a letter on his return to the United States to Senator William Fulbright. In it he warned that, 'if the United States government continues with its policy of believing that all national insurrections are manipulated by Moscow or Peking, then it is going to find itself in more than one Vietnam in Latin America'. Events in Central America today amply bear out his prediction.

The Nixon Doctrine

In late 1967 the United States' failing fortunes in Vietnam, dramatically underlined by the successful Tet offensive in February 1968, led to a basic reappraisal of its involvement in this and other theatres of conflict. The powerful Council on Foreign Relations played a key role in these deliberations. Cyrus Vance, one of the directors of the Council, explained the Council's thinking: 'We were weighing not only what was happening in Vietnam, but the social and political effects in the United States, the impact on the US economy, the attitude of other nations. The divisiveness in the country was growing with such acuteness that it was threatening to tear the US apart.'

Growing opposition at home together with the increasingly apparent military failure encouraged the Americans to consider ways of reducing their direct involvement in counter-insurgency wars while not abandoning their objectives. The new strategy emerged from a statement made by President Nixon in 1969: '. . . We shall furnish military and economic assistance when requested and as appropriate. But we shall look to the nation directly threatened to assume the primary responsibility of providing the manpower for its defence.'

The Military Assistance Program (MAP) doubled in the early Nixon years to enable local armies to cope with their new responsibility. But following the debacle in Vietnam, Congress was less willing to grant the ever increasing number of MAP requests and Nixon turned to arms sales as a means of fulfilling his commitments as military sales are less subject to congressional scrutiny. This also involved reversing the Johnson administration's decision to limit high technology military sales to Latin America and in 1973 the ban on these sales was lifted. United States arms sales to Latin America increased from an average of US$30 million a year in the 1960s to US$118 million in fiscal year 1974.

The new policy was partly aimed at building up mini-powers to police troubled regions on the Americans' behalf; in Latin America this role was to be played by Brazil. But the United States did not neglect the smaller countries. Central America and the Caribbean, which had previously been dependent on MAP grants, were now given licences to purchase arms and equipment, which they were quick to take advantage of. Although most of the equipment sold under the Foreign Military Sales programme consists of major combat systems for external defence it also includes, like MAP, counter-insurgency equipment for internal use as well as 'military technical services' such as training and technical assistance.

The Americans developed significant collaboration with Israel in these years. Under a 'memorandum of understanding' in November 1971 the United States agreed to provide technical and manufacturing assistance to Israel's arms industry. The objective was apparently to help Israel finance more of its own defence needs by developing an arms industry geared to the world market. Israel has subsequently become one of the main arms suppliers to Central America, in particular Nicaragua under Somoza, Guatemala and El Salvador.

The Nixon-Kissinger administration was also keen to replace the traditional Cold War strategies with more effective means of maintaining United States supremacy. Kissinger's realpolitik was aimed at preserving the balance of power through new diplomatic initiatives, shuttle diplomacy, rapprochement with China and the pursuit of detente. It included the maintenance of military strength and the development of new military options such as advanced capital-intensive military technology for lightning assaults on trouble spots round the world. It also included new low profile techniques, covert operations and methods of destabilizing 'unfriendly' regimes. In October 1970, for example, Henry Kissinger stated that the United States would give any backing 'short of a Dominican-style intervention' to the overthrow of Allende in Chile.

Particular attention was given to the development of repressive techniques of social control and what was described as 'preventive medicine': identifying signs of social unrest early enough to suppress them before a Vietnam-type situation could emerge. This approach corresponded to some of the conclusions reached by Nelson Rockefeller who Nixon had sent on a fact finding mission round Latin America in 1969. Rockefeller's report, the *Quality of Life in the*

Americas, criticised Johnson for being too soft on communism. He identified the rapid urbanization in Latin America, and the unemployment and alienation which accompanied it, as one of the major threats to stability in the region. He recommended authoritarian remedies: 'The question is less one of democracy or a lack of it than it is simply of orderly ways of getting along'.

Thus, the new counter-insurgency strategy stressed the maintenance of order in urban areas from where many of the tactics of rural insurgency were said to originate. The techniques of 'disappearance', torture and assassination employed by Arana in Guatemala were to be repeated elsewhere in Central and South America. Amnesty International wrote in its 1973 *Report on Torture*: 'One can state with some assurance that the practice (of torture) is both more widespread and more intense than it was fifteen years ago . . . it is not being used for the extraction of information alone. It is also used for the control of political dissent'.

As a result of this new emphasis private US corporations became increasingly responsible for supplying repressive equipment to Latin American and other foreign governments in the early 1970s. Arms sales took place either through government-to-government transactions under the Foreign Military Sales programme, or through direct deals with arms firms under the Commercial Sales programme; the latter frequently consisted of the small arms, riot gear and communications equipment used against civilians. Between 1973 and 1976 US private firms sold Latin American police forces 24,402 pistols and revolvers, 21,715 tear gas grenades, 3,002 gas guns and 3,072 cannisters of MACE, a chemical weapon used to incapacitate people. Other supplies more difficult to document include computers, bugging devices, truncheons and electric shock batons. Among the customers for this sort of equipment were the National Guard of Nicaragua, which was almost totally equipped by the United States, and the Palace Guard of Haiti, both renowned for their ruthlessness and brutality.

But beyond the crude and well-worn strategy of reinforcing the local armies' repressive capacities the Nixon-Kissinger administration never developed a coherent policy towards Central America and the Caribbean. In common with previous administrations it failed totally to appreciate the nature of the social changes taking place in the region — the emergence of a new middle and working class and their growing demands for access to political and economic power. The United States' neglect and ignorance of the region over the years and its failure to develop appropriate policies in response to changing circumstances was to have serious consequences for its future interests.

It was the Nixon-Kissinger administration which let slip almost the last opportunity to force the Central American oligarchies through peaceful means to share some of their economic and poltical power. In Guatemala in the early 1970's it tolerated the violent excesses of President Arana and his allies and the wave of repression during the electoral campaign from November 1973 to March 1974 aimed at preventing opposition headed by the Guatemalan Christian Democrat Party from winning the elections. The murder of about a dozen middle level leaders of the party, death threats and bomb attacks on the homes of the party leaders, and the subsequent electoral fraud went unchallenged by the United States. In Nicaragua in 1970, rather than give support to the anti-Somoza Liberals, Nixon appointed Turner Shelton as ambassador who arranged a Somoza-Conservative Party pact which assured the continuation of the Somoza regime. In El Salvador in 1972 the United States made no protest against the electoral fraud in that year which prevented the victory of the coalition of reformist parties headed by the Christian Democrat, Jose Napoleon Duarte, and subsequently opposed the attempt by Duarte and a group of constitutionalist officers to install the defrauded candidate. By refusing to back the potential or actual electoral gains of the reformist centre in Central America, the United States paved the way for its demise as a viable channel for political change and strengthened the revolutionary movements which demanded basic structural transformation.

Caribbean Sea or American Lake?

In 1972 Robert Crassweller wrote an influential book entitled *The Caribbean Community*, published by the Council on Foreign Relations. In it he wrote:

Power is intolerant of a vacuum. British influence and activity is now waning in the Caribbean; by some natural law of the international process, not so much by conscious design as by the nature of power itself, other influences, that of the dollar area and the United States in particular, is coming to replace it, thereby serving existing interests of the United States and creating new ones as well.

European colonization had left the Caribbean with few options for its future. Its economy and society had evolved around the European-owned sugar plantations, condemning it to an external dependence and economic specialization from which there were few easy avenues of escape. Similarly, class structure and racial differences were the legacy of the divisions and stratifications imposed by the Europeans. According to the Jamaican economist, Norman Girvan, the black slaves from Africa and, following the abolition of slavery, indentured workers from Asia brought in by the European plantation owners to cut sugar cane subsequently formed the basis of an independent peasantry and artisan class. The remnants of the white planter class, together with mulattoes and immigrants from the Middle East, formed a small commercial elite while political control fell increasingly to the few privileged blacks and mulattoes who had been granted the benefits of a European education.

The four major colonies of the English-speaking Caribbean became independent in the 1960s: Jamaica and Trinidad in 1962, Barbados and Guyana in 1966. As direct British control was withdrawn, these countries fell naturally under the more informal but no less pervasive influence of the United States. Bauxite, oil and tourism became the economic spearhead of America's penetration of the Commonwealth Caribbean.

Political independence coincided with the dramatic post-war expansion of United States multinational corporations who began to invest heavily in the mineral industries of the Caribbean. It was after the Second World War that Reynalds Metals, Kaiser Aluminium and Alcan discovered the large deposits of bauxite in Jamaica (as well as in Haiti and the Dominican Republic). The United States government provided much of the initial capital for them to start operations.

US Direct Investment in the Caribbean 1966-1976
(in millions of US dollars at year end)

Year	Barbados	Guyana	Trinidad and Tobago	Jamaica
1966	3	n.a.	207	163
1967	3	n.a.	217	204
1968	6	40	215	295
1969	6	40	185	392
1970	9	40	198	507
1971	12	35	262	618
1972	18	36	280	624
1973	20	—	433	618
1974	20	20	549	609
1975	19	22	656	654
1976	20	21	713	577

Source: *R.W. Palmer,* Caribbean Dependence on the United States Economy, *Praeger Special Studies, New York 1979.*

US Share of Caribbean Exports and Imports 1973-74

I: percentage of imports supplied by US
E: percentage of exports shipped to the US

	Jamaica		Guyana		Trinidad and Tobago		Barbados	
Year	I	E	I	E	I	E	I	E
1973	38.6	41.1	24.2	21.0	16.2	52.6	21.1	16.56
1974	35.3	47.8	25.7	27.5	10.6	60.8	19.3	27.05

Source: *R.W. Palmer,* Caribbean Dependence on the United States Economy, *Praeger Special Studies, New York 1979.*

Mineral exports were largely responsible for the rapid growth in US trade with the Caribbean in the 1950s and 1960s and the emergence of the United States as the major trading partner in the region. Until the 1950s over half of Jamaica's trade was with Britain and 50% of its export earnings came from sugar. By 1976 over half of Jamaica's exports went to the United States and bauxite accounted for 46% of export earnings. The United States is the major market for Caribbean bauxite. In 1977 Jamaica and Guyana together supplied 65% of the United States bauxite imports, while Haiti, Suriname and the Dominican Republic supplied a further 25%.

The mining of bauxite in the world is controlled by six multinational corporations. Norman Girvan has studied their activities in the Caribbean and shown the almost total lack of contributions made by the companies to the national economies they dominate.

Virtually all capital goods and equipment are imported and companies often provide their own services such as transport and electric power. The technology they use is capital-intensive and has created relatively few jobs. The US$300 million invested by the bauxite companies in Jamaica from 1950 to 1970 created only about 6,000 permanent jobs. The main contribution of the companies is in the form of royalties and taxes paid to the governments. But even these represent only a fraction of what the companies earn from their operations. Because the companies control the entire process of mining, refining and smelting the bauxite into aluminium, the ore is never sold on the open market but by the subsidiary to the parent company. By undervaluing the price of the ore the companies can keep their tax payments to the local government to a minimum, a mechanism known as transfer-pricing.

The real profits to be gained from bauxite mining lie in the process of smelting the ore into high value aluminium and subsequently turning it into semi-fabricated products to be used in industry. Most of this takes place in the United States and Canada and although plants to refine the ore into alumina (the stage prior to smelting into aluminium) were built in Jamaica, Guyana and Suriname in the 1950s and 1960s, the bulk of Caribbean bauxite production is exported without processing. In 1972 the region accounted for 38% of total world bauxite production but only 16% of alumina production and a mere 0.5% of primary aluminium production.

The Caribbean's 'red gold' has thus contributed very little to economic development in the Caribbean. It has helped neither to diversify the economies by forming the basis of local industry nor to improve the living standards of the populations of the region. Although Guyanese bauxite turned Alcan into the world's second largest aluminium company, the Guyanese economy stagnated: between 1940 and 1960 the average per capita income actually declined, by 1970 per capita income was only US$308 while unemployment affected an estimated 18% of the labour force.

In Jamaica bauxite production aggravated the acute problem of land shortage as the bauxite companies bought over 100,000 acres of land from local small farmers to secure control of the ore. This fuelled the process of rural migration to the cities and the neglect of agriculture and production of food for local consumption. Over half a million rural Jamaicans migrated to urban centres between 1943 and 1970. There they found few job opportunities despite an attempt in the 1950s and 1960s to apply Puerto Rico's Operation Bootstrap to the country. In Jamaica it was called 'industrialization by invitation'. The invitations were very tempting, including generous tax exemptions and an abundant supply of cheap labour. Between 1956 and 1968 the many firms who came to the country to set up assembly plants and light industries producing luxury items for the few Jamaicans who could afford them, provided only 13,000 jobs for a labour force which had increased by more than 100,000. By the late 1960s over half of all economic activity on the island was foreign-owned; mining was 100% in foreign hands; three-quarters of manufacturing and two-thirds of all financial institutions were owned by foreign, mostly American, companies.

The Caribbean basin also became important to the United States as an oil refining centre, although Trinidad and Tobago is the only significant oil producing country of those under study here. The basin is ideally located between the main oil producing areas of the Middle East, North Africa and Venezuela and North America. Refining underwent a major expansion in the post-war period. The original impetus was the European market but in 1948 the United States became a net importer of oil for the first time and by the 1970s had become the main market for refined oil from the Caribbean.

But as with bauxite production, oil refining has remained a modern enclave with few benefits for the local economy. In the Dutch Antilles oil refineries are responsible for 80% of all imports, 95% of all exports and only 8% of total employment.

Trinidad became the location of Texaco's largest refinery outside the United States. The American oil companies expanded their control over Trinidad's economy with the assistance of the pragmatic and studious politician, Eric Williams, who was Prime Minister of the country from 1956 until his death in 1981. The white planters and the commercial elite saw their influence decline as agriculture became less important to the economy. The black professional middle class which Williams's party, the People's National Movement, represented saw its power rise correspondingly. In the process it deliberately fomented racial tensions between the mostly rurally based Indian workers and the urban African industrial workers.

Williams emerged as a strong ally of foreign capital and continued a policy of promoting industrialization through incentives to foreign investors which had begun under British rule. In Trinidad, Operation Bootstrap was called 'Aid to Pioneer Industries' and the usual tax-free incentives and duty free imports were offered. By 1970 the achievements of this strategy were as minimal as elsewhere in the region. The US$257 million which had been invested created a mere 7,000 jobs while 20-25% of the workforce remained unemployed. The oil sector was the main recipient of investment and had come to dominate the economy. Social unrest grew and in 1970 exploded as workers and unemployed took to the streets to protest at the appalling social conditions and foreign domination of the economy. The United States sent in arms and stationed two warships offshore 'to protect its citizens'. They were not needed, as Williams was able to crush the revolt himself.

Williams announced a change in strategy. 'Aid to Pioneer Industries', he declared, 'is now a laughing stock even in Puerto Rico. Our goals in Trinidad, by contrast, are the highest levels of technological development based on hydrocarbons, leading to petrochemicals and steel. Our inspiration is the OPEC countries.'

In other words, it was a strategy based on oil money. In 1961 Amoco, a subsidiary of Standard Oil, began investing, unlike Texaco, in Trinidad's own crude oil reserves and soon came to dominate Trinidad's oil production. By 1976, following the rise in oil prices, 90% of US investment in Trinidad went into the petroleum industry. By 1974 oil was supplying 70% of government revenues compared with 20% in 1970, and by 1979 oil accounted for 90% of all exports, for which the major market was the United States. Today, a mere 14% of oil production is controlled by one state-owned and one state-partnered company; the private sector remains dominant with Amoco alone controlling 56% of oil output.

United States multinationals have become key partners in Williams's massive industrialization programme. A huge US$4 billion investment in an industrial park in Point Lisas is planned, which will become one of the biggest manufacturing complexes in the world. While Williams spends millions to develop roads, housing, water and other infrastructural services for the multinationals involved in the Point Lisas project, the mass of the population still lacks these essential services. Despite five boom years, some areas of Trinidad still have no water or electricity supply, poorly maintained roads and inadequate housing. Official unemployment stood at 12% in 1979, a problem which is unlikely to be solved by the sophisticated capital-intensive industries planned for Point Lisas.

The other major income earners of the main countries of the Commonwealth Caribbean are sugar, tourism and the export of people. Only in sugar does the United States not have a dominant position. Sugar exports from the region are still significant (some 54% of the total exports of Barbados, 50% for Guyana, 20% for Jamaica and 4% for Trinidad) but traditionally the United States has never been the major market. The sugar industry in the region is now in serious difficulties due to low productivity and fluctuating world market conditions. A number of Caribbean countries, especially the smaller ones such as Barbados, have come to see tourism as an alternative earner of foreign exchange.

The real expansion in United States tourism in the Caribbean occurred in the 1960s following the demise of Cuba as the playground of rich Americans. In Jamaica the volume of tourism more than doubled between 1964 and 1974. Foreign, mainly American, companies usually own the large, luxury hotels which, while fewer in number than the small, mostly locally-owned guest houses, account for over half the hotel capacity in Jamaica and Barbados. Much of the earnings from tourism are lost to the local economies through American penetration of the industry and the importation of food and consumer goods to cater for the tourists. However, it is still considered a major foreign exchange earner, and some of the small islands depend on it for over half their income.

Tourism, however, is a volatile industry, depending on economic conditions in the United States and such factors as the cost of air travel. A bad season can have a devastating effect. But it is the social impact of tourism which has come in for most criticism. The typical tourist to the Caribbean is a white, middle or upper class American,

who will spend his vacation in a luxury enclave ('the tourist plantation' as one Caribbean writer has described it) which contrasts strik-
ingly with the squalor in which most of the local population live.

In every respect the Caribbean islands are dependent on external
forces, having closer ties with the United States than with each other.
Their major exports are owned by American companies and decisions
affecting the lives of the people are made in US boardrooms. It is very
difficult for mechanisms of regional integration to function adequate-
ly in these conditions. In such circumstances, suspicions arise that
United States encouragement for regional institutions such as the
Caribbean Community and Common Market (CARICOM) which
replaced the Caribbean Free Trade Association (CARIFTA) in 1973 is
merely in order to provide large markets for American multinationals
rather than to promote regional development through planning and
controls on trade and investment.

It is difficult to identify any concrete benefits accruing to the people
of the region from their dependence on the United States. Poverty and
deprivation characterize the Caribbean islands as much as the Central
American isthmus. These mainly agricultural countries are increasingly dependent on food imports due to a US-inspired development
strategy which has encouraged rural populations to look to the cities
and promoted the interests of the large landowners producing cash
crops for export rather than the small peasant farmers producing for
local consumption. Ironically, such policies, which are designed to improve balance of payments problems, have exacerbated the drain on
foreign exchange earnings through food imports. In 1974 the import
of food represented around 7% of total imports in Trinidad and
Tobago, 13% in Guyana, 21% in Jamaica and 23% in Barbados; the
United States supplies one-third of the imports of the first three countries. The Caribbean is almost totally dependent on the United States
for wheat and corn.

An even more striking indictment of the development policies pursued is their failure to support the region's growing population. The
migration of people from the Caribbean in search of a future began in
the 1950s. While thousands of Puerto Ricans, victims of that
country's economic 'miracle', flooded into the United States, the majority of West Indians went to the United Kingdom. Britain encouraged the exodus as part of an implicit employment strategy at a time of
economic boom at home and to relieve the Caribbean of potential
social upheaval from its 'surplus' unemployed population.

In 1962 Britain banned West Indian immigration while the United
States Immigration Act of 1965 removed the national origins quota
and allowed West Indians into the country at a time of labour shortages in certain sectors of the American economy. Between 1962 and

Guyana's Police

'Along with the routine courses in police work American-style at the CIA-run International Police Academy, a number of Guyana's finest went to special training courses operated by the CIA's proprietary, the International Police Services Inc. (INPOLSE) out of a residential townhouse in Washington, D.C. At least one officer, Eustace V. Kendall, attended the Texas Border Patrol "technical course" in bombing, arson, and assassination. This Texas facility was so dirty that even the Department of Defense refused to staff the operation. Information so far available shows notable graduates of the Washington INPOLSE program to include Cecil "Skip" Roberts, present head of Guyana's Criminal Investigation Division and Norman McClean, now Chief of Staff of the Guyana Defence Force.'

Covert Action, *August-September 1980.*

1976 nearly a quarter of a million immigrants from Jamaica, Trinidad and Tobago, Guyana and Barbados were admitted to the United States, accounting for 6% of the population of those countries and 17% of the natural population increase during those years. Initially, the main demand for labour in the United States was for its expanding service sector and many of the migrants were skilled workers, including 7,700 people from the medical profession, creating serious local shortages. A second category of migrants has been young, unskilled workers and small farmers unable to survive on their tiny plots of land. Temporary migration has been the main safety valve for this category of migrants and they have provided United States agriculture, now a multi-billion dollar industry, with a steady flow of cheap labour.

Ten to fifteen thousand workers a year, mostly from Jamaica but some from the smaller islands of the Caribbean, migrate to the United States for periods ranging from one to nine months. Most head for the Florida sugar cane fields. Two-thirds of these workers are hired by three large corporations: the US Sugar Company, the Okeelanta Sugar Division of the Gulf and Western Food Products Company, and the Sugar Cane Growers Cooperative of Florida. The companies negotiate contracts with Caribbean governments through the British West Indies Central Labour Organization. They can virtually impose the conditions of contract; high unemployment, social tensions, economic stagnation and the desperate need for foreign exchange give the Caribbean governments little bargaining power and the workers concerned none at all. The contracts thus give no protection with respect to work conditions and workers can be sacked at the least sign of militancy. Today, West Indians join the tens of thousands of Puerto Ricans and illegal Mexicans (Mexicans are still subject to the quota system) who each year undertake gruelling, grossly underpaid labour for American agribusiness.

Finally, in assessing the United States' impact on this region, the records show that its economic penetration is inevitably associated with political manipulation of one sort or another. In 1971 Frank McDonald wrote in an essay on US relations with the West Indies:

American corporations and AID programs . . . represent only two sides of a triangular penetration of the Commonwealth Caribbean economy. The third side, without which the ease of this process would be severely threatened, is the organized 'Americanization' of the Caribbean trade union movement's role in Caribbean politics. With the sole exception of Trinidad, most major political parties are rooted in a labour union and the vast majority of premiers, prime ministers, and even leaders of the opposition are themselves trade unionists. Thus, the axiom holds that the politics or ideology of the trade union movement will affect the policies of the regional governments and that the more receptive Caribbean labour is to the presence of American investment and management patterns, the more so will be the regional politicians.

Infiltration of the labour movement has indeed been one of the most important techniques of American intervention in the Caribbean. It is mostly carried out through AIFLD which trains local labour leaders in the American style of trade unionism, requiring close collaboration between workers and management. But AIFLD has also acted as a channel for CIA activities. Just one example is the events which took place in Guyana in the early 1960s while it was still a British colony.

AIFLD participated in a CIA campaign to overthrow the government of Cheddi Jagan, considered by the Americans and British to be dangerously close to the Soviet bloc and apparently destined to lead the country to independence. AIFLD exploited racial tensions in the country between the pro-Jagan East Indians and the African workers who supported Jagan's opponent, Forbes Burnham, considered a more moderate, pragmatic socialist. This campaign led to a series of strikes and outbreaks of racial violence from 1962 to 1964 which finally brought down the Jagan government, enabling the British to call new elections which were rigged to ensure Jagan's defeat. The way was clear for independence under Forbes Burnham in 1966. The London *Sunday Times* commented that Jagan's ouster was 'relatively inexpensive for the CIA and accomplished with around US$250,000. The price for Guyana was 170 dead and hundreds wounded, £10 million worth of damage to the economy and a legacy of racial bitterness.' The Office of Public Safety of USAID followed up the CIA's achievements in Guyana by supplying generous amounts of aid and equipment to the Guyanese police force, 921 of whom received US training between 1966 and 1970.

Modernization US-Style

In the 1970s the United States tightened and extended its economic stranglehold over its traditional dependencies in Central America. This was part of a so-called strategy of 'modernization'.

The banana companies were the first to 'modernize'. United Fruit had been under pressure to modify its operations since the 1950s. Its direct involvement in the 1954 coup to overthrow Arbenz in Guatemala had discredited it considerably. In 1958 an anti-trust ruling in the United States found it guilty of monopolizing the banana trade and it was ordered to sell off 10% of its banana operations; at the time it controlled 75% of the world banana trade. Then, in the 1960s, it lost its holdings in Cuba, an event which raised again the fearful spectre of nationalization.

In the 1960s United Fruit began diversifying its holdings, though still in the area of food production. It took advantage of the Central American Common Market to produce oil and margarine for the regional market and it began to sell off some of its land. Land was sold to middle and upper class local landowners who were called 'associate producers'; they sold their entire output to United Fruit which still controlled marketing and distribution but had reduced the risks of nationalization. In addition, as the chairman of the company pointed out in 1962: 'By encouraging nationals to enter the banana industry we do not only contribute to the development of stable conditions in the tropics — and the creation of a growing middle class — but also gain partners who will be valuable allies in developing our own interests . . .'

In the late 1960s United Fruit began to face competition in the banana trade. In 1968 Del Monte entered the business and in 1972 bought up United Fruit's Guatemalan plantations and some of its lands in Costa Rica. The sale had originally been opposed by the Arana government in Guatemala, but Del Monte hired a right-wing Cuban-born Guatemalan businessman, who, with US$5 million, managed to change the government's mind. Another competitor in the banana industry expanded its interests in these years: the Standard Fruit and Steamship Company, which overtook the other companies in terms of market share. United Fruit meanwhile amalgamated with another company in 1970 and became United Brands. Together, these three companies own over 135,000 hectares of the best land in Central America and control 70% of the banana trade, worth over US$2.6 billion.

While the banana companies rationalized and reorganized their operations there were other changes in American investment strategy in the 1970s which corresponded to the gradual demise of the Central American Common Market. Further expansion of that market would require reforms and some redistribution of income. Yet there was still an alternative which would avoid the political implications of such a strategy. It involved the encouragement of new exports aimed at the world market rather than the restricted regional one. *Business Latin America* summed up the new approach in 1970:

It seems to be a pattern that whenever the problems of operating in the . . . CACM mount to a point where companies begin to think the game is not worth the candle, something happens to provide a new lure to investors. The latest siren song in CACM is a jumbo loan package amounting to about $140 million ($30 million from ROCAP) which will be available over the next three years to companies going into non-traditional exports, particularly in agribusiness, or into tourism.

It was the sunbelt economic interests of Texas, Florida and Southern California rather than the Wall Street financial groups which took particular interest in the new strategy. These interests had first begun to expand their economic influence in Central America after the overthrow of Arbenz in Guatemala. They had helped construct a powerful right-wing lobby in Washington in support of 'liberated' Guatemala. A number of the people involved in this lobby were close associates of President Nixon and were subsequently involved in Watergate and other scandals of the Nixon era: men such as Patrick Hillings and Senator George Smathers.

Close relations developed between right-wing Guatemalan and American businessmen and political figures. According to NACLA, in 1971 Governor Wallace of Alabama invited Arana on a visit to discuss their 'mutual problems of being misunderstood on the question of law and order'. The visit was eventually cancelled due to objections from the State Department, but meetings did take place between Arana and Vice-President Spiro Agnew in 1970. In addition unusual economic and political partnerships emerged in Central America in the early 1970s between the fugitive financier Robert Vesco and President Figueres in Costa Rica, and millionaire Nixon-supporter Howard Hughes and President Somoza in Nicaragua. Another connection is that between fanatically anti-communist Cuban exiles, many of whom participated in the Bay of Pigs invasion, and the sunbelt business com-

Multinational corporations (MNC) in Central America and the number of firms by country of origin and host country, 1976-80

	USA		Holland		Britain		Japan		West Germany		Canada- USA		France		Switzerland		Luxembourg		Belgium- Luxembourg	
	MNC	Subs.	MNC	Subs.	MNC	Subs.	MNC	Subs.	MNC	Subs.	MNC	Subs.	MNC	Subs.	MNC	Subs.	MNC	Subs.	MNC	Subs.
Guatemala	101	159	3	7	4	4	4	4	7	7	4	4	1	1	1	1	—	—	—	—
El Salvador	36	40	3	8	3	3	5	6	5	6	2	2	1	1	—	—	—	—	—	—
Honduras	23	60	2	4	1	1	1	1	—	—	4	4	—	—	—	—	1	1	1	1
Nicaragua	63	70	3	5	5	5	1	1	2	2	3	4	2	2	2	2	1	2	1	2
Costa Rica	143	175	3	5	6	6	4	5	1	1	2	2	2	2	—	—	—	—	—	—
% of firms by country of origin	82.1		4.8		3.0		2.8		2.6		2.6		1.0		0.5				0.5	

Source: *Donald Castillo Rivas, Acumulacion de Capital y Empresas Transnacionales en Centroamerica, Siglo XXI, Mexico 1980.*

US Direct Investment in Central America by Sector
(in millions of US dollars year ending 1979)

Sector	US investment
Mining and smelting	24
Petroleum	72
Transport, communication and public utilities	75
Trade	102
Finance and Insurance	56
Manufacturing	304
Other sectors	262
Total	895*

Source: *US Department of Commerce,* Survey of Current Business.
*Compares with CEPAL estimates of US$501m in 1967 and US$704m in 1975.

Direct accumulated investment by OECD countries in Central America
(in millions of US dollars at year end)

	Amount		Percentage	
	1967	**1975**	**1967**	**1975**
Costa Rica	136	250	22.6	26.0
El Salvador	77	130	12.8	13.5
Guatemala	146	260	24.3	27.1
Honduras	169	230	28.1	24.0
Nicaragua	73	90	12.2	9.4
Total	601	960	100.0	100.0

Source: *Donald Castillo Rivas,* Acumulacion de Capital y Empresas Transnacionales en Centroamerica, *Siglo XXI, Mexico 1980.*

US Share of Total Central America Exports and Imports

I: percentage of imports supplied by US
E: percentage of exports shipped to the US

| | El Salvador | | Guatemala | | Honduras | | Nicaragua | |
Year	I	E	I	E	I	E	I	E
1973	29	33	32	34	40	56	34	34
1974	31	25	32	33	40	47	32	19
1975	31	27	34	23	42	52	32	28
1976	29	33	36	35	44	56	31	31
1977	29	32	39	33	43	49	29	24
1978	31	15	30	29	not available		33	23

Source: South, *15 March-April 1981*.

munity. Nixon's close friend Bebe Rebozo had many business deals with the Cuban exiles, a number of whom emerged as entrepreneurs in Central America or as managers of American companies in the region. The participation of Cuban Bay of Pigs veterans in the Watergate break-in and many CIA-sponsored clandestine operations is well known; in Cuba these activities have earned them the name *'gusanos'* (worms).

Export promotion and diversification were the cornerstone of the new strategy. American cattle investors began penetrating the cattle industry throughout Central America, particularly in Costa Rica, and Texas ranchers came to own large estates as beef exports increased. In the early 1970s the list of non-traditional exports also grew to include fruit, vegetables and seafood aimed at a single market, the United States. Encouraged by loans and grants from international lending agencies such as the World Bank and AID, those who have benefited most from this growth have frequently been the ones least in need — large-scale local producers and agri-business multinationals. In addition to their involvement in production and processing, the latter also have a firm grip on the marketing and distribution of the produce.

The Latin American Agribusiness Development Corporation (LAAD) is the main source of capital for non-traditional export industries in the region. Its principal founder is the Bank of America but it includes thirteen of the largest American agribusiness corporations. The Bank of America is a powerful institution in the region and in particular in Guatemala where it is the major source of agricultural capital. It is the only corporate member of *Amigos del Pais*, a right-

Comparison of Average Hourly Wages in the United States and El Salvador, 1977
(in US dollars)

Country	Mechanics	Electricians	Unskilled
El Salvador	between 0.41 and 0.86	between 0.58 and 0.86	between 0.31 and 0.58
United States	over 7.50	over 8.00	between 3.10 and 5.80

Source: *Donald Castillo Rivas,* Acumulacion de Capital y Empresas Transnacionales en Centroamerica, *Siglo XXI, Mexico 1980.*

wing Guatemalan business group (see page 175).

In the mid-1970s Central America began to attract 'offshore' light assembly industries geared to the export or re-export of manufactured goods from tax-exempt industrial zones. Low labour costs and generous government incentives made it cheaper for American companies to transport goods to Central America for elaboration and re-export to the United States than to pay the high wages at home. Costa Rica and El Salvador until 1980 were the most favoured countries for these investments. Despite these investments however, few jobs were created, and as the industries which were established usually concentrated on one productive process, they have done little to stimulate other areas of the local economy.

By 1978 60% of Central America's exports still came from coffee, cotton and bananas but the contribution of non-traditional exports such as beef, sugar, light manufactures and fruit and vegetables had grown considerably. However, despite such diversification, the region's dependence on the United States has increased rather than diminished, both in terms of the market for its products and the expansion of American agribusiness and other multinationals into new areas of the economy.

Twentieth Century Slavery

Haiti, the poorest nation in the Western Hemisphere, is another country where the United States has attempted to apply its strategy of 'modernization'.

The United States had pinned a lot of hopes on the accession to power of Jean Claude Duvalier following the death of his father François Duvalier in 1971, known to the world as Papa Doc. Papa Doc had come to power in 1957 with the help of the American-trained army. In the early years of his tyrannical rule he had used Haiti's close proximity to Cuba to secure considerable amounts of US military aid which were to be used to modernize the army. However Duvalier channelled it into his own private security force, the *'tonton macoutes'*, over which the United States had no control. Duvalier's son Baby Doc was reputed to have closer connections with the more modernizing branch of the ruling elite and to be more warmly disposed toward the United States. In late 1970 the Nixon administration lifted the ban imposed by Kennedy in 1962 on the sale of arms and equipment to Haiti and between 1971 and 1976 Haiti received over US$4 million in military arms and training. A new elite corps, the Leopards, was created at Washington's instigation to fight against 'guerrillas, invaders and Communist subversion'. The Leopards were trained and equipped by former marines, employed by a Miami-based front company, Aerotrade.

This attempt to reassert United States military influence in the country was followed by renewed economic penetration. The United States controls four out of Haiti's five main exports: sugar, bauxite, sisal and light manufactures, only coffee is owned locally, but it remains dependent on the American market. Between 1970 and 1976 American companies installed 230 new industrial plants in the country attracted by the exceptionally cheap labour. By 1978 United States investment in Haiti was estimated at US$60 million, three times what it was in 1975. The official minimum wage in Haiti is just over one dollar a day, while at least 70% of the population is unemployed. It is hardly surprising that with this incentive the so-called runaway industries which had first moved from the United States to Puerto Rico and from there to the Dominican Republic now began to set up shop in Haiti. The number of jobs provided by the late 1970s have had only a marginal impact on the appalling level of unemployment.

The United States has also considered plans to modernize the agricultural sector in Haiti. Approximately 76% of the population live in rural areas where 1% of Haiti's population own 60% of the land. A 1976 World Bank report on economic prospects for Haiti suggested plans to 'develop' the countryside through infrastructural projects which would help open it up to big business:

With the completion of the northern and southern routes and reconstruction of irrigation systems, it should become possible to establish agro-industries to service export and domestic markets. A private industrial group envisages construction of a vegetable and fruit canning plant in the southwest of Haiti to supply Port-au-Prince. It should also be possible to export canned fruits and

Big Business

'Almost all the baseballs used in the United States, including those of the major leagues, now come from Haiti . . . Haiti has a monopoly not because of any special skill or resources. The monopoly is there because of cheap labour . . . Tomar Industries, one of several American companies that put baseballs together in Haiti, pays its workers 38 cents for every dozen baseballs sewn. The average girl can sew 3½ to 4 dozen baseballs a day. That's $1.33 to $1.52 a day. Baseballs are sewn in Haiti because of desperation . . .

The sewing of clothing from American textiles is the largest assembly industry in Haiti. Baseballs are next. In third place is the assembly of transformers and other electronic equipment.'

Los Angeles Times, *8 July 1974.*

'All right, so I punched him a couple of times. No big deal. He's my worker and it's my factory. If you wanta get some work out of a Haitian, you gotta *step* on him — not literally, of course, *but step on* him. Anyway, the next day there's a headline in the paper: "Foreign Industrialist Beats Local Peasant." Do I need that kinda crap? Hell, no! And I'll tell you something else I don't need: all those goddamn chicken feet they keep hanging on my door. Not that it bothers me; I just don't need it, is all. I mean, I'm in *electronics*!'

Harpers Magazine, *February 1976*

vegetables to the US and possibly to the Jamaican market.

However the United States' plans have been thwarted by the continued power of the Haitian feudal oligarchy, known as the dinosaurs, who have resisted the introduction of large-scale production of this sort in the countryside. Despite brief periods of liberalization the power of the dinosaurs has not been broken and Jean Claude's own position towards agribusiness remains ambivalent. Under his rule the extreme corruption of the Duvalier dynasty has continued, with an estimated 20-40% of the government's income going directly into the family coffers. External assistance on which the poverty stricken country relies is frequently diverted into the pockets of the ruling elite. Waves of repression carried out by the still powerful *tonton macoutes* continue to terrorize the population.

In Haiti today half of all children die before they reach the age of five, a child of two is called in creole *'youn ti chape'* (a little escapee

Haitian Reality

'For the reality of Haiti today is the mountains of American semi-luxury goods dumped in Port-au-Prince and hawked around the streets by ragged peasant women. It is the insult of American dollars and coins always being preferred over the local currency in any commercial exchange. It is the obsequiousness to rich American tourists by Haitians whose women long for light-skinned children. It is the shady-looking American wheeler-dealers who flip chips across the green felt tables of the casino in Port-au-Prince alongside Duvalierist self-made millionaires and members of the light-skinned mulatto élite during visits to Haiti to prove the chances of exploiting Haiti's massive body of readily and above all cheaply bought unemployed by setting up business for which the government has guaranteed that there will be no strikes. It is the US naval base at Guantanamo 50 miles away across the sea. It is the giant US aircraft carrier which "coincidentally" appeared in the bay off Port-au-Prince as a warning on the day Papa Doc's death was announced. It is US ambassador Clinton Knox, a fervent admirer of the Duvalier family, arranging and guiding events up at the presidential palace in the middle of the night when Papa Doc's son Jean-Claude was sworn into office on the old dictator's death. It is Andrew Tangalos, the commercial attaché at the US embassy who a few months ago ended his term by extracting a personal 15-year concession from the government to build another casino in Port-au-Prince, to enable the well-heeled members of the élite he came to know during his stay to continue to fritter away the country's resources to the profit of foreigners.'

Greg Chamberlain, 'Patterns of Crisis', Latin America Review of Books, *London 1973.*

' "Without Duvalier, the whole structure would collapse", says a United States businessman. And without United States support, Mr Duvalier could not remain in power. He serves United States interests well by preserving stability in his strategically situated country. To Haiti's south lies South America, a rapidly growing market and a rich preserve of vital minerals; eastward is the Dominican Republic, with huge corporate investments; to the west lies Cuba, a persistent threat to United States business interests in Latin America (New York bankers are as terrified of socialism as Haitian farmers are of Baron Samedi).

Washington is content to retain Mr Duvalier, for he takes no nonsense from his starving peasants, and selfishly binds his Government to Washington. His reward takes three forms: military support,

> food aid, financial assistance. For fiscal year 1981, the Pentagon has offered Haiti $300 million in military sales credits and $199 million for military training. Last July, the Agriculture Department agreed to provide Haiti with $9 million worth of wheat, rice, soybeans, and cottonseed oil. In 1980, the United States gave Haiti $2 million for hurricane relief and $10 million for development projects. An anthropologist involved in development work estimated that only 10 percent of an aid project's funds reached their target — the rest wound up in personal accounts, according to a *Christian Science Monitor* article.'
>
> George G. Cotter, 'Haiti Under Duvalier II: It is the Same Situation', New York Times, *March 7 1981.*

from death). Life expectancy is only 53 years, 96% of the population is illiterate and per capita income is a mere US$260 a year. An estimated 0.8% of the population receives 43% of the national income while 61% of Haitians subsist on an average of US$60 a year.

Every year the Duvalier regime exports 15,000 Haitian workers to harvest sugar on plantations in neighbouring Dominican Republic. According to one estimate, in 1979 it received US$1.6 million from the Dominican government for 'recruitment costs'. Apart from this contracted labour, an estimated 285,000 Haitians cross the border illegally every year to work on the plantations. Dominican soldiers and immigration officials lie in wait for the migrants and deliver them for a fee of US$11 a head to local landowners. These Haitian labourers receive approximately half the wage of the Dominicans and are controlled by Haitian government 'supervisors' closely linked to the *tonton macoutes*. This twentieth century slave trade has attracted little international attention.

Thousands of Haitians have tried to leave the island to escape repression and starvation. More than 21,000 have risked their lives since 1972, making the sea voyage in small leaky boats to the Bahamas or the United States. An estimated 8,000 Haitians survived the sea voyage to the United States between 1972 and 1980; in 1981 the exodus of Haitians increased still further, and the United States has become increasingly concerned. The Carter administration classified the Haitian 'boat people' as economic refugees as this makes it easier to exclude them from the United States than if they were given the legal rights and guarantees of political refugees, although there is ample evidence of the torture, imprisonment or even death which could await them in Haiti. The United States embassy in Port-au-Prince has

93

estimated that if the United States relaxed its immigration laws a million Haitians — one-fifth of the population — would flee to the United States.

Wherever the Haitians go it seems they face degradation, exploitation and misery. The deep involvement of the United States in their country since the beginning of the century has done little to alleviate their condition; the main concern of the United States has been Haiti's strategic position rather than the needs of its people. In this context American strategies for economic modernization and the occasional expression of concern at human rights violations seem particularly inappropriate. While Haiti's oppressive social structure remains intact, 'modernization' for the majority of Haitians will simply mean a new form of exploitation.

Bauxite Battles and Banana Wars

In the early 1970s American corporations faced a growing challenge from the region they had dominated so unquestioningly for decades.

In Guyana in 1971, Forbes Burnham, hitherto looked upon as an ally of the West, proclaimed a 'cooperative republic', a term deliberately selected to distinguish it from the brand of Marxism espoused by his rival, Cheddi Jagan. The scheme was partly an attempt to reinforce Burnham's support among the black middle class by expanding the state sector to provide them with employment. It included the adoption of an anti-imperialist posture and the nationalization of a number of key foreign owned enterprises so that the state came to control 80% of the economy.

The nationalizations began in 1971 with the Demerara Bauxite Company (DEMBA), a subsidiary of Alcan Aluminium, to be followed in 1975 by the smaller bauxite holdings of Reynalds Aluminium and in 1976 by the sugar investments of the British multinational, Booker McConnell.

The nationalization of DEMBA was heralded by Caribbean nationalists as a major step forward in the struggle against foreign economic domination. But it also contained lessons of another kind: namely, the ability of powerful multinationals to minimize the effect of such expropriations on their global operations.

Alcan had in fact been shifting away from Guyana as its major bauxite supplier since the 1950s. Guyana's surface deposits had been gradually depleted and more accessible large deposits became available first in Jamaica and in the 1970s in Guinea and Australia. The company had also become increasingly nervous at the political situation and racial violence in Guyana. Nevertheless, Alcan was determined to secure a favourable compensation settlement and the United States government readily gave its support. In June 1971 for instance the United States abstained from voting on a Guyanese application to the World Bank for a sea defence loan, explaining that 'The World Bank has a long-established policy of not lending to countries that have expropriated foreign investments unless there is evidence that satisfactory progress is being made toward settlement of the expropriation dispute . . .' Eventually the Burnham government agreed to pay a compensation higher than the book value of the companies' assets. Alcan, the US State Department and the World Bank all expressed satisfaction at the settlement. After all, the aluminium multinationals still controlled the industry as a whole.

In 1973 the OPEC offensive encouraged Jamaica to take action against the bauxite companies. While on the one hand it had shown the potential strength of joint action by exporting nations, on the other it tripled the country's oil import bill.

Jamaica earned 64% of its export income from bauxite and alumina, and only 20% from sugar and bananas. The industry — including mining, processing and transportation — was owned by six United States and Canadian aluminium corporations; they also owned 13% of Jamaican land. Jamaica received only 2% of the final value of the aluminium on the world market thanks to the mechanism of transfer-pricing described earlier which enabled the companies to keep their tax payments to a minimum.

In 1974 a negotiating team made up of the country's wealthiest businessmen, who in no way sought a radical confrontation with the companies, demanded an increase in government revenues from bauxite and alumina and at least a 51% share in the companies' operations. When the companies refused the government imposed a 7½% production levy on all bauxite. In March of that year the International Bauxite Association was established linking the major bauxite producers.

The companies, anxious to avoid full expropriation at a time when Jamaican bauxite was still crucial to the aluminium industry, capitulated after a short struggle. They agreed to sell 51% of their mining assets and lands at the market price. Jamaica in return guaranteed a forty-year supply of bauxite. Jamaica increased its income six-fold while the companies merely passed the tax and more onto the consumer and maintained their profit margins. They retained key management roles in the local bauxite companies and their dominance in technology, capital and market control ensured that they had lost little while gaining a certain degree of security against total nationalization. At the same time they began to transfer their operations to other countries, especially Australia, Guinea and Brazil.

Third World nationalism and producer cartels were viewed with particular alarm by the United States as they represented a serious potential threat to supplies of essential raw materials. In Jamaica this threat was intensified by the election in 1972 of a progressive government which challenged US interests in a number of other ways. In late 1974 Michael Manley's People's National Party (PNP) announced its commitment to 'democratic socialism'. It was a response to the growing demands for social change in the country. The Manley government began to pursue strategies involving public works to provide jobs for the increasing number of unemployed, the nationalization of public utilities, transport and manufacturing enterprises and the establishment of agricultural cooperatives. In foreign policy Jamaica adopted a policy of non-alignment and began to develop close ties with Cuba.

The alarm of the United States was matched by that of local business interests who had supported the bauxite levy but wanted to see the proceeds benefiting them rather than being used to raise the living standards of the poor. They allied with the United States government and the bauxite companies in a tacit agreement to oust the PNP. The methods used had only recently been tested against the socialist government of Allende in Chile. They included political destabilization and economic sabotage.

In 1975, following the introduction of the bauxite levy, the aluminium companies cut back production of bauxite and alumina and reduced their imports by a third. The official reason was the world-wide recession, but the companies had doubled their imports from Guinea at the same time. The number of strikes in the industry rose four times from 1974 to 1976 which many observers attributed to deliberate provocation of the workforce by the companies, aimed at disrupting the island's economy. United States investment in the country came to a virtual standstill while US government assistance dropped from US$13.2 million in 1974 to US$2.2 million in 1976. USAID refused a request for a US$2.5 million food grant in 1975. Henry Kissinger visited the country in 1975 for a 'holiday'. He is reported to have offered to resume aid if Manley refused to support the MPLA in Angola and broke off relations with Cuba.

The *New York Times* and *Newsweek* began to print articles suggesting that Jamaica was moving towards communism and was a dangerous and unstable place to visit. Locally, the *Daily Gleaner* played a similar role to the right-wing *El Mercurio* under Allende in Chile, and repeated these allegations and other scares about the government. The number of tourists visiting Jamaica dropped 23% between 1974 and 1976. Local businesses cut back production or closed down; it was estimated that J$200 million had been smuggled out of the country between 1975 and 1976.

The opposition Jamaican Labour Party (JLP) led by Edward Seaga, who represented the business, financial and landowning class in Jamaica, became a major vehicle for the political destabilization of Manley's government. Seaga had close links with the United States. The party's affiliate in Miami, the Jamaica Freedom League, played an important role in the US campaign against the government. Within Jamaica the party was directly involved in the violence which escalated in the country just before the 1976 election. In June 1976 Herb Rose, a top JLP official, resigned from the party accusing it of using violence and arson to gain power. In the same month a JLP parliamentary candidate, Peter Whittingham was arrested on suspicion of involvement in the political violence. Handwritten documents were found in his briefcase which referred to the operations of a secret paramilitary organization called 'Werewolf', it was described as a 'militant underground movement . . . willing to take up arms against the communist regime and purge them from our shores'. In September 1976 Philip Agee, a former CIA agent in Latin America, identified a CIA team of seven officers and four collaborators working under cover in the US embassy in Kingston. A few days later three of those named left the island.

Manley won the election despite what his government had officially recognized as a systematic destabilization campaign to stop him. But the country was in a state of economic bankruptcy through loss of earnings due to the cut backs of the bauxite companies and a drop in world sugar prices, together with the flight of capital and inability to raise international loans. Manley's victory over the bauxite companies seemed a Pyrrhic one, and would not prove long-lived.

Until the 1970s the banana companies in Central America had had more trouble from labour than from governments. Indeed the governments had been very cooperative towards the companies and particularly so during their labour disputes. The Guatemalan army even maintained a post in the middle of Del Monte's plantations and AIFLD was given free access to plantation workers whom they attempted to train in US labour practices. They were not always successful: in 1975 18,000 workers on the United Brands plantations in Honduras voted to oust their pro-US leadership.

But a more serious challenge emerged in the 1970s from the wave of Third World nationalism. In 1972 the major banana exporting countries of Guatemala, Costa Rica, Panama, Honduras, Nicaragua, Colombia and Ecuador proposed a producers' cartel, the Union of Banana Exporting Countries (UPEB). The world market price for bananas had changed little for the past twenty years while the cost of manufactured goods had rocketed. The countries concerned received only 11.5 cents from every dollar of bananas sold by the companies.

In 1974 UPEB proposed a one dollar tax on each box of bananas exported.

The might of the three giant multinationals who control the industry was mobilized against the exporting nations. Standard Fruit cut back production in Honduras and Costa Rica and destroyed 145,000 boxes of bananas rather than pay the tax. It was also alleged to have plotted to assassinate General Omar Torrijos of Panama, one of the most militant advocates of the tax. In Guatemala right-wing allies of Del Monte blocked attempts to pass the tax amidst allegations of bribery. When the tax was finally passed the company avoided paying it by declaring very low export figures. In Panama the government was forced to reduce the tax to 35 cents a box.

In Honduras, both United Brands and Standard Fruit felt threatened by the government of Lopez Arellano who came to power after a coup in 1972 and who not only supported the tax but also talked about agrarian reform as a means of modernizing the economy. At the same time the companies were having to deal with increased labour unrest and militancy. In 1975 United Brands offered Lopez Arellano US$1.5 plotted to assassinate General Omar Torrijos of Panama, one of the million in return for lowering the export tax and it was dropped to 25 cents. When an American investigation team discovered the bribe it was used by the army as an excuse to overthrow the government and another army officer, Melgar Castro, took power in December 1976. The senior legal advisor to the new government was the head of the law firm representing Standard Fruit and United Brands in Honduras. The new government was very helpful with respect to the companies' labour problems: in March 1977 the army arrested and tortured 200 of the most militant union leaders and a new union leadership was installed.

The banana companies emerged unscathed from the banana war. Only one country, Panama, imposed the full tax while Nicaragua decided not even to join UPEB. Where a lower tax was introduced it had no effect on the companies' profits as they simply raised the price of a box of bananas to the consumer. The companies have thus maintained their economic position in Central America, and although there has been an increase in the use of associate local producers to avoid the risks of nationalization, most notably by Del Monte in Costa Rica, the control of marketing and distribution ensures their continued domination of the banana industry.

PART 3
The Eagle Retrenches

WINTER 1974-75, No. 6

Trialogue

A Bulletin of North American · European · Japanese Affairs

COMMISSION RECOMMENDS COOPERATION WITH OIL-EXPORTERS, PROPOSES NEW AID AGENCY, CONSULTS WITH FORD AND KISSINGER

"The international system is undergoing a drastic transformation through a number of crises. Worldwide inflation reflects, transmits and magnifies the tensions of many societies, while the difficulties produced by the abrupt change in oil prices are accompanied by the entry of major new participants onto the world scene.

"Confrontation in an attempt to maintain the under-lying assumptions of the old system could lead to a general breakdown. On the other hand, creative policies to adapt it to the new partners and conditions could extend the area of effective cooperation more widely than ever before. Such cooperation must be based on the principle of equality. This is the core of any future political understanding."

Members of the Executive Committee meeting with President Ford about Trilateral Commission recommendations. From the President's left, they are as follows: David Rockefeller, Chairman, The Chase Manhattan Bank, N.A.; Zbigniew Brzezinski, Director, The Trilateral Commission; Robert W. Bonner, Q.C., Bonner & Fookes, Vancouver; Tadashi Yamamoto, Japanese Secretary of The Trilateral Commission; George S. Franklin, North American Secretary, The Trilateral Commission; François Duchêne, European Deputy Chairman, The Trilateral Commission; Karuzshige Harasawa, Radio-TV news commentator, Japan Broadcasting Inc.; Harold Brown, President, California Institute of Technology; Chujiro Fujino, President, Mitsubishi Corporation; Cesare Merlini, Director, Italian Institute for International Affairs; Gerard C. Smith, North American Chairman, The Trilateral Commission; Mary T. W. Robinson, Member of the Senate of the Irish Republic; Umberto Colombo, Director of the Committee for Scientific Policy, OECD; Jean-Luc Pepin, P.C., President, interimco, Ltd.; Georges Berthoin, former Chief Representative of the Commission of the European Community to the U.K.; Max Kohnstamm, European Chairman, The Trilateral Commission; Nobuhiko Ushiba, former Ambassador of Japan to the United States; Marc Eyskens, Commissary General of the Catholic University of Louvain; Elliot L. Richardson, Fellow, Woodrow Wilson International Center for Scholars, Smithsonian Institution; Otto Grieg Tidemand, former Norwegian Minister of Defense and Minister of Economic Affairs; Lord Patrick Gordon Walker, former British Foreign Secretary.

Published by: **THE TRILATERAL COMMISSION (N.A.)** *GERARD C. SMITH/GEORGE S. FRANKLIN/CHARLES B. HECK*
Chairman   Secretary   Editor

Contents

1971	Nixon suspends convertibility of dollar into gold and imposes surcharge on imports into the US
1973	US recognizes defeat in Vietnam
	OPEC oil embargo and price increases
	Trilateral Commission is founded
1974	Nixon resigns following Watergate scandal
	Grenada becomes independent
1975	Harkin Amendment links US economic aid to recipients' human rights record
1976	Congressional hearings on human rights in Nicaragua, Guatemala and El Salvador
	Carter elected President
	Manley re-elected in Jamaica
1977	Guatemala and El Salvador reject US military aid with human rights strings
	Jamaica seeks help from IMF
	Panama Canal Treaty signed
1978	Civil war breaks out in Nicaragua
	Dominica becomes independent
1979	Maurice Bishop's New Jewel Movement overthrows US-backed Gairy in Grenada
	Sandinistas overthrow Somoza in Nicaragua
	St Lucia and St Vincent become independent

The Nixon Shocks

By 1971 the post war international monetary system based on the supremacy of the dollar was disintegrating. In that year the United States registered a net trade deficit, and in August 1971 Nixon suspended the convertability of the dollar into gold and violated the rules of free trade enshrined in Bretton Woods by putting a 10% surcharge on imports into the United States. By 1974 American capitalism had reached its worst economic crisis since the war with simultaneous stagnation, inflation and growing unemployment.

In 1973 the United States formally recognized defeat in Vietnam; the Paris treaty was signed in that year and the Thieu regime fell in April 1975.

In October 1973 the Arab nations imposed an oil embargo against the United States because of its support for Israel during the October war; this was followed by the OPEC price increases of 1973-74 which more than quadrupled the price of oil.

In June 1972 a team of hired burglars were arrested while breaking into the Democratic National Committee headquarters in Washington. They were all products of the Cuban exile community in Miami and along with other Watergate conspirators, had a long history of involvement in CIA sponsored 'dirty tricks' in Latin America. The Watergate break-in and subsequent cover-up led to the White House resignations and finally that of Nixon himself in 1974. This sequence of events heralded the most serious crisis in the American system since it had first asserted its global economic, military and political supremacy after the Second World War. The maintenance of this dominant position had proved a costly business.

Even before 1971 it was clear that United States trade and overseas investment were insufficient to finance the American empire. In 1958 the United States experienced its first balance of payments deficit since the war; from then on the economic deterioration was steady. This was due to a combination of factors: firstly, the continuous outflow of American capital in search of profitable overseas investments; secondly, the economic aid programmes and huge military expenditure abroad which provided the means by which multinational corporations could move freely round the world and America could confront the challenge from national liberation movements in the Third World; and thirdly, the deteriorating balance of trade as a result of increased competition from Western Europe and Japan.

The United States had met the costs of extending and policing its empire by simply printing more dollars, which under the Bretton Woods system had to be accepted as if they were 'as good as gold'. While Europe and Japan struggled to stabilize their balance of payments, the global dominance of the dollar enabled the United States to avoid this obligation and to pursue its economic expansionism unimpeded. The German mark and the Japanese yen grew in strength while confidence in the dollar fell, leading in 1971 to the international monetary crisis, the Nixon shocks and the decline of the dollar as a reserve currency.

Apart from their impact on the international economy, Nixon's economic measures had profound domestic consequences. While protection and devaluation benefited certain business interests in the mid-west, south and south-west more oriented towards the domestic market, they horrifed the leaders of United States corporate capitalism, the so-called 'eastern establishment' of leading multinational corporations and banks. The Nixon presidency had originally been supported by a coalition of all these economic groups, but such a coalition could not survive the betrayal of such sacred principles of multinational capital as free trade, free investment and a cooperative interdependent world economy. Nixon seemed to be reasserting American supremacy through economic confrontation with its Cold War allies at the same time as he sought a *modus vivendi* with the Soviet Union.

The traditional consensus over foreign policy was breaking up; defeat in Vietnam and the rise of Third World nationalism symbolized by OPEC's new militancy created a new international panorama which accelerated its collapse.

It had always been assumed that the United States' pursuit of its national security objectives could only have a positive effect both on its own economy and society and on it global prestige and power. But Vietnam challenged these assumptions. Rather than stimulate the economy through increased defence expenditure the enormous cost of the war had aggravated the balance of payments crisis. Rather than promote internal social unity, the war had provoked deep antagonisms which led to the emergence of a strong anti-war movement radicalizing many sectors of the population. And instead of enhancing United States prestige, defeat had seriously undermined its international credibility to the extent that, for the near future at least, the United States would be unable to pursue the interventionist policies of the past. At the same time, American moral authority, on which it had tried to rest its foreign policy for so many years, received a dramatic reverse with the Watergate revelations and the Nixon resignation. It was time for a reassessment of American foreign policy in the post-Vietnam age.

Trilateralism

There are various influences upon the formulation of foreign policy in the United States: they include big business, big labour unions, the Pentagon, the State Department and other government departments, the President and Congress, the press, and the academic community. There is much debate over who exerts most influence.

If the structure of economic power in a society is some guide to political influence then it is clear that the extreme concentration of such power in the United States is an important factor influencing its foreign policy. Manuel Castells, in a recent study of American society, concluded that, 'the United States economy relies on a very small number of large corporations that concentrate and centralize capital, labor and resources'. Other studies have shown the interlocking network of interests which link corporate directors, the mass media, the most prestigious universities and the social elite, and which give big business unique access to top decision-makers.

Big business influences US foreign policy in a variety of ways. Lobbying through its associations is one way. Two business associations are particularly effective on Latin America: the Council of the Americas (COA) and the Association of American Chambers of Commerce in Latin America. COA is especially powerful; its membership consists of 200 corporations representing 90% of US investments in Latin America. Almost every major US multinational is included and David Rockefeller, president of the Chase Manhattan Bank, is the single most influential figure in the organization and was COA chairman from 1965 to 1970. Each of the sixty-five members of the Council's board is a president, chairman or senior vice-president of a large multinational. The Council has direct access to every executive branch policy maker in the US government, including the President. In May 1973 the COA chairman and executive vice-president briefed Secretary of State William Rogers and Assistant Secretary of State for Inter-American Affairs Jack Kubisch, prior to an official tour of Latin America; no other organization interested in US policy toward Latin America would have had such an opportunity. In 1976 the COA president reported that 'the trustees, advisory boards and staff met regularly over the year with senior officials of the United States Government Departments of State and Commerce, the White House, and with leaders of the US Congress'.

The lack of any strong economic interest in Central America on the part of the most powerful American multinationals — smaller enterprises, mostly from the south and south-west of the United States account for most of the investment in the region — may well have contributed to the lack of serious consideration given to developing a coherent policy toward the region by successive administrations.

Another means by which business exerts its influence is through the elite planning institutions and 'think-tanks' it sponsors. The most powerful of these are associated with the economic interests of the eastern establishment, for instance the Business Roundtable, the Committee for Economic Development, the Atlantic Council, the Brookings Institute and, most influential of all in the field of foreign policy, the Council on Foreign Relations.

The Council, which was set up in 1918, has been described by *Newsweek* as 'the foreign policy establishment of the United States'. Allen Dulles, who helped set up the CIA, was a director for over forty years and his brother, John Foster, who ran the State Department at the same time, was also a Council member. Their names have already appeared in this book in connection with US intervention in Guatemala. Henry Kissinger was a Council protege, and Zbigniew Brzezinski and Cyrus Vance, who rose to key foreign policy positions under President Carter, were both Council directors. David Rockefeller has been one of the key leaders of the Council since 1949.

The Council has formulated foreign policy, provided personnel for government, and acted as a major forum for contacts and discussion between big business, the media and the universities. It was the Council which helped plan America's role in the new international order which emerged after the Second World War, and in the early 1970s it turned its attention to the post-Vietnam era, embarking on what it called the '1980s project'.

In 1973 many of those involved in this project, together with other Council members, joined a new planning institution with a complementary role to that of the Council. The new body was called the Trilateral Commission and it was set up by David Rockefeller who invited the most powerful multinational businessmen and corporate lawyers to join him. Brzezinski, a director of the Council, became director of the Commission from 1973 to 1976.

The new dimension of the Commission was the inclusion of political and business leaders from Western Europe and Japan, hence 'trilateral'. *Newsweek* described the Commissioners as 'movers and shakers . . . a remarkable cross section of the interlocking establishments of the world's leading industrial nations'. European commissioners include Giovanni Agnelli, the president of Fiat, and John Loudon, chairman of Royal Dutch Shell; British members include Lord Carrington, Denis Healey, Edward Heath, Roy Jenkins, David Owen and Sir Mark Turner, former chairman of Rio Tinto Zinc.

The Commission, which has published a steady stream of documents and books on its objectives, was a response to the increasing interdependence of the world and the tensions and uncertainties which came to threaten it in the 1970s. It sought a 'broad global strategy for the management of interdependence', the promotion of liberal trade policies and international monetary reform. It reflected the major concerns of the giant multinational corporations which dominate the world economy and which seek above all a stable, secure environment in which to operate. In pursuit of this objective they have proved pragmatic and highly adaptable to changing national and international conditions.

The degree of cohesiveness and coherence amongst trilateralists should not be exaggerated either in the theory or in the implementation of their objectives. But their approach was to become particularly influential in the United States in the 1970s, and had certain implications for US policy towards Central America and the Caribbean.

It is Brzezinski himself who offers one of the clearest expositions of the trilateral approach to US foreign policy in the various books and articles he wrote in the late 1960s and early 1970s. He recognized that the United States had to adapt itself to the loss of its previously undisputed supremacy following the Vietnam debacle. This did not mean an abandonment of its expansionist traditions — on the contrary, Brzezinski maintained, 'it is only America that has the power to shape a hostile world for itself'. But he rejected Kissinger's nationalist approach which implied retrenchment behind the old frontiers of the Cold War in the pursuit of a balance of power. Brzezinski was committed to 'global consciousness', a world in which the nation state lost its centrality and a network of like-minded technocrats and businessmen from the three regions addressed themselves, under American supervision, to world problems. It was a view which led him to play down the old 'spheres of influence' approach to world politics and he even suggested abandoning the Monroe Doctrine as it was necessary 'to concede that in the new global age, geographic or hemispheric contiguity no longer need be politically decisive'.

Brzezinski also criticised Kissinger for his over-emphasis on East-West relations to the neglect of the North-South dimension. Trilateralism was particularly concerned with the growing demands of the Third World, which it saw as a major source of instability in the world. In 1975 Brzezinski wrote:

. . . today we find the international scene dominated on its overt plane more by conflict between the advanced world and the developing world than by conflict between trilateral democracies and the communist states . . . the new aspirations of the Third and Fourth Worlds united together seem to me to pose a very major threat to the nature of the international system and ultimately to our own societies. That threat is the threat of denial of cooperation.'

The need to guarantee a stable supply of raw materials, cheap labour and an expanding market for multinational corporations, and the repayment of the ever growing Third World debt to the private international banks was clearly uppermost in Brzezinski's mind and that of other trilateralists. Their response was a strategy of divide-and-rule, to incorporate the more advanced 'Third World' countries such as Brazil and Mexico into international management, while the poorer countries of the 'Fourth World' would receive aid and loans, preferably through recycled OPEC petrodollars administered by Western-dominated agencies. In 1975 Tom Farer, then serving as special assistant to the Assistant Secretary of State for Inter-American Affairs, described the approach as a 'strategy of accommodation' and he compared it to the tactics used to defuse class conflict in the industrialized West in the early twentieth century.

Within each underdeveloped country the trilateralists recognized the need to preserve conservative pro-Western elites. But where possible these elites should be encouraged to move towards new, viable democracies including middle sector entrepreneurs and consumers and providing the minimum of social justice necessary for stability; an approach with more than a passing resemblance to the Alliance for Progress. By encouraging gradual social change the trilateralists believed they would avoid revolutionary upheavals that would really challenge the United States' interests. In an address before the Foreign Policy Association in New York in September 1979, Cyrus Vance made this point in specific relation to Latin America: 'These moves toward more democratic and open societies in Latin America are distinctly in our interest. The great strength of democracy is its flexibility and resilience. It opens opportunities for broadly based political and economic participation. By encouraging compromise and accommodation, it fosters evolutionary change.'

There were some differences between American trilateralists on East-West relations. There was broad agreement that the new world order should incorporate the Eastern bloc (and China) into the community of developed nations and that this should involve both detente and deterrence; but there was disagreement concerning how much of each. Brzezinski was particularly concerned with Soviet influence in the Third World and preferred to take a more combative position on US-Soviet relations; when revolutionary upheaval broke out in Central America in the late 1970s he emphasized the role of Soviet intervention and the need for the United States to escalate its military presence in the region in response. Cyrus Vance on the other hand, while equally concerned with Soviet objectives, took a more cautious approach and was prepared to consider internal causes to conflicts in Central America and elsewhere in the Third World as well as the possibility of Soviet manipulation. He favoured a more measured response which would include reforms within the countries concerned.

These different approaches help explain why it was possible for someone like David Packard to be a member of the Trilateral Commission and also a founder member in 1976 of the right-wing Committee for the Present Danger which represented the Cold War hardliners. There was still a strong Cold War lobby in the United States, particularly in the Pentagon and Congress and amongst certain sectors of public opinion which had absorbed a barrage of Cold War propaganda over the years.

Jeff Frieden, who has made a study of trilateralism, has summed up the Commission as 'not a cabal or conspiracy as some would have it. It is the international forum for discussion and decision making of imperialist finance in an unstable age. With ties to every major imperialist government, every transnational bank and corporation, and every imperialist think-tank, its power is significant — a concerted power based on a commonality of interests and concerns rather than a blood oath.'

William Greider writing in the *Washington Post* placed the Commission in the context of changing realities in the post-Vietnam world:

In the simplest terms the Trilateral Commission is an establishment booster club, a floating seminar for business and academic leaders . . . on a deeper level the Trilateral Commission is an effort to re-establish consensus in the American foreign policy community where even the harmony of that small club was shattered by Vietnam.

Without indulging in conspiracy theories, it is possible to appreciate the potential influence of such an elite planning body, even though influence does not guarantee effectiveness. The Commission did make a considerable contribution to the formulation of US foreign policy in the mid 1970s. Kissinger, serving under Ford, became a member of the Commission. In its third annual report for 1975-76 the Commission was able to write: 'In the United States, there was noticeably increased emphasis on trilateral ties as the cornerstone of American foreign policy — as evidenced in the pronouncements of both Secretary of State Henry Kissinger and presidential candidate Jimmy Carter, an active Commission member — and "trilateralism" seems to have become a recognized word in the foreign policy lexicon.'

It was Jimmy Carter who presented the trilateralists with their greatest opportunity for promoting their vision of the world. Politicians are the vehicles for trilateral policies, taking them to the wider public, and Carter's image of the honest, moral family man, politically conservative but not extreme, impressed David Rockefeller and other trilateralists who mobilized their network of wealthy and powerful individuals in his support. Carter joined the Commission which he wrote in his autobiography, 'gave me an excellent opportunity to know national and international leaders in many fields of study concerning foreign affairs'.

Almost his entire foreign policy was elaborated by Brzezinski who wrote most of his major speeches. When Carter came to form a government he turned primarily to the liberals of the eastern establishment and included twenty members of the Trilateral Commission and at least fifty-four members of the Council on Foreign Relations. Five of the six members of the National Security Council, the key foreign policy coordinating body, were members of the Trilateral Commission. Brzezinski became his National Security Advisor and Cyrus Vance his Secretary of State. In its fourth annual report the Commission wrote: 'An increase in the Trilateral Commission's impact, resulting in large part from the number of Commissioners entering various governments was perhaps the principal feature of the year 1976-1977'.

Carter and the Strategy of Accommodation

Long before Jimmy Carter was elected President, Congress had shown increasing resentment at presidential monopoly over foreign policy and growing unease at its cynical implementation by the Nixon-Kissinger administration. Its attempts to restrain presidential power and redirect policies led to continuous conflict between the President and Congress under Nixon and Ford, who were unprepared to accept any restriction on their freedom to pursue what they considered to be the imperatives of national security.

In 1973 the Congressional Foreign Affairs Subcommittee on International Organizations began to hold hearings on the human rights situation in individual countries, raising the question of the role of US military assistance and AID programmes. In March 1974 the Congressional Committee on Foreign Affairs published a report, *Human Rights in the World Community: A Call for US Leadership*. The report maintained that hitherto US policy had 'led the United States into embracing governments which practise torture and unabashedly violate almost every human rights guarantee pronounced by the world community'; this, it concluded, damaged both American prestige and its long-term interests as right-wing dictatorships are inherently unstable.

Congress began to seek ways of incorporating human rights considerations into foreign policy. Foreign aid programmes were the major channel for American support of right-wing governments and Congress inserted clauses into the Foreign Assistance Acts of 1973 and 1974 urging the President to deny economic or military assistance to foreign governments which consistently violated human rights. Section 502(b) of the 1974 Act also called on the President to explain to Congress if, despite evidence of violations, he continued to send military aid. Section 660 made it illegal to use aid funds to 'provide training or advice, or provide any financial support, for police, prisons or other law enforcement forces for any foreign government'. In 1974, following revelations of abuses carried out under it, the Public Safety Program was abolished altogether. The Harkin Amendment to the Foreign Assistance Act of 1975 gave Congress the power to limit economic assistance to any government responsible for gross violations of human rights unless it could be shown that the aid 'will directly benefit the needy people' in the country concerned. In 1976 Congress enacted legislation enabling them to terminate military assistance on human rights grounds by a joint resolution of both houses. Congress also began to phase out Military Assistance Program grants, except for training programmes. By the time Carter took office, a government administrative structure for formulating human rights policy had been set up and the State Department had commissioned a report on the human rights situation in eighty-two countries receiving US military aid.

Apart from the issue of human rights, some of the key elements of Carter's policy towards Latin America also emerged prior to his election. In 1974 a report requested by Kissinger entitled *The Americas in a Changing World* was published. It had been compiled by the Commission on United States-Latin American Relations. A second report by the same commission published in December 1976 stated that, 'Covert US involvement in the domestic politics of Latin America such as occurred more recently in Chile, is indefensible and should be ended'. It recommended respect for ideological diversities in economic and social organization, a move towards more normal relations with Cuba, a Panama Canal Treaty and investigations of reports of human rights violations. Even Kissinger tried, unsuccessfully, to initiate a 'new dialogue' with Latin America, and it was reported that only Nixon's intransigence prevented a thaw in relations with Cuba.

Carter took over Congress's lead in introducing human rights considerations into foreign policy. This reflected the process of reassessment of US foreign policy described earlier and the need to restore legitimacy to the American presidency both internally and externally. It did not represent a change in US objectives but merely an adaptation of tactics and strategies to changing realities. The American writer James Petras places Carter's approach within the context of the history of US foreign policy: 'Morality is the recurring ideological expression of US imperialism in a period of crisis, it is what is offered to the world in place of substantive changes in the world's economic and social order'. Human rights was at the centre of a strategy to restore credibility to American foreign policy.

This is not to deny that the strategy had some meaningful if somewhat marginal impact. The Carter administration began to identify itself with democratic, broadly centre-right governments and political movements rather than with the authoritarian regimes of the past. It sought to encourage Central American dictators to liberalize through the offer of increased aid and to dissuade them from repression by threats, occasionally backed up by action, to withhold military and economic assistance. In the Caribbean it meant a new attempt to deal with the colonial enclaves of Puerto Rico and Panama and a rapprochement with Cuba and Manley's Jamaica. It also saw a move away from the confrontational politics involving CIA dirty tricks and covert operations to more subtle economic manipulation through international agencies such as the IMF.

But this 'strategy of accommodation' could not overcome some basic contradictions. Sincere advocates of human rights and real as opposed to cosmetic changes in US-Latin American relations struggled continuously against national security considerations which never lost their pre-eminence amongst American foreign policy objectives. Indeed, Deputy Secretary of State Warren Christopher suggested that they could never lose that centrality when he wrote in a State Department policy document in 1978: 'Nearly ten million American jobs depend upon our exports. Two-thirds of our imports are raw materials that we do not or cannot readily produce. One out of every three dollars of US corporate profits is derived from international activities. These economic issues are crucial to our national security.' Human rights policy and accommodation to Third World demands were acceptable in so far as they were seen to coincide with and even promote national security interests but they would not survive any real conflict between them.

Carter and the Caribbean

Terence Todman, Assistant Secretary of State for Inter-American Affairs, explained in hearings before the House Subcommittee on Inter-American Affairs in June 1977:

We no longer see the Caribbean in quite the same stark military security context that we once viewed it. Rather our security concerns in the Caribbean are increasingly political in nature. The threat is not simply foreign military bases on our doorstep. It is possibly an even more troublesome prospect: proliferation of impoverished Third World states whose economic and political problems blend with our own.

The shift was towards political rather than military strategies, cooperation rather than confrontation. It involved the acceptance of a certain degree of ideological pluralism as represented by the governments of Guyana and Jamaica; Sally Shelton, Deputy Assistant Secretary of State for Inter-American Affairs spoke of 'this Administration's willingness to tolerate economic models which are not necessarily our own and which we would not advocate but with which we are prepared to live'. There was a reassessment of the non-Marxist left in the Caribbean, whose closeness to Cuba some came to interpret as pragmatic opportunism rather than ideological affinity: 'The fact is', the Deputy Assistant Secretary of State for Inter-American Affairs told a congressional subcommittee in 1976, 'that Manley is a Social Democrat, Fidel is a Communist, two people who do not get along in serious politics are Social Democrats and Communists.'

The Carter administration launched a diplomatic, political and economic offensive in the Caribbean, beginning with a series of visits to the region by high-ranking government officials as well as the President's wife. A rapprochement with Cuba was heralded, with the support of many businessmen who glimpsed profitable economic opportunities on the island.

Reconsideration was given to the status of Puerto Rico, where economic crisis in the mid-1970s, growing unrest and demands for independence from inside and outside the island made it an increasingly pressing issue. In 1972 the UN Committee on Decolonization had approved a resolution recognizing the inalienable right of the Puerto Rican people to self-determination and independence, and in 1978 this was reinforced with a call by the UN for the transfer of power to the people of Puerto Rico so that they could decide their future without interference from the United States. However, two reports which appeared early in the Carter presidency came out in favour of statehood rather than independence, suggesting that the only solution to Puerto Rico's anachronistic colonial status acceptable to the United States would be to turn it into the 51st state.

In the meantime the Carter administration continued to treat Puerto Rico as a colony. The small island of Vieques for instance is a militarized zone where the US navy tests and evaluates weapon systems and trains the Atlantic Fleet forces. Three-quarters of the island's area is restricted by the navy for these purposes and all day long naval ships and aircraft bombard the island. The environmental damage both to the island and to the local waters is slowly destroying the livelihood of the fishermen and farmers who live on the island. In February 1977 the local population had their first victory over the US navy when a flotilla of forty wooden fishing boats prevented 'Operation Springboard', a series of war manoeuvres by NATO forces involving missile launching and anti submarine and aircraft fire, from taking place. In 1978 they forced the navy to cancel 'Operation Solid Shield' another large-scale military operation.

A reassessment of previous political strategies was apparent in the Carter administration's reaction to events in the Dominican Republic. When it looked as if pro-Balaguer members of the armed forces were about to rig the 1978 elections to prevent the victory of the opposition Dominican Revolutionary Party (PRD) led by Antonio Guzman, the United States responded immediately to ensure a free election. According to Richard Feinberg, a former State Department official, General Dennis McAuliffe of the Southern Command in Panama telephoned one of the leading military plotters and Cyrus Vance telephoned Balaguer. Guzman was allowed to assume the presidency.

While this gesture was a significant public relations exercise in keeping with the United States' new commitment to democratic processes in the Third World, the Carter administration was not in fact risking any of America's considerable stake in the country. Guzman, a wealthy cattle rancher, was known to Vance who in 1965 had been part of a mission to the country which had identified Guzman as a possible future President. The PRD was no longer seen as a major threat to US interests, despite its affiliation to the Socialist International; indeed, since coming to power Guzman has offered no real challenge to foreign capital. Nevertheless, the liberalization which has taken place has resulted in growing labour unrest and social protest in the country and the PRD has become increasingly divided over Guzman's failure to follow some of the more radical measures in the party programme.

The economic element of the Carter administration's offensive included the encouragement of an international approach to tackling the economic stagnation in the Caribbean. In 1977 a Caribbean economic task force was set up by the administration aimed at tackling the economic problems of the region, and this was followed in 1978 by the establishment of the Group for Cooperation in Economic Development, under World Bank sponsorship, to channel and coordinate international aid flows to the region. Philip Wheaton of the Washington-based EPICA Task Force has suggested that the strategy was aimed at pre-empting local regional development plans which might have been carried out through an independent, revitalized CARICOM focusing on locally perceived needs rather than the

112

priorities imposed by Western governments.

Suspicions that Carter's economic strategy in the region was aimed at promoting sufficient reforms to preserve the status quo and to prevent Caribbean nations from abandoning the capitalist model of development are reinforced by events in Jamaica. According to the American social scientist, James Philips, 'Under Carter the IMF became the vehicle for implementing trilateral policy toward Jamaica rather than the CIA. The IMF set out to complete the job which the destabilization campaign had begun.'

By 1977 the Jamaican economy was in a state of acute crisis and Manley was forced to enter into negotiations with the IMF for assistance with the growing balance of payments deficit. The austerity programme demanded by the IMF, which included wage and budget controls, a 40% devaluation and severe cutbacks in subsidies on basic foods and government social service spending, fell most heavily upon the poor and attacked the very basis of Manley's original programme of democratic socialism. In March 1980 Manley broke off negotiations with the IMF when it began demanding even harsher terms for further credit. By that time the country was in a worse economic condition than in 1977, before the IMF stabilization plan. Some have suggested that the economic objectives of the IMF were secondary to the political aim of bringing Jamaica back into the fold of Western capitalism and obliging acceptance of its recipe for growth through unlimited foreign investment.

Carter and the Canal

The Panama Canal Treaty provides a particularly clear example of the trilateral strategy of making concessions to Third World demands while preserving American interests.

Ever since the 1903 treaty Panamanian resentment at United States control over the Canal Zone had been growing and in 1964 it broke out into open confrontation between unarmed Panamanian students and US marines. Twenty-one Panamanians died and 400 were wounded. General Torrijos who came to power in 1968 made the Canal issue a major rallying point for nationalist sentiment within the country.

The Canal Zone is a country within a country. The American legal system, police force and education system prevail in the 640 square miles of the Zone. 40% of Panama's foreign earnings come from the Canal, 80% of its commerce is based in or around the Canal Zone as are 50% of the population and 70% of its industry. It has been estimated that between 1903 and 1970 Panama received US$55 million in direct benefits from the canal while the United States received

US$1,221 million less operating costs.

The United States began to reconsider its control over the Canal in the late 1960s. The Linowitz Report had concluded that the United States 'does not need perpetual control of the Canal for exclusive jurisdiction over it', and even military strategists came to believe that direct control of the Canal was not as essential to United States security as previously thought. The joint chiefs of staff of the American armed forces decided that 'basic US military interest is in the use of the Canal not in ownership or presence'.

American economic interests in Panama had also changed. Very little United States trade passes through the Canal which cannot take very large ships. However, Panama has grown in importance as a centre which services the operations and transactions of multinational corporations. The Colon Free Zone is a ninety-four acre piece of land in the city of Colon which has become an 'offshore' tax-free haven for multinationals. They use the zone to import, store and repack goods for distribution to Central and South America. They also use it to set up paper companies which act as tax free channels for executive salary benefits and facilitate transfer pricing and other dubious accounting devises used by multinationals to boost their profits.

The Panamanian Bank Act of 1970 provided the conditions for offshore banking activities in the country which led to a dramatic boom in banking. Before the boom Panama had five banks with US$125 million in deposits, by 1976 it had seventy-four banks with combined deposits of nearly US$10,000 million. In 1974 David Rockefeller while visiting Panama City responded enthusiastically to Panama's new role: 'Our increasingly interrelated global economy needs additional stable money centers to mobilize efficiently the very vast amounts of productive capital now flowing around the world . . . Panama is an ideal new center in the Western Hemisphere.' It is interesting to note that the conservative Council of the Americas, in which Rockefeller plays a major role, became one of the leading protagonists in favour of the Canal Treaty. Stable conditions and friendly relations with the Panamanian government were of more interest to multinational corporations than direct control of the Canal Zone.

Nevertheless, a number of right-wing groups in the United States fought vigorously against the Treaty, amongst the most vocal opponents being Ronald Reagan.

When the Treaty was finally signed in 1977 it was clear that the United States had successfully modified its colonial relationship with the country while relinquishing little of substance.

Panama regained sovereignty over its entire national territory and full control of the Canal by the year 2000. But it had made some important concessions. For the first time the United States was given the

The Banks of the Canal

'Most of Panama's growth as a banking center occurred in the latter half of the past decade, bankers explain, largely because of the sudden supply of Eurodollars created by OPEC's oil hikes. Panama's Swiss-style banking secrecy rules and its exemption of offshore loan operations from taxation made the country an attractive harbor for this capital, they say.

The country's other selling points included its use of US currency, a strong US military presence, and, more recently, its image as the one nation in the isthmus least tainted by terrorism and political unrest.

Still another asset was Panama's reputation for good labor relations. While the national labor code adopted in 1972 severely restricted an employer's freedom to terminate employees, an amended version passed in 1976 — known as Law 95 — brought personnel practices closer to the US-European norm. Businessmen pointed to Law 95 as a key factor in the resurgence of foreign investment in the last several years.

Last month's repeal of the law by the Legislative Council, controlled by the government's Revolutionary Democratic Party, raised private sector fears of a return to the 1972 code requiring companies to defend all dismissals in labor court. However, the minister of labor has been given three months to submit an alternative bill to the Council.

Although the foreign banks rarely step into local politics, they should be in a strong position to influence the shape of that legislation. Stopping short of a public threat to abandon the country, bankers can point out that Panama's banking center is not as permanent as it may seem: most major banks lease rather than own their office buildings; Panama is still not viewed as offering the security of Switzerland or Hong Kong; and rival offshore banking centers planned for New York and Puerto Rico will soon be advertising comparable or superior legal enticements.

Underscoring the financial center's vulnerability is the fact that Panama's five largest banks — respectively the Banco de la Nación Argentina, First National of Chicago, BankAmerica, Citibank and Banker's Trust — control more than half of the 110 banks' total asserts, or nearly $19 billion. If this economic muscle can be translated into local political clout, the labor minister's new legislation could closely resemble the discarded Law 95.'

This Week — Central America and Panama, *March 16, 1981.*

legal right to maintain military bases in the country which would be reduced from fourteen to three by the year 2000. After that date the United States will still be able to keep combat troops in Panama, while the School of the Americas will remain until 1984 as an elite training centre for high ranking Latin American officers.

Under the Treaty of Neutrality and the De Concini Amendment the United States has the right in perpetuity to intervene if the neutrality of the Canal is threatened. Panama must also charge 'just and reasonable' tolls for use of the Canal, so that by raising the tolls for the mostly American ships which pass through it, Panama could be open to accusations of violating the neutrality agreement.

An economic aid package also accompanied the Treaty, but mostly in the form of credit guarantees to American businesses wishing to invest in Panama for the first time and loans which would only add to Panama's considerable debt burden. The National Guard would receive US$50 million in military aid.

The nationalist issue of American control over Panamanian territory has been resolved, but the country's economic dependence on the United States is as strong as ever. Panama's banana producing and service enclaves, both dominated by American capital, have contributed to the kind of distortions apparent in all the other countries of the region: high levels of rural and urban unemployment, unequal distribution of wealth, neglect of food production for local consumption, dependence on foreign loans (Panama has the highest per capita foreign debt in Latin America) and slow economic growth. Panama's socio-economic profile remains the same with or without the Canal Treaty.

Carter and the Dictators

In May 1977 Brzezinski stated: 'American longer range interests would be harmed by continuing indifference to the mounting desire in Central America for greater social justice and national dignity, as our indifference will only make it easier for Castro's Cuba to exploit that desire.'

In 1976 congressional hearings had been held on the human rights situation in Nicaragua, Guatemala and El Salvador, and these were followed in early 1977 by a State Department report on Guatemala. It was the first time that the United States had publicly criticised the Guatemalan government's human rights record. The response of the Guatemalan government, followed shortly by El Salvador, was immediately to reject in advance further supplies of US military equipment or military assistance. The Foreign Assistance and Related Pro-

116

grams Appropriations Act of 1978 prohibited foreign military sales to Guatemala and El Salvador.

But the Carter administration's outspoken concern with human rights ('The soul of our foreign policy' claimed Carter) was never as unconditional and straightforward as it appeared. Carter was no less determined than his predecessors to retain maximum flexibility and control over foreign policy.

Cyrus Vance echoed the sentiments of Henry Kissinger when he advocated caution in promoting human rights: 'The means available range from quiet diplomacy in its many forms through public pronouncements to withholding of assistance. Whenever possible we will use positive steps of encouragement . . . We must be realistic . . . It is not our purpose to intervene in the internal affairs of other countries.'

So when Congress tried to strengthen America's ability to control economic assistance to repressive regimes through the Harkin Amendment to the 1977 Foreign Aid Bill (requiring US representatives to vote against loans from international lending agencies to countries violating human rights) it was actively opposed by the Carter administration. When the amendment was finally passed it contained sufficient loopholes, as a result of administration lobbying, to allow the government to continue supporting its allies where 'national security interests were involved'.

Carter's human rights policy always distinguished between America's friends and enemies, leading to some of its most blatant inconsistencies. This is particularly clearly illustrated by its application to Somoza's Nicaragua. The Somoza dynasty was in serious trouble by the late 1970s. Until then it had served the United States reasonably well. Nicaragua's importance to the United States was always more strategic than economic. American companies dominated some of the most dynamic sectors of the economy, such as food processing, lumber and tourism, and had set up some assembly plants in tax-free zones, but Somoza himself monopolized most of the economic opportunities. One American businessman was quoted in *Business Week* in 1978: 'You just don't do business here without offering the General a share in it from the beginning'. But since Somoza presented himself as a bastion of anti-communism in the region his inordinate greed was tolerated.

However, by the mid-1970s Somoza's autocratic rule was becoming a liability, threatening Nicaragua's long term stability. The Sandinista National Liberation Front (FSLN) was gaining in strength while Somoza's refusal to broaden his social base and expand economic opportunities had alienated the middle class and many businessmen. In 1976 the congressional subcommittee hearings on human rights in Nicaragua produced a real indictment of his regime with its revela-

Nicaragua's Tragedy

'The ongoing tragedy of Nicaragua represents not only the final result of over 42 years of corrupt and predatory rule by the Somoza family, but also a crucial failure of United States policy and influence in a strategically proximate area where we have been the dominant power throughout the century. Few nations in the world have been so strongly influenced by us as Nicaragua. This influence, created in part by two major United States military interventions, has produced a wide variety of effects, ranging from the adoption of baseball as Nicaragua's national sport to the fact that more of their military personnel have attended our military schools than have soldiers from any other Latin American nation. The current dictator, General Anastasio Somoza Debayle, is a graduate of the United States Military Academy, his brother, who earlier served as President, was a graduate of Louisiana State University, and all of his sons attended American universities. His wife is even a United States citizen.'

From the statement of Professor R.L. Millett before the Subcommittee on Inter-American Affairs of the House Committee on Foreign Affairs, United States Policy toward Nicaragua, *June 1979.*

tions of arbitrary arrest, torture, murder and other atrocities.

Even so the United States would not abandon its traditional ally until there was a clear anti-communist alternative. The Carter administration therefore opted for a policy of using its leverage — the carrot and the stick — to persuade Somoza to see the necessity for change. His personal wealth would be guaranteed, the National Guard preserved and there would, it was hoped, be a gradual transition to a more stable, less authoritarian and broader-based government.

Between 1968 and 1978 the United States provided Nicaragua with almost US$20 million in military aid. It became the largest per capita recipient of US aid in Central America. Somoza had also maintained a powerful lobby of friends in Congress and under Carter this lobby fought to retain the aid programme to Nicaragua despite the evidence of human rights violations. The Carter administration also supported the programme claiming that the aid was necessary in order to convince Somoza to improve his human rights record. In 1977 US$3 million in military aid and US$15 million in humanitarian aid was approved, but its release was subject to the discretion of the administration and an improvement in human rights. In September 1977, following the arrival of the new US ambassador to Nicaragua, Somoza lifted martial law and press censorship and a US$2.5 million credit agreement was signed. From then on the State Department oscillated between reinstating and suspending aid, a policy which reflected its dilemma caused by the assassination in January 1978 of Pedro Joaquin Chamorro, the only liberal alternative to Somoza acceptable to Washington. This policy only served to reinforce Somoza's conviction that he would not be abandoned by Washington.

Even when restrictions on economic and military aid to dictatorships were unequivocally applied by the Carter administration, there were a number of ways in which they were circumvented or their significance diminished.

According to a Center for International Policy report at the beginning of 1977 entitled *Foreign Aid: Evading the Control of Congress*, 69% of American and international foreign aid reaching the Third World was not subject to congressional review. In fact United States aid was increasingly channelled through large American and international financial institutions such as the Export-Import Bank, the World Bank and the IMF.

In any case, bilateral US assistance, over which Congress does have some control, represents a very small percentage of total United States financial flows to Central America, and withholding such assistance on human rights grounds has an insignificant effect compared with the much greater volumes of private investment which continue to flow uninterrupted.

However, President Carter made it quite clear during a visit to Brazil that he in no way opposed private investment and bank loans to repressive regimes:

It would be inconceivable to me that any act of Congress would try to restrict the lending of money by American private banks . . . under any circumstances. This would violate the principles of our own free enterprise system. And if such an act was passed by Congress I would not approve it . . . I don't see any incompatibility between a belief in the free enterprise system where a government does not dominate the banks . . . and a deep and consistent and permanent and strong belief in enhancing human rights around the world . . . the American business community . . . support(s) completely a commitment of our nation to human rights.

There were also ways of avoiding congressional restrictions on military and police assistance. By the mid-1970s Military Assistance Program (MAP) grants were of limited significance. In Guatemala, for instance, they were down from US$1,864,000 in 1971 to $200,000 in 1976. Military sales on the other hand had increased and are less open to congressional control as they do not involve the American taxpayer in the same way as MAP grants. The Foreign Military Sales

119

Israel Steps In

In 1973 the Israeli Ministry of Defence began actively to encourage arms sales abroad. Latin America became its best customer. Israel seems to have specialized in supplying countries involved in territorial disputes and right wing dictatorships. Those countries which refused or were refused US military supplies as a result of Carter's human rights policy were thus able to continue to purchase the arms they needed.

Somoza's Nicaragua, El Salvador, Guatemala and Honduras are amongst Israel's best clients. According to the Stockholm International Peace Research Institute, Israel supplied Somoza with 98% of his arms imports until the Sandinista victory. Between 1972 and 1977 El Salvador purchased 81% of its arms from Israel, making up nearly 15% of total Israeli sales. One of the most popular Israeli exports is the *Arava* short take-off-and-landing military transport aircraft used in counter-insurgency. Between 1972 and 1977, 25 of these aircraft were sold to El Salvador. Guatemala has bought 15 of these aircraft in recent years in addition to 50,000 Ghalil rifles, 5 Asimo helicopters and 1,000 machine guns. Israel has also supplied technicians and experts in counter-insurgency and security to all these countries. There are reports that Israeli mercenary pilots fly for Guatemala's armed forces.

credit programme does come under the Foreign Assistance Act and the various restrictions imposed by Congress, but again control is hampered by the fact that the State Department does not have to inform Congress in advance of sales under US$7 million.

Despite Section 660 of the 1974 Foreign Assistance Act banning aid to police forces abroad, the United States continued to do this through the International Narcotics Control Program which permits the provision of very similar equipment and training to local police forces as under the Public Safety Program but with the supposed aim of stemming the drug traffic. Michael Klare, an expert on US arms transfers, has shown how the Pentagon has used this and a variety of other methods to continue its support for repressive police operations in foreign countries.

It has also found ways of continuing its links with the armed forces of these countries. The American writer Nancy Stein has shown how the United States increasingly makes use of 'white collar mercenaries', civilian technicians and advisors, often ex-servicemen, to provide training and servicing for equipment sold under the Foreign Military Sales programme. The complexity of modern technology ensures a continuation of the dependent relationship of the past. The vice-president of Lockheed made this point himself during an interview with Stein: 'When you buy an airplane you also buy a supplier and a supply line — in other words you buy a political partner.'

It is not surprising that progressive organizations in Central America expressed scepticism about the intentions and effectiveness of Carter's human rights policy. For example, in Guatemala the National Committee of Trade Union Unity (CNUS), representing all the major unions in the country, produced a document in June 1977 accusing their government of implementing a systematic plan of repression against the people, and the United States of continued complicity in this plan, particularly through its promotion of a Central American army. CNUS pointed to the unpublicized presence of Pentagon officials in Guatemala even after the Guatemalan government had rejected US military aid, the continued training of Central American soldiers in Panama and the USA, and to the simultaneous emergence of right-wing paramilitary organizations throughout the region, namely: the reorganized *Mano Blanca* death squad in Guatemala, an organization with the same name in Nicaragua, and the *White Warriors' Union* in El Salvador.

Hurricane of Change in the Caribbean

In March 1979 the New Jewel Movement (Joint Endeavour for Welfare, Education and Liberation) of Grenada led by Maurice Bishop overthrew the American and British-backed government of Eric Gairy in an almost bloodless coup. Gairy was out of the country at the time but he had left orders with his personal security force, the Mongoose Gang, to execute leaders of the NJM who were alerted just in time.

Gairy and his Grenada United Labour Party had enjoyed power since the 1950s except for the years from 1962 to 1967 when Gairy had been removed from office for unauthorized use of public funds. In 1974 the country became independent and Gairy used his thugs in the Mongoose Gang and his power of patronage to control the island, suppress all opposition and amass for himself a personal fortune.

Grenada is one of the poorest countries in the Western Hemisphere with a per capita income in 1975 of US$390. It is totally dependent on export agriculture based on bananas, cocoa and spices. The price it receives for its bananas is bound by an agreement signed in 1953 with the British company, Geest Industries Ltd.

Agriculture for local consumption slumped under Gairy so that the island has to import most of its food. Unemployment is estimated at

15-20% of the labour force, though some sources put it nearer 50%. Tourism, another major foreign exchange earner, also declined during the 1970s. At the same time the balance of payments deficit increased along with the foreign debt and inflation. By the time of Gairy's overthrow the economic crisis and the Prime Minister's idiosyncratic and despotic political behaviour had created a powerful opposition movement. His removal was greeted with enthusiasm by most sectors of the population.

Shortly after the coup, Bishop proclaimed: 'People of Grenada, this revolution is for work, for food, for decent housing and health facilities and for a bright future for our children and great-grand children'. Bishop's development programme for Grenada is based on meeting the needs of the population and promoting education and what Bishop has called a genuine participatory democracy.

It is a social democratic and nationalist programme. Foreign capital is accepted as a necessary component although investors will have to agree to guidelines laid down by an overall economic plan: priority is given to labour-intensive investments and casinos are banned. Foreign banks have also been allowed to stay although the NJM's 1973 programme had called for their nationalization.

The development plan includes increasing food production for local consumption through a policy of 'idle hands for idle lands'; over one-third of Grenada's productive land was found to be idle at the time of the revolution. There are also plans to modernize the fishing industry and to develop an agro-industrial sector based on local products, such as fruit canning and processing.

Tourism is to be encouraged, although the government has expressed concern at some of its social and economic implications, as Bishop himself made clear: 'We are very concerned about the real possibility that bringing in 200,000 tourists a year can cause the rest of the rural population to abandon the land to work in a tourist sector, as has happened in Barbados where they now have to import labour to work in the cane fields. Tourism has to develop in a phased and orderly way and to be carefully linked to local production.' Foreign and local hotel owners are to be urged to make use of local goods and services rather than import them as frequently occurs in the Caribbean tourist industry. The construction of an international airport is considered an essential feature of the government's economic plans to promote tourism and export agriculture (see page 190).

However, the pro-American governments in the Caribbean including Trinidad and a number of the smaller islands of the Eastern Caribbean reacted with considerable hostility to the new government in Grenada. The premier of St Vincent asked Britain to send troops to overthrow it. Although the requests was rejected, neither Britain nor the United States and Canada responded to Bishop's request for military aid against a possible invasion by Gairy and his supporters.

Bishop appealed to both capitalist and socialist countries for aid, but in the first month of his government only Cuba and Guyana had responded by sending high level missions of military and economic experts to the country, while Jamaica expressed its willingness to do so.

The United States sent what Bishop described as the 'paltry sum' of US$5,000 for each of a series of small aid projects, while the American ambassador Frank Ortiz informed him that the United States would 'view with displeasure any tendency on the part of Grenada to develop closer ties with Cuba'. It did not bode well for the future when shortly afterwards the State Department described the Caribbean as the world's newest trouble spot. For the United States the events in Grenada were seen as the beginnings of a hurricane that, if unchecked, would sweep through the Caribbean. One official in the Carter government stated that Grenada 'has made us realize how vulnerable the islands are. All it takes is a small armed group to install a very distasteful government.'

Central American Political Volcano

In July 1979 the Sandinista Front for National Liberation (FSLN) succeeded in overthrowing the Somoza dictatorship in Nicaragua. This was precisely the outcome the United States had most wanted to avoid. Its failure to do so highlighted the many contradictions in Carter's strategy of accommodation and accelerated its demise.

After the assassination of Pedro Joaquin Chamorro, Washington had oscillated between supporting Somoza and trying to preserve Somoza-ism without him. One State Department official admitted in September 1978: 'We've been looking everywhere for another Balaguer but we can't seem to locate him'. During the strikes which followed the assassination, and which were supported by anti-Somoza businessmen, the United States threatened to cut off military aid to Somoza for the rest of the year. But as the movement against Somoza grew in strength and out of the control of the business sector, Washington announced that it would not suspend aid for 1978 after all, only for 1979.

In May 1978 the Inter-American Development Bank approved a US$32 million loan to build a road connecting two military garrisons in an area where 600 peasants had been killed in National Guard operations since 1975. In July 1978 Carter sent a personal letter to Somoza praising him for the improvement in the human rights situation in Nicaragua. In August, following a visit to Washington by

Mediation and Marines

'The mediation failed for a variety of interrelated reasons. One basic reason was that it was founded on essentially false premises. We allowed our hopes that Somoza would willingly acquiesce in a process which might result in a loss of his control over Nicaragua to be translated into an actual policy goal. Past history provided no basis for this belief. We further expected that more radical elements, including the Sandinistas, would accept or at least not disrupt a mediation designed to exclude them from any meaningful share in power. We further assumed that the Somoza-dominated Liberal Party represented a legitimate and at least semi-independent entity, assumptions for which there was no basis in reality. Finally, we assumed that virtually all major issues were amenable to some form of compromise. In at least two critical areas this was obviously impossible. The first of these related to control by General Somoza, his relatives and his close supporters over the *Guardia Nacional* . . . Related to this were efforts to provide guarantees for protection of at least a major share of the massive ill-gotten wealth of the Somoza family within Nicaragua.

Among the more ludicrous aspects of the mediation was its efforts to promote a virtual carbon copy of the settlement formula which Henry Stimson, supported by several thousand Marines, had imposed on Nicaragua in 1927 in an effort to end a previous civil war . . . The major difference was that (in 1978) Ambassador Bowdler was accompanied by one Dominican and one Guatemalan instead of by several thousand Marines, a factor which diminished his ability to force acceptance of this formula.

The use of the tri-partite mediation only served to further handicap the entire process. It . . . conspicuously failed to convince any Nicaraguans or, indeed, virtually anyone else in Latin America that the United States was not actually the totally dominant party.'

Professor Richard Millet, United States Policy Toward Nicaragua, *op.cit.*

Somoza, three loans of US$40, 50 and 60 million were negotiated by private Nicaraguan banks.

In October, following the failure of the first major Sandinista offensive, the United States persuaded the OAS to agree to send a mission to Nicaragua to mediate between Somoza and the broad opposition front (the FAO) which included businessmen and a group of prominent intellectuals with close ties to the Sandinistas known as 'the Group of 12' *(Los Doce)*. The mediation team was from Guatemala, the Dominican Republic and the United States and was led by the State Department's William Bowdler.

The United States had clearly decided that Somoza had to go, and its main consideration now was to ensure that a new provisional government would include members of Somoza's Liberal Party and exclude the Sandinistas, and that the National Guard would be preserved. This pro-American army would ensure continued US military influence in a post-Somoza Nicaragua. The United States rejected the opposition proposal that Somoza and representatives of his family in the National Guard resign and the FAO form a government, although such a government would have been much more favourable to American interests than the one which finally emerged. Its own proposals coincided with the views of the most conservative anti-Somoza businessmen in the FAO who in no way wished to see a Sandinista victory and Somoza's assets taken over by the state. The Americans seemed intent on creating a split in the FAO and the Group of 12 soon withdrew from the negotiations, claiming that the American plan 'would leave practically intact the corrupt structures of the Somoza apparatus'.

The mediation team continued its efforts to secure Somoza's resignation. The United States even persuaded the IMF to postpone an important US$20 million stand-by credit to Nicaragua. But the efforts collapsed by January 1979 through Somoza's persistent refusal to accept a proposal for an internationally supervised referendum to determine whether he had any support among the people.

Within the United States the pro-Somoza lobby remained strong. Although in September 1978 eighty-six members of Congress had asked the President to postpone all aid to Somoza and to withdraw the US ambassador and the five-man military advisory team in Nicaragua, seventy-eight right-wing congressmen had at the same time urged Carter to continue supporting the dictator, and they were strengthened by a number of right-wing victories in the November US congressional elections.

Internationally support for the FSLN was mounting; regionally it came from Costa Rica, Panama, Mexico and Venezuela and elsewhere from several Western European social democrat parties. Support for Somoza rested with his fellow members of the Central American military alliance CONDECA, Guatemala and El Salvador, while he also received important supplies of arms from Israel. In April 1979 Israel sent a team of military experts to Nicaragua to install an air defence system. By April 1979 American fears of a new Sandinista offensive were growing. In that month the IMF approved a loan of US$40 million to Somoza, and in May a further US$25 million. In May also there were reports that US military aircraft from the

Setting up Pluralism

'From May onward it became clear that Somoza could not survive until the oft-proclaimed end of his term in 1981, and that a military collapse was entirely likely. It was our view that a purely military solution would provide the least auspicious prospect for true self-determination and an enduring democratic outcome to Nicaragua's agony. The growing power of the Marxist leadership in the Sandinista army also raised increasing concerns that the final outcome might be determined by these elements on the basis of their control of coercive military power. We therefore again sought ways to promote an end to the conflict, and a transition that would maximize the possibility for all elements of the opposition to have a say in the transition. A pluralistic set-up appeared to be the best bet for avoiding an ''ideological or military imposition'' of a final outcome . . . our purpose in June was to seek an end to the bloodshed and suffering and to avoid radical control.'

Letter from Viron P. Vaky, Sept. 8, 1979, United States Policy Toward Nicaragua, *op.cit.*

Panama Canal Zone were flying in weapons for the National Guard, although military assistance had officially been cut off in September 1978.

In June the Sandinistas launched their final offensive. The United States was faced with the prospect of a Sandinista victory or direct intervention to stop it. Brzezinski and his assistant, Robert Pastor, were reported to favour intervention, while Harold Brown, the Defense Secretary, publicly stated that it was not 'inconceivable'. Cyrus Vance on the other hand was said to be against it, though even he had begun to talk about growing evidence of Cuban involvement in Nicaragua. Other State Department officials referred to 'hard' intelligence that such involvement existed. When pressed they admitted it was 'soft' intelligence, but this was just the kind of propaganda that had in the past preceded or accompanied direct US intervention.

However, later that month the film of an ABC correspondent being shot in cold blood by Somoza's National Guard was shown on American television, horrifying the American public and making it more difficult for the United States to consider intervention. In any case, unilateral intervention by the US at this stage would have been extremely difficult. Carter tried to persuade the OAS to agree to send a 'peacekeeping force' — which would have been in fact a military intervention to prevent a FSLN victory — but the OAS refused to comply. Mexico led the opposition to the proposal; it was the first time the OAS had failed to approve intervention by the United States.

The United States had little option but to intensify its diplomatic manoeuvres in an attempt to influence the provisional government the Sandinistas were setting up in Costa Rica and to ensure that the National Guard remained intact. In so doing it delayed Somoza's departure still further and prolonged the war.

The Sandinistas, aware of their vulnerability to United States action, had in fact set up a provisional government in which conservative and social democrat opinion were well represented, and a five-person junta which included a businessman and the non-aligned wife of the murdered newspaper editor, Pedro Joaquin Chamorro. The United States nominated five others to be included in the government, amongst them was Ernesto Fernandez, the financial secretary of Somoza's Liberal Party and a close confidante of the dictator. Venezuela and Costa Rica supported the United States' attempts to introduce more 'moderate' elements into the new government.

On 17 July Somoza left Nicaragua; an agreement had been made whereby Francisco Urcuyo, head of the Nicaraguan Congress, would act as President until the provisional government of the FSLN arrived from Costa Rica. The older officers of the National Guard were to leave the country, allowing younger officers to take their place.

This agreement, which had been laboriously worked out in discussions between Bowdler and the provisional government, broke down to the United States' fury when Urcuyo made it clear that he intended to stay on as President. While Washington was persuading him to change his mind, the National Guard, leaderless and demoralized, collapsed. The Sandinistas were able to push forward and win an all-out military victory.

Under Somoza infant mortality was 46 per thousand live births, life expectancy was 53 years, at least 57% of the population was illiterate and unemployment was officially 22% (by the end of the war it was 33-40% of the labour force). The bottom 50% of the population shared 15% of GDP while the top 5% took 30%. Such was the structure of exploitation and deprivation which the United States had helped sustain.

The struggle for social justice cost the Nicaraguan people 35-40,000 dead, 100,000 wounded (an estimated 40,000 requiring continued medical care), 40,000 orphaned, 200,000 families made homeless and a total material damage to the economy, estimated by the Washington-based Center for International Policy at US$1,810 million. This included physical damage to housing, livestock, industry and infrastructure, reduction in Gross Domestic Product as a result of the war and losses in foreign exchange reserves from capital flight and

127

illegal withdrawals. In addition, Somoza had left a crushing national debt of US$1.5 billion.

These statistics convey nothing of the human misery which Somoza created and which the United States tolerated until it had absolutely no alternative but to abandon its traditional ally. Even then it did everything in its power to prevent a Sandinista victory and subsequently to weaken its effectiveness, although there was no doubt in the minds of most observers that the outcome could not have been a clearer expression of the Nicaraguan people's will.

The programme of the Sandinista government was aimed initially at reconstruction of the devastated economy. In the first year of the revolution the emphasis was on raising the social wage — i.e. improvements in housing, education, health and welfare — rather than raising real incomes, While the state was considered the main agent for development, the private sector has retained considerable influence; two years after the revolution it still controls 75% of industrial production and 80-85% of the main exports (coffee, cotton and cattle).

But from the outset many Americans considered they had 'lost' Nicaragua. They began to talk of preventing 'another Nicaragua' in the same way they had talked of preventing 'another Cuba' in 1959.

America's very presence is an inescapable constraint on the social experiment both in Grenada and Nicaragua. One American official coined a neat phrase which well describes the United States presence in the region. 'We're like an elephant in a sitting room. Even if we don't move you can't ignore us.' Of course the elephant is never completely stationary, and after the Nicaraguan revolution it began to stir itself rather rapidly.

PART 4
The Eagle Reborn

Contents

1979	Caribbean Joint Task Force set up in Florida
	Young officers overthrow General Romero in El Salvador
1980	Jamaica breaks off negotiations with IMF
	Seaga defeats Manley in Jamaican elections
	US-sponsored peace treaty signed between El Salvador and Honduras
	Reagan elected President
1981	President Reagan inaugurated
	US aid to Nicaragua suspended
	Military aid to El Salvador increased
	Belize becomes independent

Cold War II

By July 1979 the trilateral strategy for global cooperation pursued by the Carter administration had become entangled in its own contradictions.

Many reasons have been put forward for the strategy's failure to achieve its major goals under Carter and for the gradual abandonment or modification of those goals by at least some of its main exponents. The American social scientist Alan Wolfe, for example, has suggested that trilateralism was unable to transform public opinion which was still deeply imbued with the ideology of the Cold War. This was partly a reflection of the elitism and anti-democratic sentiments of many trilateralists who disdained the views of the ordinary public. 'Effective operation of a democratic political system usually requires some measure of apathy and non-involvement on the part of some individuals and groups', wrote Samuel Huntingdon in the book *The Crisis of Democracy* which was a major subject of discussion at the first plenary session of the Commission in 1975. There was a feeling that presidential authority, particularly in the field of international economics and foreign policy, should not be restrained by public opinion or by the parochial interests of Congress, and that the social unrest in the United States in the 1960s had in fact been a result of an 'excess of democracy'.

The trilateralists also failed to convince powerful state and private interests, who clung to more traditional approaches to foreign policy, of the need to adjust the United States' role to changing world realities. As Wolfe points out, the trilateralists could not afford to alienate these strong vested interests:

In post-war United States conservative vested interests had entrenched themselves in the Pentagon, the armed services, the intelligence agencies, and other important bureaus. They had a self-interest in keeping the Cold War alive, to be sure, but they were also ideologues who genuinely believed in their anti-communism and were willing to pursue their passion whatever the economic consequences. And in the private sector, defense contractors and other major manufacturing industries connected to them (rubber, steel, etc.) could be counted on to support high defense budgets and Cold War assumptions.

Cold War militants had in fact been on the offensive since at least 1976 and they had an ideological weapon, the national security threat, which Carter lacked. The Committee on the Present Danger emerged as a powerful lobby, including in its ranks such prestigious names from the American foreign policy establishment as Eugene Rostow, Dean Rusk, Maxwell Taylor and Richard Allen. As it failed to persuade the Carter administration to stimulate the economy through increased defence expenditure and to adopt a harder line towards the Soviet bloc it began to appeal to the American people for support and increasingly to ally itself with other right-wing organizations. These included traditional advocates of the Cold War like the American Security Council, referred to by one author as 'the soul if not the heart of the military industrial complex', as well as the more recently formed grassroots movements of the New Right which embraced such causes as anti-abortion, anti-homosexuality and an evangelical fundamentalist Christianity in addition to the Cold War. Such a coalition of anti-communist, jingoistic movements almost succeeded in blocking the Panama Canal Treaty.

The trilateral strategy, which stressed accommodation to Third World demands, the peaceful resolution of conflict, and the preservation of the military balance with the Soviet Union through Salt II, could hardly compete with the impact of resurgent Cold War sentiment and the emotional appeal and economic interests which fuelled it. It was even more difficult for a President facing an election year to ignore the potential electoral gains from Cold War rhetoric, especially as by the end of 1979 he was being accused of having lost both Nicaragua and Iran.

Carter's dilemma

'. . . Even those who decry the call for a resurgent America, and insistently remind us that we no longer have the power to shape the world according to our desires, appear uneasy over accepting the prospect of a world in which American influence would decline. This, at least, is what they have repeatedly declared. The officials of the Carter Administration, including the President, were no doubt quite sincere in expressing the desire to see the developing world move in a manner that would ultimately prove congenial to us. To be sure they advocated the need for America "to get on the side of change". But they did so presumably in order to guide and to manage the great changes they found sweeping the world. Through different and more congenial methods than those that were often employed in the past, they nonetheless aspired to achieve the goals of the past.

This strategy inevitably failed. The goals of the past could not be achieved while foreswearing the methods that once attended those goals. Even a policy of moderate containment cannot escape incurring the risk of intervention.'

Robert Tucker, Foreign Affairs, *Winter 1980/81.*

Internationally as well as domestically events highlighted the contradictions in trilateralism and contributed to its failure. Partnership amongst Western nations in a period of economic stagnation became increasingly difficult to sustain. As economic rivalries grew, so did the protectionist tendencies which struck at the very heart of trilateralism. Politically too events revealed that 'partnership' was never intended to be interpreted literally, rather that it meant cooperation under American guidance. When crises occurred, America's 'partners' were expected to follow the United States' lead, often without prior consultation. The most serious crises of the last two years of the Carter presidency, the Soviet invasion of Afghanistan and events in Iran, indicated, however, that most of Western Europe was reluctant, if not actually unwilling, to echo America's policy directives (the exception being Britain under the Conservative government). Carter and Brzezinski's bungled attempt to rescue the American hostages in Iran and restore American self-respect was viewed with particular alarm by the allies. Both Carter and Brzezinski began to lose support even amongst committed trilateralists, and Cyrus Vance resigned in protest at the confrontational direction of foreign policy during Carter's last year in office.

In the Third World, trilateralism was continuously torn between its stated aims of promoting reforms and more stable democratic governments, and its perceptions of America's national security interests which tended to involve it in support for repressive dictatorships, lest their sudden removal unleash a revolutionary upheaval.

The Nicaraguan revolution brought into focus many of these tensions within the trilateral strategy. It also highlighted the failure of both the traditional 'marines, money and munitions' approach to preserving United States' supremacy in its backyard as well as the more accommodationist strategies of the trilateralists. Neither had in fact succeeded in stemming the tide of revolution.

Having historically backed repressive, corrupt regimes in Central America and helped create powerful, politicized armed forces, the United States could hardly expect them to relinquish voluntarily their political and economic power. Not only did the dictators refuse to introduce political reforms, they considerably reduced the United States' room for manoeuvre by systematically eliminating moderate alternatives whom the Americans might have backed to replace them. Nicaragua's Pedro Joaquin Chamorro was not the only victim of this process in Central America; in Guatemala the leaders of the country's two social democrat parties, Alberto Fuentes Mohr and Manuel Colom Argueta, were gunned down in early 1979, and the following year the relatively liberal Vice-President, Villagran Kramer, had to leave the country for fear of being assassinated by the extreme right. In El

Salvador the process of polarization which characterized the region as a whole had eroded most of the support once held by the Christian Democrat leader, Jose Napoleon Duarte, who had been forced into exile in 1972.

By the late 1970s there was no viable 'centre' position left in Central America. The electoral process, nearly always fraudulent and inevitably carried out in a climate of repression and corruption, had proved a totally inadequate vehicle for change. The political initiative passed to those who advocated direct forms of political action including armed struggle. It was no longer a question of small guerrilla bands trying to 'create the conditions for revolution' as in the 1960s; the political-military movements which emerged in the 1970s were based on a genuine mobilization of the people as peasants, urban workers and sectors of the middle classes saw they had no option but to fight for social justice. The intransigence of the dictatorships was partly due to an awareness that any relaxation in their iron rule would result in an explosion of this mass movement.

Nevertheless, some of the more consistent adherents to the trilateral strategy in the Carter administration continued to stress the internal causes of regional unrest and the need for reform. They believed that post-revolutionary Nicaragua could still be prevented from falling into the Cuban camp while elsewhere in the region they clung to the illusion that a political centre still existed capable of preserving US interests while simultaneously diffusing social tensions. They were concerned at the spread of Cuban influence but, while not excluding a military response, they still emphasized political, diplomatic and economic initiatives and a process of gradual change which they believed might still pre-empt revolutionary upheaval and further risks to United States interests in the region.

State Department representatives such as Viron Vaky, the Assistant Secretary of State for Inter-American Affairs, and Lawrence Pezzullo, the US ambassador to Nicaragua, fought hard against mounting congressional hysteria at Cuba's supposed intentions in Nicaragua in order to secure a US$75 million aid package to the country, 60% of which was destined for the private sector. Vaky told the House Foreign Affairs Committee in December 1979: '. . . I think the ball game is still on in Nicaragua. I think it is not closing the barn door. I think that we would have desired a different outcome than that which occurred, but given the situation, it is possible in my view for the United States to have a major and significant influence over what evolves there. I think we can do no less than try.'

In the same vein, Under Secretary of State Warren Christopher explained to a House Committee: 'We recognize some elements of the present government in Nicaragua might prefer a closed Marxist society. We recognize as well that Cuba is already providing substantial advice and assistance. The moderate outcome that we seek will not come about if we walk away now. Precisely because others are assisting Nicaragua and may seek to exploit the situation there, I feel we must not turn our backs.'

Immediately after the Nicaraguan revolution, the State Department embarked on a diplomatic offensive in Central America to wring political reforms from the region's other dictators in exchange for military aid. Viron Vaky went on such a mission in August 1979 and tried to persuade President Romero of El Salvador to resign and bring forward elections scheduled for 1982. He was followed by special envoy William Bowdler, but the only concessions they managed to gain were the return of some political exiles and a commitment to hold municipal and legislative elections in 1980.

Meanwhile the Pentagon, the CIA and the National Security Council were making a different assessment of the regional situation. Brzezinski and his supporters placed the Grenadan and Nicaraguan revolutions within the sphere of 'Soviet-Cuban military activism in the Third World'. The internal causes of these revolutions were less important than the perceived determination of Cuba to exploit them for its own ends. It was a return to Cold War assumptions. The strategy of accommodation was no longer considered adequate to deal with the new and dangerous challenge to United States supremacy from within its own backyard. A firm response was required.

The domino theory was resurrected. In the Caribbean, the Grenadan revolution was linked to the emergence of small left-wing movements throughout the region, such as the victory of the St Lucian Labour Party in the July 1979 elections. The escalating struggle in El Salvador was seen as a sign that the Sandinista victory and Cuban supervision would threaten the stability of every Central American republic.

The differences within the Carter administration over tactics and assessments of the regional conflict (though not over the ultimate objectives of US foreign policy) resulted in a noticeable lack of coherence and many inconsistencies when translated into policy. Carter's own ineptitude and lack of leadership undoubtedly contributed to the confusion.

In Central America there were attempts, where possible, to bolster up parties of the centre-right despite their lack of political base, partly because of the misconception that these still represented an alternative and partly to persuade international opinion of the United States' democratic intentions. At the same time, however, the United States increased its backing for military attempts to crush the movement for change.

135

In the Caribbean, policy statements continued to reflect an apparent awareness of the social and economic difficulties of the region, while the United States escalated its military presence there and sought to isolate those countries attempting to pursue an alternative model of development. Such was the confusion over precisely how the administration interpreted the regional situation that the *Washington Post* wrote in September 1980:

The US view on whether Cuba and the Soviet Union poses a military threat in the Caribbean that ought to be met with a military response varies depending on which administration official is asked and when. In many instances, administration and defense officials note that the primary problem in the Caribbean is an economic one, and that high unemployment and falling gross national product will lead to destabilization long before Cuba imposes it.

Nevertheless, the trend was clear, Cold War II was approaching.

United States foreign policy seen over time seems to be more about shifts in emphasis than dramatic changes in direction. The last year of the Carter administration recalls the gradual modifications in the Alliance for Progress in the 1960s. Then, a strategy which began by stressing economic and social reform was soon overtaken by military concerns as these reforms began to threaten American interests. In the same way, Carter in his last year introduced a military dimension into his political strategy, which under his successor has once again become the dominant feature of US policy toward the region.

The Caribbean Basin in the Eighties

During the last year of Carter's presidency the Caribbean basin, which includes the Central American mainland as well as the islands of the Caribbean itself, became one of the administration's major preoccupations. The region was emerging as one of the most volatile and conflictive in the world, alongside the traditional trouble spots of the Middle East and South-East Asia. The threat posed by events in the Caribbean basin demanded that the United States give serious attention to defining a more detailed and coherent policy towards its backyard. For the United States the Caribbean basin is of strategic, commercial, economic and psychological importance.

Strategically the region's proximity to the United States gives it a unique position in America's national security considerations. US bases in Guantanamo Bay on Cuba, San Juan and Roosevelt Roads in Puerto Rico, and in the Panama Canal Zone as well as dozens of smaller air and naval bases in the region are considered vital to

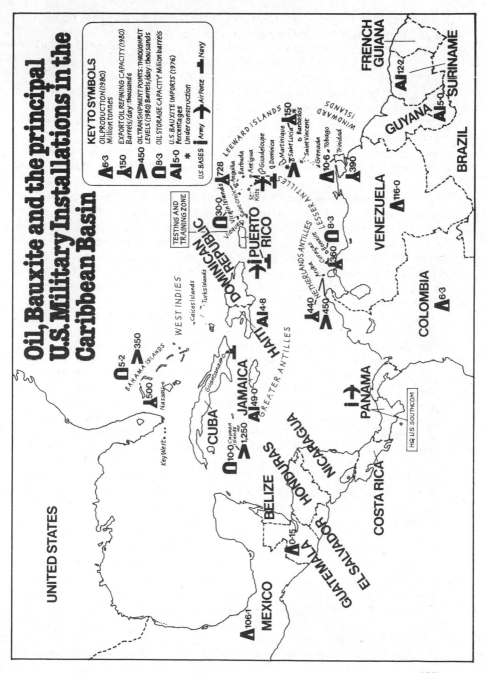

Oil, Bauxite and the principal U.S. Military Installations in the Caribbean Basin

KEY TO SYMBOLS

▲63   OIL PRODUCTION (1980) *Million tonnes*

▲150   EXPORT OIL REFINING CAPACITY (1980) *Barrels/day: thousands*

➤450   OIL TRANSHIPMENT POINTS: THROUGHPUT LEVELS (1980) *Barrels/day: thousands*

◘8·3   OIL STORAGE CAPACITY *Million barrels*

AI5·0   U.S. BAUXITE IMPORTS (1976) *Percentages*

✱   *Under construction*

U.S. BASES ⚓ Army ✈ Air Force ⚓ Navy

UNITED STATES

BAHAMA ISLANDS   ◘5·2   ➤350

▲500   Nassau·

WEST INDIES

·Caicos Islands

: Turks Islands

KeyWest ··

CUBA   ◘10·0   Cayman Islands ⌒

▲1,250

Guantánamo ⚓

JAMAICA   AI49·0

GREATER ANTILLES

MEXICO   ▲106·1

BELIZE

GUATEMALA   ▲0·15

EL SALVADOR

HONDURAS

NICARAGUA

COSTA RICA

PANAMA ⚓✈

HQ U.S. SOUTHCOM

DOMINICAN REPUBLIC   ◘30·0

HAITI   AI4·8

TESTING AND TRAINING ZONE

Vieques   Virgin Islands ⚓   PUERTO ⚓✈ RICO

St. Kitts · Saint Croix · Anguilla · ▲28

LEEWARD ISLANDS

Barbuda ·

· Antigua

◘Guadeloupe

0 Dominica

· Martinique ▲150

· Saint Lucia ✱

D Barbados

· Saint Vincent

LESSER ANTILLES

· Grenada

AI0·6 · Tobago

Trinidad ▲390

WINDWARD ISLANDS

Bonaire   Curaçao ◘8·3

NETHERLANDS ANTILLES   ➤360

Aruba   ➤440   ➤450

COLOMBIA   ▲63

VENEZUELA   ▲116·0

GUYANA   AI5·0

SURINAME   AI12·2

FRENCH GUIANA

BRAZIL

137

American defence. The permanent right to defend the Panama Canal was an important feature of the Panama Canal treaties.

Puerto Rico is a key centre for naval control over the Caribbean and the South Atlantic. United States military installations cover nearly 100 square miles of Puerto Rican territory. The Roosevelt Roads naval base is one of the most important testing and training areas for the US military in the world. Large quantities of weapons are stored on the island of Vieques for use by the Atlantic Fleet in any conflict involving Africa, Central or South America.

According to the US naval commander in the Caribbean, Rear-Admiral Arthur Knoizen, the US navy's presence in Puerto Rico ensures that there will be no revolution on the island. Just in case, however, the National Guard was reinforced, following the country's economic crisis of 1973-75, from 7,500 troops to 9,000 in 1977. It is directly dependent on the US Defense Department and receives most of its funds from the US government. The Guard has been used to suppress student unrest and strikes. According to a study by John Enders of the US military presence in Puerto Rico, the Fort Buchanon US army base in San Juan is kept open almost entirely for reasons of Puerto Rican internal security.

Another aspect of the American military presence in the Caribbean is the undersea surveillance system in the Eastern Caribbean. The Navy's Atlantic Underseas Test and Evaluation Center in the Bahamas is crucial to the development of anti-submarine warfare capabilities. The United States is worried by Soviet attempts to expand its naval presence in the Caribbean, which began in 1969 with the appearance of a seven-ship naval squadron in the area. In particular it is concerned with Soviet submarine facilities in the region. The Caribbean basin would be one of the main supply routes between Europe and the USA in the event of a war in Europe. Soviet submarines able to use the Cienfuegos base on Cuba or other Caribbean ports could threaten this supply line. According to a study in 1980 by the right-wing London-based Institute for the Study of Conflict: 'Soviet efforts are . . . now directed more at extending political influence in the Caribbean as a vital area of communications to be controlled or interrupted rather than as an area from which military operations are to be conducted against the mainland.'

Crassweller in *The Caribbean Community* forcefully emphasized the strategic significance of the region when he wrote in 1972: 'The nature of the security interest can be simply stated: no part of the Caribbean may safely be permitted through conquest or subversion or *even orderly process*, to serve as a military power base hostile to the United States.' (my italics.)

Nevertheless, there are others who suggest that the strategic significance of proximity is less relevant in the nuclear age when a conventional global war is less likely. Many also argue that only the loss of Mexico which actually borders on the United States would really threaten its security. But there are other psychological and emotional reasons why the region is considered vital to the United States. Ultimately, if the United States cannot maintain its supremacy in its own backyard, its ability to do so elsewhere in the world is open to serious doubt. The presence of Cuba is seen as a permanent affront to American dignity as well as to its national security.

Commercially the Caribbean basin is an important trade route through which essential raw materials are shipped from Africa and Latin America to the United States and American manufactured goods are exported in return. The islands of the Caribbean are scattered across the major shipping lanes as well as the approaches to the Panama Canal. Particularly important is the strait between Cuba and Haiti, enhancing the United States concern with the defence of that country and its neighbour, the Dominican Republic.

The economic importance of the basin is considerably less than its geopolitical significance. United States investments in the Caribbean itself have been estimated at US$2 billion, with a further US$2,756 million in 'book value' direct investments in Panama and US$895 million in the rest of Central America, although this latter figure may well be an underestimate.

The Caribbean also supplies the United States with vital minerals, the most important of which is bauxite. But it is its role as an oil refining centre and its actual and potential oil and gas reserves which have increased the region's importance to the United States.

The Caribbean basin became a major oil refining area in the 1950s due to its useful location between the sources of supply and the market, its deepwater anchorages — suitable, unlike most American ports, for oil supertankers — and its cheap labour. In addition, the small size and colonial status of the islands enabled the powerful oil companies to exert their influence and ensure that environmental constraints and other government controls were not imposed.

By 1979 56% of United States refined oil imports were being refined in the Caribbean and plans were underway to expand refining facilities in the area still further; the American corporation Amerada Hess had begun work on a transshipment terminal and refinery on St Lucia and was negotiating an agreement to construct a terminal and refinery on Bonaire.

But the region also has considerable unexplored oil and gas reserves of its own. At present the main producers in the Caribbean basin are Venezuela, Trinidad, and Mexico making these countries particularly important to the United States. But geologists suspect that Central

139

America is part of the same oil rich belt that includes Mexico and Venezuela's large deposits. Mexico's largest reserve is located only nine kilometres from the Guatemalan border. A conglomerate headed by Basic Resources International and another led by Hispanoil, Spain's state-owned company, are already operating in west-central Guatemala and in April 1981 the American oil companies Texaco and Amoco announced finds in northern Guatemala. According to the *Journal of Commerce*, 'independent oil experts estimate the nation could be producing one million barrels of oil a day in five to eight years, a development significant not only for Guatemala but for the United States as well. "That kind of production would make it like Alaska's North Slope" and could eventually account for a significant part of US daily oil imports of ten million barrels, said one analyst.' A US State Department official has called Guatemala 'the plum of Central America'. Texaco, Esso, Union Oil and other US companies are also exploring for oil in Honduras.

It is known that two broad strata of rock likely to bear oil run the length of the Caribbean basin, but much of the oil is far below the Caribbean sea making recovery difficult and costly. However, with the rise in oil prices, the advances of offshore deep drilling techniques and the continued uncertainty in the Middle East, it is becoming increasingly viable to exploit the deep water reserves of the Caribbean itself. Two major US oil companies are already exploring in the region, Gulf Oil in Suriname and Mobil in Barbados; other large Canadian and United States independent oil companies are exploring in the Dominican Republic and Guyana; Jamaica, Antigua and Cuba are also looking for oil. The region's vast potential oil wealth will add a new, more urgent, dimension to the United States' search for stability in the Caribbean basin.

Targets of Opportunity

The United States has found the pursuit of stability in its backyard particularly elusive. By the late 1970s a new factor of instability had been added to regional politics. Four of the six islands of the Eastern Caribbean which had become semi-autonomous Associated States in 1967 gained their full independence from Britain: Grenada in 1974, Dominica in 1978, and St Vincent and St Lucia in 1979. The gradual withdrawal of Britain from the Caribbean and the economic vulnerability of the tiny, impoverished islands it has left behind has created what the Institute for the Study of Conflict calls a 'strategic vacuum' in the area, unsettling the balance of power and raising Washington's fears that Cuba might take advantage of the situation to extend its influence.

In August 1979 Philip Habib, a former Under Secretary of State, was despatched to Trinidad, Guyana, Jamaica, Barbados and Antigua. His report concluded that economic and social instability in the Caribbean would provide Cuba with 'targets of opportunity' in the region. This partly explains the relentless hostility of the United States (and Britain) to the Grenadan revolution.

At the root of Washington's concern is the realization that not all the islands of the Caribbean accept the model of development promoted by the United States as appropriate to their needs and they have therefore not fallen as naturally into the American orbit as expected. However, the United States has chosen to interpret the search for an economic system capable of meeting peoples' basic needs in Cold War terms.

The traditional economic role of the Eastern Caribbean islands under colonial rule was to supply Britain with a limited number of raw materials. They are all heavily dependent on export agriculture, mostly bananas and, increasingly, tourism. These activities can hardly sustain a heathly economy and all the islands suffer from high levels of unemployment and poverty and chronic foreign exchange shortages, exacerbated not only by rising oil prices but also by their dependence on imports of food and most other basic requirements. In August 1979 Hurricane Allen swept through the region devastating the islands and underlining their vulnerability. 97% of St Lucia's banana plantations were destroyed, 95% of St Vincent's, 75% of Dominica's and 40% of Grenada's. The Geest company which markets the produce estimated that exports would not resume in the three most devastated islands until April 1981, allowing other banana exporting countries to further erode the market share of the Caribbean islands.

The State Department clearly sees the weakness of the islands' economies as a danger to regional stability. Viron Vaky told the House Foreign Affairs Committee in December 1979:

As to the Eastern Caribbean as a whole, with the exception of Barbados, which is in pretty good shape economically, you have a number of deep-seated socio-economic problems which create vulnerabilities. These in turn create political problems. You have situations in which small states, because of their smallness, have trouble being viable economically. Unemployment in many of these areas runs as high as 50 or 60 percent. The Deputy Prime Minister of St Lucia told me, for example, that among the young, under 25, the unemployment rate was 60 percent in his country. Opportunities for education, for advancement, are very limited. These create very difficult, very traumatic kinds of vulnerabilities. It is for that reason, in fact, that you have seen these tremendous problems. You see a tendency, particularly among the young political leaders to seek other ways and systems to try to overcome these im-

Opposing Camps

'It is patently obvious that the development strategies that we have espoused and tried in the region over the last 25-30 years have not worked . . . The failure of the strategy of inviting in foreign capital and espousing domestic capitalist development has led to the rejection, in some quarters, of not just the whole system and the philosophies that provided its intellectual justification, but of the relationship with the international system which had developed, and particularly the nature and forms of the relationship with the West. In some quarters, therefore, (and it is stronger in some countries than in others), there is the search for new forms of social and economic organization and for new relationships. Thus capitalism is rejected, socialism espoused, the West and imperialism denounced and rejected, and new relationships sought and developed with the Socialist countries or with other states. In other quarters the old ideologies and strategies continue to hold sway, and even intensify their hold. The result, however, is intense and even bitter conflict within and between states of the region. Further, and what is even more dangerous, is the form in which the debate is posed — in terms of ideology and alliances. This excites the attention of extra-regional powers and invites a stepped-up penetration of the region by them as they seek to influence its direction in their own interests. The opposition of socialism to capitalism and East to West brings the cold war into the region with seriously invidious consequences. American penetration of the region has, for example, increased sharply over the last year. There is stepped-up American military activity; greatly stepped-up intelligence activity; increased penetration by the foundations and other arms of the American politico-military machinery; increased manipulation of domestic politics. This is in clear response to the direction that is being taken in some areas of the region and to US perceptions and fears of increased Russian and Cuban influence. In precisely the same way, there is increased Venezuelan concern in the region.'

Dr Trevor Farrell, economist at the University of the West Indies, in Caribbean Contact, *March 1981.*

mediate problems. Cuba plays to that. Cuba does not cause the problems, but they surely take advantage of them, holding themselves forwards as the way to solve illiteracy or ill health and so on.

Two months later, in February 1980, John Bushnell, Deputy Assistant Secretary of State for Inter-American Affairs, told a House subcommittee how Cuban influence could be countered:

Seeking Help from the Devil

'In economic desperation, these Caribbean territories are really prepared to seek help from the devil himself. But as countries try all kinds of different expedients, the result is intensified fragmentation in the region, since the wooing of different aid sources stimulates the taking of different political stances! In some territories it is the welcoming of offshore banks and offshore medical schools. In some it is the surrender to the Mafia, to casinos and to the rip-off of the people by fly-by-night investors. The relationship between such people and the politicians leads inevitably to the corruption of the politicians and the political process, to the destruction of the social fabric and to the banditry that passes for government in some of the smaller islands. Walthers' Antigua and Patrick John's Dominica are two easy examples. Other territories embittered and disillusioned by the mask for exploitation that US and European aid has turned out to be, feel forced to seek aid from the socialist bloc. They believe, not always correctly, that they will get a better deal here. This encourages them to take certain kinds of political positions, at least rhetorically. That it is often pure posture can be seen by contrasting what they say with their actual domestic policies. The result, though, is to excite American reaction. The Americans, of course, want the region to be "stable" — meaning apparently, that we should lie down quietly so that we can be better and more effectively penetrated.'

Dr Trevor Farrell, Caribbean Contact, *November 1979.*

. . . The rapid reduction in the British role in the Caribbean requires us to open the door to cooperative security relationships with them. Our security assistance proposals, principally for military training, are modest. But they can have a significant impact in providing security for development. To do otherwise is to leave the field to Cuba, which is aggressively expanding its influence with its smaller Caribbean neighbors.

However, it is precisely Cuba's record of achievements in the field of social welfare and education which has earned the respect of many people in the Caribbean and Central America who simply are looking for ways out of their endemic poverty.

In 1972 there was the beginning of a collective regional acceptance of Cuba's presence in the Caribbean. In that year despite United States threats to cut off aid, Guyana, Jamaica, Barbados and Trinidad and Tobago recognized Cuba. In 1975 the McIntyre Report on Windward-Leeward island independence recognized the positive value of Cuba's presence: 'Four of the independent Commonwealth

Treasure Island

The Caribbean as a whole has attracted a number of unscrupulous American businessmen, but lately the small island of Dominica has become a particular focus for their activities. In January 1979, the island's Prime Minister, Patrick John, made an agreement with a Texan called Ronald Pierson, the owner of the Caribbean Southern Corporation. Pierson was given a 45 square mile duty free zone in the northern part of this 109 square mile island on a 99 year lease which was to cost him a mere US$100 a year. He planned to use the land to build a casino. A public outcry forced John to cancel the deal, and he was led to resign as Prime Minister in May 1979. A caretaker government followed, led by Oliver Seraphin who signed a similar agreement with the Los Angeles based Intercontinental Development and Management Company at the beginning of 1980. The deal would have given the company complete tax free control of Dominica's tourist industry, banking interests, timber exploitation, and a large share in its own industries. It also, through overseas tourist offices, could offer Dominican passports to whoever it pleased, which was widely interpreted as a manoeuvre to enable Iranian exiles to live in the United States. Seraphin's election campaign in July 1980 was financed by a group of Miami businessmen. According to the magazine *Covert Action*: 'Seraphin flew from constituency to constituency by helicopter, piloted by Executive Air Services from the US Virgin Islands; he gave away Texan ten-gallon hats, Caribbean "stingy brim" hats, and tams, and he handed out wristwatches which, when you pressed a button, flashed a picture of him. His full-color brochures, printed in Miami, were in stark contrast to the mimeographed and off-set materials distributed by the other parties.'

Seraphin lost the election to the right-wing Freedom Party led by Eugenia Charles. On 27 April 1981 eight American and two Canadian mercenaries, members of the Ku Klux Klan and various neonazi organizations in North America, were arrested in the United States for attempting to mount an invasion of Dominica. According to the island's Attorney-General, the plotters hoped to gain control of the island so that they could market its marijuana or set up gambling casinos. The leader of the group, Michael Perdue, was reported to have close links with former Prime Minister Patrick John and the head of the army, both in jail on charges of plotting a coup.

Caribbean countries have announced policies of trade and diplomatic relations with Cuba. It is just a matter of time before the Associated States will have to make a similar response. It is becoming increasingly recognized that countries with different ideologies can develop mutually beneficial trade, technical assistance . . . and that much can be gained from the Cuban experience.'

Cuban aid to the region mostly takes the form of technical assistance using its most abundant and cheapest resource: people. It has provided medical teams, construction workers and teachers to Guyana, Jamaica, Nicaragua and Grenada. It has a small team of military advisors in Grenada helping to train that country's police force. It undoubtedly hopes to expand its influence and create regional friendships through this assistance, but in view of the United States' persistent antagonism to the island this is hardly surprising. As Anthony Payne, a specialist on Caribbean affairs, points out: '. . . Cuban foreign policy in the region is dominated by the realization that any weakening of American power strengthens Cuban security.'

Nevertheless, Cuba's cultivation of allies in the Caribbean clashes head on with the United States's determination to isolate it and to preserve a commitment to capitalism in its backyard. It has therefore done its utmost to undermine the incipient links forged between Cuba and other Caribbean nations. A number of Caribbean political leaders have responded favourably to inducements offered by American capital and US-dominated international lending agencies. They have opted for a close alliance with the United States and accepted its recipe for economic growth, despite the economic and political dependency this entails, the uneven distribution of wealth it promotes, and its total failure to date to meet the needs of the region's people (see box page 143).

The search for an economic future has thus divided the Caribbean into opposing camps. Following the Grenadan revolution the process of fragmentation accelerated still further, fuelled by the United States' determination to isolate Grenada as it had tried to isolate Cuba. Guyana, Jamaica and St Lucia responded sympathetically to Grenada's assertion of its right to pursue an independent path of development while Trinidad, Barbados, Antigua, St Kitts and St Vincent reacted with considerable hostility. Such polarization has severely handicapped any moves towards independent regional cooperation through a regenerated CARICOM or other regional institutions and has facilitated American economic and political penetration of the Caribbean.

Allies and Rivals

The complexities and uncertainties of regional politics have been exacerbated still further by the fact that the United States is not the only power with interests in the region. In some cases it has found useful allies but in others it has seen its room for manoeuvre considerably reduced.

145

Britain and Holland have for a long time wished to disengage from their colonial commitments in the Caribbean. Britain has collaborated closely with the United States to allay America's fears that by departing from the area it was allowing its former dependencies to fall into the clutches of Cuba. Meetings took place in May, July and October 1979 between the two countries to discuss their policy toward the region and the containment of radical movements there.

The Dutch granted independence to Suriname in 1975. Since a sergeants' coup there in February 1980, the country has experienced continuous instability. A strong left-wing movement within the army has added to the United States' alarm that it might lose another Caribbean country as a consequence of colonial withdrawal. The independence of the Dutch Antilles has been delayed, partly because some of the islands oppose it and partly, it may be assumed, to await a more auspicious political moment. The United States has considerable interests in the islands which house a number of strategically important oil refineries. The island of Aruba is virtually controlled by two American multinationals, Exxon and W.R. Grace.

France is determined to retain a hold on its territories in the Caribbean. Martinique, Guadeloupe and Guyane (French Guiana) were made administrative departments of metropolitan France after the Second World War. Typical of the French attitude is the statement of Paul Dijoud, the French minister for overseas territories, during a visit to Guyane in 1979: 'It is necessary once and for all that Guianese understand that it is home territory for France, that they are French and that they must look neither backwards nor question the future.'

The economies of these territories are totally dependent on France and are maintained by massive aid flows. France has deliberately run down the traditional plantation economy of the two islands as their sugar exports competed with the European sugar beet industry. Martinique and Guadeloupe are destined to become tourist playgrounds for Europeans while France has decided after years of neglect to develop some of the timber and other resources of Guyane. Unemployment in these territories is 20-30%. An estimated 400,000 French West Indians have emigrated to France, while white immigrants are encouraged to take up jobs in the territories.

In the late 1970s independence movements emerged in the French territories. A guerrilla organization appeared in Guadeloupe in March 1980 and unrest was particularly marked in Martinique. Paul Dijoud accused Cuba of fomenting unrest: 'International communism is on the march in the Caribbean, and Cuba is the staging post for Soviet action'. He announced that France would take firm action to protect its territories: 'If there is any disorder and with all means possible . . . France is one of the rare countries in the world which is capable of

146

transporting to the Antilles and Guiana, in ten hours, a division and a half of crack troops.' He also announced France's willingness to collaborate with other 'West and free' nations to halt Cuban penetration in the region.

Since then France has been on the offensive in the Caribbean. It supplemented its 3,000 strong regional garrison with 220 riot police in March 1980. They 'inspire good behaviour', remarked Dijoud. It has also made an effort to extend its influence to the English-speaking Caribbean, particularly Dominica which is sandwiched between the two French islands. It has offered technical assistance to a number of islands of the eastern Caribbean and has sought observer status with CARICOM. It remains to be seen whether the new French President, Francois Mitterrand will adopt a more progressive policy towards the colonies.

Another active power in the Commonwealth Caribbean is Canada. Canadian interests in the Caribbean are substantial: the Commonwealth Caribbean is the largest single recipient of Canadian aid and Canadian investment in the region is an estimated US$500 million. Canada has avoided the image of an imperial power in the region despite its traditional support for American positions in international affairs.

But Canada's investment and banking strategies differ very little from those of the United States. Many large multinationals with interests in the Caribbean which are considered Canadian, such as

---

The Canadian Connection

'(Canada) acts through its extensive investments in both Latin America and the Caribbean, laundering American capital through Canadian-based multinational corporations. In a continent which has a long-standing anti-Yankee tradition, the "Canadian" front (Brascan, Alcan) and low profile (has Canada ever landed Marines in Latin America?) help to mystify Latin American sentiment about the actual bonds of dependency and control which continue to exist. Nations, conscious of their overriding dependency upon the US, see the diversification towards foreign investment from other countries as a way of altering that deleterious primary relationship. By welcoming Canadian capital as if it is very different from American capital, they become victims of covert mechanisms which camouflage US control of the major Canadian multinationals.'

Tim Draimin and Jamie Swift, quoted in R. Chodos, The Caribbean Connection, *James Lorimer & Company, Toronto 1977.*

Alcan, Falconbridge Nickel and Inco, are in fact controlled by United States capital. The chief officers of Inco, for example, are American and its headquarters remained in New York even when Canadian ownership went above 50%. Two Canadian writers Tim Draimin and Jamie Swift, have suggested that there is a political pay-off to the United States in making use of Canada's more acceptable profile to gain control over the Caribbean's natural resources (see box). In terms of foreign policy, Canada remains a firm ally of the United States.

A number of Latin American countries have attempted to assert their influence in the Caribbean. Venezuela in particular has tried to present itself as a Caribbean power and to use its oil wealth to extend its influence in the area. Between 1978 and 1980 Venezuela provided more than US$450 million for aid and cooperation programmes in the region. It has given loans to Barbados, Guyana and Jamaica and negotiated economic and technical assistance programmes with Antigua, St Kitts and Grenada. In 1980 it signed an agreement with Mexico to provide jointly low interest loans and oil for some of the Caribbean countries worst hit by rising oil prices, including Nicaragua. Venezuelan private banks and investment companies are also increasingly active in the region.

Venezuela is undoubtedly partly motivated by a desire to counteract Cuban influence in the Caribbean, as the Venezuelan Foreign Minister Jose Zambrano implied when he said: 'Venezuela is cooperating with all the nations in the region and strengthening democracy and freedom there. The region must be kept at peace and away from unacceptable totalitarian systems.'

Under the Christian Democrat government of Luis Herrera Campins, which came to power in 1978, Venezuela has joined the conservative axis in the region and is considered one of the United States' allies. Whereras, under the previous government of Carlos Andres Perez's social democratic party *Accion Democratica*, Venezuela was one of the leading champions of Third World demands in the North-South dialogue, Herrera Campins has limited himself much more to South-South relations. The differences between the two are particularly marked by the present government's response to the civil war in El Salvador. *Accion Democratica* supports the opposition front in El Salvador while the Christian Democrat government of Herrera Campins supports the Christian Democrat junta. The President of El Salvador, Jose Napoleon Duarte, lived in Venezuela for seven years following his exile in 1972 when he formed close friendships with ex-President Rafael Caldera of the Venezuelan Christian Democrat party (COPEI) and Aristides Calvani, deputy Secretary General of COPEI and a prominent advisor to President Herrera on Central America. They argue that the civilian-military junta in El Salvador represents

148

the political centre and is the only hope of a moderate solution to the conflict.

However, there are members of the party and the government who are not happy with this support for the junta. Under its democratically elected Presidents, Venezuelan foreign policy has traditionally opposed authoritarian regimes. But it now finds itself identified with a government which is widely held responsible for the deaths of many thousands of Salvadoreans. Although United States policy-makers view Venezuela as a major ally in the region the Venezuelans do not totally agree with the direction of US foreign policy under Reagan and there are many who are uncomfortable with the close association between the two. Venezuela would like to see an end to military regimes and oligarchic domination in the region. It would not support direct US intervention and would prefer not to see the Caribbean basin become an arena for East-West conflict. Venezuela still gives aid to Grenada and Nicaragua. Nevertheless, these differences have not yet affected Venezuela's identification with and material support for the junta in El Salvador and this has been extremely useful to the United States.

Trinidad is particularly resentful of Venezuela's role in the Caribbean, for geopolitical rather than ideological reasons. The exploitation of its oil wealth in the 1970s dramatically changed Trinidad's status in the region and it has harboured its own ambitions for regional influence and a claim to be the Caribbean alternative to Cuba. Prime Minister Eric Williams accused Venezuela of attempting a neo-colonization of the region, but his own offers of aid with strings attached alienated a number of Caribbean countries. Trinidad has become increasingly isolated in the region although it is one of the anti-communist bastions of the area and its hostility toward Grenada rivals even that of Barbados. Eric Williams died in March 1981. Elections for his successor are scheduled for late 1981 and it is not yet clear how this will affect Trinidad's policy towards the rest of the Caribbean.

The discovery of vast oil deposits in Mexico has considerably enhanced that country's international stature and has encouraged it to initiate a more active foreign policy than ever before. Mexico's history and geographical position have made it one of the most nationalist countries in the region, strongly opposed to American intervention. Although it has never been able to ignore the powerful presence of its neighbour, Mexico has consistently maintained a more independent foreign policy than any other country in Latin America. In 1964 Mexico was the only member of the Organization of American States to oppose the breaking off of relations with Cuba, and in 1965 Mexico voted against the creation of an inter-American force to intervene in

149

the Dominican Republic and introduced resolutions in the OAS and the UN calling for the US to withdraw. In that year the United States Congress voted to reduce the Mexican sugar quota, a decision which, according to the Mexican ambassador in Washington at the time, was 'based on inappropriate criticism in our international policy, with reference to the attitude adopted by our country with respect to Cuba, with respect to the armed intervention in the Dominican Republic, and for our supposed lack of support for the Alliance for Progress'.

While the Mexican government's foreign policy is far more radical than its domestic policies, Mexico's support for the Sandinistas, its subsequent economic assistance to the Sandinista government, and its backing for the opposition front in El Salvador have been very important to those movements. Mexico is not motivated by a desire to see radical socialist governments on its doorstep. It is undoubtedly much closer to the political parties of the centre who have joined the armed struggle than to the guerrilla movements in the region. But it acknowledges that change in Central America will now only come about through force of arms. Its main objective is to secure long-term stability on its frontiers which it does not consider can best be achieved through support for unpopular dictators. It is anxious to promote a negotiated settlement in El Salvador and to prevent an outbreak of a civil war in the region which might drag it more directly into the struggle and force it to channel its oil wealth into an arms build-up rather than to deal with the country's own serious socio-economic problems. 'The crisis that has as its temporal epicentre the Salvadorean conflict', warned President Lopez Portillo, 'has become a spiral that threatens to envelop all the states of the area. It is necessary to avoid the internationalization of the crisis. We are certain that a military solution is not viable and that only a political solution will permit the re-establishment of peace.' The possibility of civil war on the other side of its border with Guatemala and increased American involvement in the region must be viewed with great alarm by Mexico.

Many suspect that Mexico is also trying to carve out its own sphere of influence in Central America by supporting progressive movements which it believes will sooner or later come to power.

The United States is evidently perturbed by Mexico's support for the movements for change in the region. There is a body of opinion in the United States which believes that Mexico itself is in danger from the regional unrest. Unequal distribution of wealth (about 45% of the population still lives in the countryside and earns only 6% of national income), poverty (75% of the population earns less than the legal minimum wage) and unemployment (less than 50% of the population is fully employed) affect Mexico as much as the other countries in the region. William Colby, former director of the CIA, told a US congressional conference on national security in 1977, 'We don't have to go over to Asia or Europe to look for a crisis when Mexico is in our backyard'. The right in the United States sees Mexico as particularly vulnerable to 'communist subversion'; Daniel James wrote in the *Washington Quarterly* in the summer of 1980:

The area's largest, richest and most advanced country, Mexico, is the big prize. Certainly it has been Moscow's most important Caribbean objective since Constantine A. Oumansky, its ambassador to Mexico during World War II, had the foresight to utilize it as a 'window' to probe and exploit American weaknesses. Mexico today, needless to point out, is far more than a window: it is a growing industrial power in its own right with 72 million people. The United States could no more afford to let it fall into Soviet hands than, say, Texas or California.

To those familiar with the Mexican ruling elite's sophisticated management of social conflict, the suggestion that Mexico is likely to be affected in the short term by regional upheaval is absurd. But clearly the United States has several reasons for wanting to remain on good terms with its southern neighbour, not least of which is Mexico's very considerable oil reserves. Indeed, after Canada, Mexico is the United States' second most important supplier of essential raw materials and its main source of many rare metals.

It is not certain, however, whether this will give Mexico any special leverage in modifying United States policy toward the region. The Mexican economy is vulnerable and dependent, particularly on the United States. In 1980 the United States accounted for 69% of total foreign investment in the country and is Mexico's major trading partner. The migration of hundreds of thousands of Mexicans, many illegally, to the United States each year in search of temporary employment is very important to the Mexican government in relieving the pressures of unemployment in the country. In addition, thousands of Mexicans now live permanently in the United States. It is possible that with the intelligent use of its oil revenues Mexico may reduce some of this dependence, but in the meantime it has to balance its radical foreign policy with the need to avoid alienating the United States too much. Mexico has begun to strengthen its position by sponsoring a regional grouping of Latin American and Caribbean nationalist and social democratic parties, the Permanent Conference of the Political Parties of Latin America (COPPPAL). It has also tried to forge stronger links with Europe as a counterweight to the United States and in this it has found useful allies among the European social democrat parties.

In the mid-1970s the European social democrat movement began to take an increasing interest in Latin America and the Caribbean. According to Francois Mitterrand, the movement aims to promote a third way 'between the regimes of Pinochet and Videla and the system of Castro'. The Socialist International, which is led by the European social democrat parties, has set up a Committee for Latin America and the Caribbean which at its 1980 conference in Santo Domingo declared its firm support for the Puerto Rican independence struggle, for the Sandinista government in Nicaragua and for the opposition front in El Salvador.

The Socialist International has established close ties with the progressive forces in the region such as the New Jewel Movement in Grenada, the FSLN in Nicaragua, the Democratic Revolutionary Front (FDR) in El Salvador, Michael Manley's PNP in Jamaica and the PRD in the Dominican Republic. It recognizes that many elements in these movements are not hostile to capitalism as such but merely wish to curb its excesses, which fits in well with its own preoccupations. It therefore identifies primarily with nationalist and reformist movements, but where these have been forced to join with more radical organizations advocating the armed overthrow of corrupt dictatorships, the Socialist International has continued to offer its material and verbal support while seeking to strengthen the politically more 'moderate' elements.

Whatever its motivations, the European social democrat movement has made it more difficult for the United States to pursue an interventionist policy in Central America. Pressure from the base of the Social Democrat Party has helped persuade the sometimes reluctant West German social democrat government of Helmut Schmidt to distance itself from some of the American policy initiatives on El Salvador. The ultimate objectives of social democracy may well one day conflict with a more radical challenge to capitalism in the region, but its present posture, like that of Mexico, has helped moderate the United States' role. The election of the socialist Francois Mitterrand as President of France in 1981 will further enhance the bargaining power of the European social democrats *vis-à-vis* the United States. Mitterrand has taken a particular interest in Latin America.

The Caribbean basin has thus been a 'target of opportunity' for not one but many external interests, but the decisive influence remains that of the United States; Carter's last year in office would reinforce the point.

Carter's Last Stand

Shortly after the Nicaraguan revolution, Cyrus Vance had told Senator Richard Stone: 'there is no evidence of any substantial increase of the Soviet military presence in Cuba over the past several years or of the presence of a Soviet military base'. However, in September 1980, just two months later, there were reports that 3,000 Russian combat troops had been 'discovered' on Cuba. The troops had in fact been there for the past seventeen years as the United States was well aware, but the issue provided the pretext Carter needed to announce the tough new policy toward Central America and the Caribbean which Brzezinski had been advocating all year. Carter's 'last stand' was to comprise military, political and economic initiatives; the promotion of human rights and gradual reforms were not totally abandoned by the administration but they increasingly took secondary place to the main objective of containing 'communist expansion' in the region.

In a televised speech in early October 1979, Carter announced that he was forming a permanent Caribbean contingency task force with headquarters in Key West, Florida. The task force consists of security officers and enlisted men and is seen as a joint planning staff (see box). He also announced an 'increase (in) our economic assistance to alleviate the unmet economic and human needs in the Caribbean region and further to ensure the ability of troubled peoples to resist social turmoil and possible communist domination'. At the same time Carter declared his intention to inject more resources into rapid deployment forces 'to protect our interests and act in response to requests for help from our allies and friends'.

The Caribbean's Rotten Apple

'My people aren't meant to fight the 3,000 man Russian brigade or the Cubans, but we're meant to control the force that will fight them. That's the purpose of this headquarters, to have forces assigned to us in the event of a contingency or an emergency in this part of the world . . . I've heard rumors that it was conceived because of political motivations, but whatever brought about this task force, when Mr Carter established it, he fulfilled a longstanding extremely valid military requirement to have a group of people focus in on the Caribbean . . . We've left a rotten apple in the middle of the Caribbean basin down here, and that rotten apple is Fidel Castro.'

Rear-Admiral McKenzie, head of the Caribbean Joint Task Force, New York Times, *30 November 1980.*

In late October a memorandum drawn up by Brzezinski was leaked to the press. It called for measures to prop up anti-communist governments in the Western Hemisphere and the stepping up of a 'worldwide campaign of propaganda and political pressure' against the Russians and the Cubans.

The new policy was put into operation immediately. American warships began to be seen more frequently in the Caribbean on 'goodwill' cruises and carrying out military manoeuvres. A mock landing exercise involving 1,800 marines was held at Guantanamo Bay and spy flights over Cuba were renewed. In May 1980, Operation Solid Shield, an annual event usually confined to the south east of the United States, took place in the Caribbean under the command of the Key West Task Force. It involved 20,000 personnel, 42 ships and 350 aircraft.

In January 1980 Major General Robert Schweitzer, the US army's director of strategy, planning and policy, visited Port-au-Prince and Santo Domingo. While in Santo Domingo he announced he had come to strengthen links with 'our Dominican friends in the battle against the communist threat' and he promised the country US backing wherever that threat arose in the Caribbean or Latin America. Later in the year there were reports that a secret understanding had been reached whereby the Dominican government would intervene in the event of an insurrection against the Duvalier regime in Haiti.

In February 1980 Miguel D'Escoto, Nicaragua's Foreign Minister, told the Mexican newspaper *Excelsior*: 'If the Sandinista revolution was on the point of triumph now instead of last July, there would have been a North American intervention'.

The military build-up which took place was aimed at erecting a *cordon sanitaire* around Nicaragua and to prevent the spread of the revolution to El Salvador and in the Caribbean, to increase the military capacity of some of the smaller islands of the Eastern Caribbean.

In December 1979 the administration proposed a military package of US$10-20 million for the Eastern Caribbean, the Dominican Republic and Central America. The money was to cover International Military Education and Training (IMET) and Foreign Military Sales (FMS) credits. In Central America the main recipients were Honduras and El Salvador, though the administration made clear that it would consider resuming military aid to Guatemala, hitherto blocked by Congress and the Guatemalan government's own refusal to submit a request.

The military situation in El Salvador was one of the United States' main preoccupations during 1980 as the guerrilla movement grew in strength and the opposition political forces came together in the Democratic Revolutionary Front (see Part V).

In April 1980 the House Appropriations Subcommittee on Foreign

Operations approved the reprogramming of US$5.7 million in FMS credits to El Salvador. At the same time US$3.5 million in FMS credits to Honduras was approved together with an increase in IMET funds. The administrations' request for military assistance for Fiscal Year 1981 reflected the escalation of United States military involvement in the region as further FMS credits and IMET funds were programmed for El Salvador and Honduras. This included US$5.5 million for El Salvador, US$5 million in FMS credits to Honduras and US$498,000 in IMET to be used to train 43 Honduran officers in the United States and 207 at the US Army School of the Americas in Panama.

In the Eastern Caribbean the United States collaborated closely with Britain to promote the idea of a joint regional coastguard defence force which would supplement the islands' poor internal security forces although ostensibly it was aimed at Cuba.

In early 1979 the British government had opened discussions with Barbados about the idea of such a coastguard. Following the Grenadan revolution plans were made for the establishment of an Organization of Eastern Caribbean States (it was finally set up in July 1981) one of whose purposes would be to promote regional defence including a regional police force to deal with any internal armed threat to elected governments.

In December 1979 impetus was given to the project when Barbados helped St Vincent suppress a rebellion of Rastafarian militants on Union Island. Tom Adams, the Prime Minister of Barbados, clearly welcomed the role of regional policemen and offered to send troops to any other island which requested them. Barbados emerged as the coordinator of what was called a coastguard and fisheries protection service, which initially included Barbados, St Lucia and St Vincent, with Dominica and Trinidad as possible future members. Barbados received US$10 million worth of assistance for the coastguard from Britain and additional funds for qualified Royal Navy officers and men to serve in the boats while training coastguard personnel. In 1980 Barbados and St Vincent ordered armed patrol boats from Britain.

During a visit to the Caribbean in August 1980 Lord Carrington, the British Foreign Secretary, stated: 'The policy generally on arms sales is that each case is decided upon its merits . . . Broadly speaking we sell arms to our friends and to those whom we wish to encourage to defend themselves.'

It is not surprising, in view of United States and British hostility to the social experiment in Grenada, that Britain's Conservative government has refused to sell arms to that country. It has, however, while expressing concern over human rights and the failure to call elections in Grenada, resumed arms sales to the military dictatorship in Chile in July 1980.

Canada has also played its role in US military plans for the region. In May 1980 a story appeared in the *Winnipeg Free Press* about Canadian government pressure at the behest of the US State Department, on the Canadian International Development Agency (CIDA) 'to begin providing gunboats and other types of security assistance including police training to small Eastern Caribbean islands such as St Lucia, St Kitts and Dominica'.

Canadian and British collaboration has clearly been very useful to the United States. As the Institute for the Study of Conflict has pointed out: 'The preponderant historical relationship of the US with Central and South America virtually ensures that burgeoning local nationalism must to some extent take on an anti-US character. US naval power . . . is not readily acceptible even to Western inclined states.'

The United States did, however, step up its own military assistance to the region. The administration's package for 1981 included IMET and FMS credits for Barbados, St Lucia and St Vincent. It also increased its intelligence operations in the Caribbean. A small security team was installed in the US embassy in Bridgetown, and Antigua became the chosen site for the Barbadan Embassy's first branch office and other intelligence activities. In 1980 the US government's Voice of America radio station set up a relay transmitter on the island to broadcast specifically to the Eastern Caribbean. The Deputy Prime Minister of the island had at first rejected the proposal and had informed the State Department that 'every Caribbean government whether right, left or center in political orientation would feel that Antigua had become a bastion of US metropolitan presence in the Caribbean'. He was overruled by the Prime Minister. Subsequently, the Voice of America announced plans to bring in sixty US technicians to operate the station, although according to information gathered by the American magazine, *Covert Action*, none are required to maintain a relay station. The station is located on the large US military installation on Antigua which houses both a naval and an air force base; the naval base is the major 'secret' underwater listening post for the Eastern Caribbean already referred to. According to sources interviewed by *Covert Action* both bases are 'being beefed up because of Grenada'.

As well as military initiatives, the Carter administration took new political and diplomatic ones in its last year. There were five changes of ambassadors in Central America in the space of a year. The 'new breed of activist envoys' as *Time* magazine described them, such as Robert White in El Salvador and Lawrence Pezzullo in Nicaragua, were mostly associated with Carter's human rights policy and they continued to use its rhetoric and to pursue less overt means of preserving US influence in the region even while more confrontational policies were being promoted elsewhere in the administration.

Politically as well as militarily Honduras was considered one of the cornerstones of US strategy towards Central America. It was the one country where the movement for change was still relatively weak, though growing, and the United States had sufficient room for manoeuvre to be able to pursue its new military initiatives simultaneously with support for 'democratization'. The US ambassador to the country was reported to have played an important role in persuading the military to accept a return to civilian rule. In the elections for the Constituent Assembly which were called in April 1980 to prepare for the transition, the United States strongly backed the Liberal Party rather than the ultra conservative National Party. The victory of the Liberal Party was in fact later nullified when the army, still in control, proceeded to reduce its influence in the cabinet. However, Washington did gain sufficient leverage to enable it to arrange peace talks between El Salvador and Honduras, a major objective of its policy at the time. A peace treaty was finally signed in October 1980 opening the way for close collaboration between the two armies against the guerrilla movement in El Salvador, and for attempts to revive the Central American Common Market which Honduras agreed to rejoin.

While the struggle in Central America continued to preoccupy the administration, by the middle of 1980 the political panorama in the Caribbean was beginning to change in America's favour. It looked as

---

The Honduran Bridge

'Though each nation is different and must solve its domestic problems in its own way, the Central American isthmus is also a regional unity in some fundamental senses. The development of one country in the region is closely linked to the fate of the others. Our policy must take this into consideration . . . We are impressed by the Honduran government's demonstration of social awareness and its commitment to restore constitutional rule. Honduras' location between Nicaragua and El Salvador gives it a key geopolitical position in the "bridge building" process we hope will emerge in Central America. Additionally, it is important that Honduras not be exploited as a conduit for the infiltration of men and arms to feed conflicts in neighboring El Salvador and Nicaragua.'

William Bowdler, Assistant Secretary of State for Inter-American Affairs, Statement before the Inter-American Affairs Subcommittee of the House of Representatives, May 1980.

if the plan to build a conservative pro-American axis in the region was succeeding.

In December 1979 the right-wing party of Milton Cato in St Vincent won elections in which the left only obtained 14% of the vote and gained no seats in parliament. In St Lucia the victory of the Labour Party in July 1979 produced no radical initiatives as the party became embroiled in a bitter conflict between the Prime Minister, Allan Louisy, and his left-wing deputy, George Odlum. Louisy had agreed before the election that he would step down in Odlum's favour, but he reneged on the agreement, accusing Odlum of making unauthorized contacts with socialist countries.

In Antigua, the conservative Bird government was re-elected in April 1980. The Antigua-Caribbean Liberation movement, which at one time had seen its support grow as a result of revelations of government corruption, was routed. In St Kitts-Nevis, the elections in February 1980 also saw a victory for the right and it was reported that the new coalition government was refusing to have any formal relations with the Grenadian government. In Dominica the July 1980 election produced a victory for the right-wing Freedom Party of Eugenia Charles.

Guyana also, once considered part of the pro-Cuba camp, was now very much favoured by the United States. In 1979 the departing US ambassador had said in a farewell speech that differences between Guyana and the US were not to be taken seriously: 'The important thing is of course the existence of a bond of friendship and mutual respect of both sides which can prevent such differences from becoming acrimonious and harmful.'

United States aid increased from US$2 million in 1976 to US$24.7 million in 1978, 33% of the total US aid to the country over the past twenty-five years. Another sign of United States approval was the support Guyana received from the IMF. The cost of the IMF imposed austerity measures, which always accompany its financial assistance, was very high for the Guyanese people: it included widespread public sector lay-offs and a rapid fall in real wages and was backed up by escalating state violence and repression. Nevertheless the IMF was sufficiently pleased with the 1978 programme to negotiate a new three-year extended facility in 1979.

The resistance to the Burnham government in Guyana was led by the Working People's Alliance, a radical movement formed in 1978 and clearly of more concern to the United States than Burnham's corrupt and brutal regime. In June 1980 the leader of the party and internationally respected historian, Walter Rodney, was murdered in circumstances which pointed strongly to government responsibility. Even the State Department was forced to admit this in a report in

March 1981: 'Available information indicates that the government was implicated in the June 13 death of WPA activist Walter Rodney, and in the subsequent removal of key witnesses from the country.' This still did not shake US confidence in the Guyanese government. One week after Rodney's death, the IMF and the World Bank announced one of the first joint funding projects they had ever awarded: a US$100 million package and support for a multi-billion dollar hydro-power aluminium smelter scheme for Guyana.

Following Rodney's murder, Maurice Bishop of Grenada stated: 'If the best of our Caribbean sons can be cut down in such a manner this can usher in a new and sinister phase of Mafia and CIA-type approach to politics, by removing violently the progressive leadership of the Caribbean.' He charged the CIA with aiming to destroy the 'revolutionary process' in Cuba, Nicaragua and Grenada and suggested that 'progressive leaders' in Jamaica, Guyana, St Lucia and Suriname were also in danger.

A week after his statement, Bishop and his entire cabinet narrowly escaped death when a bomb exploded at a rally in the Grenadan capital. Bishop accused those responsible of having close connections with the CIA, particularly as the technology used to manufacture the bomb could not have come from Grenada. It was not the first time since the revolution that Grenada had been under attack. In November 1979 the government discovered plans for a three-pronged invasion of the island in American ships backed by 100 mercenaries based in Miami.

The existence of a growing body of mercenaries made up of not only anti-Castro Cubans but also former members of Somoza's National Guard is a particular threat to Grenada, Nicaragua and El Salvador. Information emerged in 1980 of training camps in Florida for these forces. In an article in the *Boston Globe* in July 1980, two journalists revealed how they had been taken to a place called *Campo Libertad* (Freedom Camp) in the Florida Everglades, where they saw platoons of Cuban exiles marching in full battle dress and carrying M-16 semi-automatic weapons. The camp commander was a former member of the US Special Forces, Major Jorge Gonzales, who explained that his troops 'will be a well-balanced invasion force . . . I think you will be surprised at how soon the invasion will be on us. We have to be very cautious. But we are well prepared now . . . very well prepared.'

A document, known as the 'Dissent Paper', which appeared in November 1980 purporting to represent the views of officials in the Carter administration who were critical of the direction of its foreign policy, spoke of the formation in 1980 of a paramilitary strike force made up of former members of the Nicaraguan National Guard, anti-Castro Cubans, Guatemalan military personnel and mercenaries.

Their intention was to intervene in El Salvador. The document stated:

It should be noted that US intelligence has kept informed of the plans and capabilities of the paramilitary strike force in Guatemala. US intelligence has been in contact with Nicaraguan exile groups in Guatemala and in Miami and it is aware of their relationship with Cuban exile terrorist groups operating in the US. Charges that the CIA has been promoting and encouraging these organizations have not been substantiated. However, no attempt has been made to restrict their mobility in and out of the US or to interfere with their activities. Their mobility and their links with the US — it seems reasonable to assume — could not be maintained without the tacit consent (or practical incompetence) of at least four agencies: INS, CIA, FBI and US Customs.

The Manley government in Jamaica was another thorn in the United States' flesh. Jamaica is one of the most important countries in the Commonwealth Caribbean. Manley had become a highly respected spokesperson for Third World demands and the democratic socialism of his party, the PNP, inspired a number of movements within the region. In May 1980 the PNP voted to break off negotiations with the IMF as its loan package would have had a devastating effect on the Jamaican poor. Elections were called for later in the year.

The 1980 elections did not begin auspiciously when in June there was an attempted coup led by a right-wing fanatic called Charles Johnson, who had served with the United States in Vietnam. Edward Seaga, leader of the opposition JLP, had been visiting Washington at the time and he denied any involvement in the attempt. His election campaign, as in 1976, was based on inflammatory statements and accusations against the government and its relations with Cuba. His economic pronouncements at first referred to the Puerto Rican model as appropriate for Jamaica, and later he suggested that Jamaica would be in a good position to attract the American manufacturers fleeing the troubles in Central America. In any case, he made clear his commitment to the free enterprise system and foreign investment and that he would support IMF proposals.

The elections were characterized by mounting violence, in which gangs of armed youths roamed the streets. 350 people were killed between February and July alone. Manley acknowledged that there were 'definite signs of destabilization' involving 'a campaign of violence and other activities to create panic and fear'. Andrew Young, the former US ambassador to the United Nations went further. He accused the National Security Council in Washington of encouraging political tensions and economic instability by persuading US investors not to put their money into Jamaica under the Manley government. Such were the suspicions that the Director of the Office of Caribbean

Affairs in the US State Department publicly declared in October that 'The United States is definitely not involved in any covert actions in this area . . . We don't have any effort anywhere in this region to destabilize the country.' He did not explain the presence in the US embassy in Kingston of fifteen CIA personnel named in July 1980 by *Covert Action* magazine. Seaga's victory in the October elections was greeted with enthusiasm by Washington.

Winning more friends and isolating its enemies was not, however a purely military or diplomatic problem for the United States. Even its closest allies in the region looked for more from Washington than displays of military force and offers of military assistance. A Barbadan Foreign Ministry official, for example, while emphasizing his anti-communist convictions, stated:

I don't think a military threat in the Caribbean exists at the moment. It's a battle of minds and more subtle means exist to combat it . . . The United States perceives that by sending us ships, that is protection. I suppose the soldiers and sailors spend money in port, but I prefer more concrete trade favours. If that kind of thing is done in the Caribbean the need for military might will be less. The primary interest in any such (defence) program is US interest, not Barbados interest.

The main concern of pro-Western Caribbean leaders was trade, aid and foreign investment. The United States was not of course unaware of the political importance of its aid programme. During 1980 US spokespersons made it clear that US economic assistance to the Caribbean was to be selective and increasingly bilateral. Sally Sheldon, US ambassador to the Eastern Caribbean and one of the most active of the 'activist envoys', pointed out: 'One reason why we support bilateral aid programmes is so that we can orient our economic aid increasingly towards progressive governments that are democratic.' According to George Roberts, the US ambassador to Guyana, US government support for Caribbean development meant specifically: 'support for systems which encourage the free flow of capital and which encourage imagination and initiative'. 'America's motive for such support', added Loren Lawrence, the US ambassador to Jamaica, 'is not solely humanitarian or altruistic but an outgrowth of Jimmy Carter's view that (we) share a common destiny'.

United States bilateral aid to the Caribbean in 1980 was US$132 million, twice as much as in 1977. The bulk of US aid was for its allies and for those countries who had not strayed too far into the enemy camp. More than half of the US$149 million requested for the Caribbean for 1981 was destined for the Dominican Republic and Haiti, two staunch American allies.

Two Views of Britain's Role

'There is now a government in Kingston whose economic philosophy is distinctly conservative. We therefore have a golden opportunity to show the world that when a country turns so decisively from East to West and from radicalism to moderation, it will not have done so in vain. If we do not seize it, conditions in Jamaica will deteriorate further; disillusionment with western-style economic management will set in; opportunities for Cuban subversion will be enhanced; and the swing to the political right could rapidly be overtaken by a movement far further to the left than Jamaica has ever known . . .

It would, of course, be politically unacceptable in today's world for the United States or for any other western country directly to intervene against (such) externally provoked subversion — although it is sobering to recall that President Johnson did so in the Dominican Republic in 1965 without provoking any challenge. There is therefore no alterantive to effective indigenous security arrangements if stability is to be maintained in the Caribbean.

This is best ensured by a system of collaboration in which elected governments are assisted by their colleagues when internal order breaks down. The West must encourage this by providing diplomatic support for the concept of regional security — cooperation and the necessary equipment for reconnaissance, policing and paramilitary intervention.

But we cannot leave our security policy in the Caribbean at that. There is no substitute for the West's own military power as a source of psychological reassurance for our friends and in deterring threats against which their own defence capabilities would not be adequate. This is particularly true at a time when the Soviet naval involvement in the Caribbean is growing rapidly and is becoming a potent source of reassurance to radical leftist regimes in the region . . .

The greatest danger for the West would be for us to use the obvious vitality of the democratic process in Jamaica to rationalize our extraordinary parsimony in the face of its enormous economic needs and our timidity in the face of dangers to its security. Democracy can never be taken for granted, let alone in a country with the problems of Jamaica today. She needs our wholehearted support as one of the beacons of freedom and hope in a fragile and brutal region of the world.'

Edward Heath, The Times, *10 December 1980.*

'British policy towards the Caribbean is at present set in an unimaginative and conservative mould. It is founded upon the assumption that the best prospect for the economic development of the Commonwealth Caribbean lies in the region's whole-hearted integration into the world economy as currently organized. It seeks to encourage private investment, sees little need for extensive aid programmes, and believes that the traditional free-enterprise policies pursued by Caribbean governments can still lead to the achievement of economic development. Regimes which reject these premises are regarded as dangerously radical and treated accordingly.

The British government entirely endorses American fears about Cuba's role in the Caribbean. At a press conference on a visit to Venezuela the Foreign Secretary, Lord Carrington, described Cuba as "a destabilizing force in the area" and accused the Castro regime of "exporting its system of government or seeking to export it by subversion to other countries". In a clear reference to Grenada and the emergence of other radical groups, particularly in the Eastern Caribbean, he also warned against the possibility of "disruptive elements" taking over the government in certain territories.

This attitude explains Britain's support for the recent scheme to create a joint Eastern Caribbean defence force to guard against the fear of insurrection, and no doubt influenced its decision to supply St Vincent with a new coastal patrol boat. It also indicates the general nature of Britain's response to the process of change that is taking place in the Caribbean. For Britain nothing is more likely to undermine its remaining influence in the Caribbean than to be perceived as a mere echo of the United States Government, ready and willing to support conservative and repressive regimes for fear of left-wing alternatives. Britain's support for Gairy until the moment of his overthrow is still remembered, and the continuation of aid to Burnham's Guyana widely noted in the region today.'

Anthony Payne, Change in the Commonwealth Caribbean, *1981.*

However, for most governments in the region this assistance was completely inadequate for their needs and Carter had made no attempt to meet the region's demands for fairer trade relations. Eugenia Charles of Dominica told Washington: 'The United States presence in our region is not enough. We are not your backyard, we are the front door and you should help us keep it clear.' Various studies commissioned by the administration came to the same conclusion. One World Bank official stated: 'What is necessary is something on a big scale with political appeal that will turn around the prospects of the region in five years.'

Grenada was deliberately excluded from bilateral aid by Britain as well as the United States. It was the only country to be left out of the banana rehabilitation scheme sponsored by the United States and Britain following Hurricane Allen.

In Central America United States economic assistance was concentrated on El Salvador, Honduras and Nicaragua. The US$75 million aid package to Nicaragua involved a bitter battle between those who believed that the country had not yet gone over to the Cuban camp and that the United States should continue to send aid in order to prevent it from so doing and the mounting chorus of opinion that it was already lost. When the package was eventually passed in July 1980 it contained various conditions, including the requirement that the President certify to Congress before releasing the assistance that the government of Nicaragua has not 'cooperated with or harbors any internationalist terrorist organizations or is aiding, abetting or supporting acts of violence or terrorism in other countries'. As we shall see, Reagan was quick to use this clause against Nicaragua following his inauguration in January 1981.

The last year of the Carter administration also saw renewed efforts to promote American investment in the region. In April 1980 the State Department encouraged the merger of the Washington-based Committee on the Caribbean, an organization of businessmen founded by Richard West, chairman of Tesoro Petroleum, into a new Caribbean/ Central American Action Committee (CCAA). The new body aims to create in the United States the 'sense that the Caribbean is a good place for business'. It includes among its members the largest multinational corporations involved in the region: Tesoro Petroleum, the Bank of America, Gulf and Western, Texaco and Amerada Hess. Bob Graham, the Governor of Florida, heads the organization and Peter Johnson, on leave from the State Department, is its executive director. President Carter himself addressed its inaugural meeting. Since then it has organized a number of conferences to discuss business opportunities in the Caribbean (see box page 166).

According to the US Commerce Department, the most attractive investment opportunities are in the Dominican Republic, Haiti, Trinidad and Tobago, Barbados and the Dutch Antilles. 'Most attractive' means of course most profitable, and some of the smaller islands of the Caribbean may not find it easy to attract the kind of foreign investment they seek. Even after the victory of Edward Seaga, Jamaica's crusader for free enterprise, at least one US diplomat expressed doubts about the region's future: 'The conservative sweep is what (the State Department) wants to believe. But the broad middle ground in the Caribbean that is pro-Britain, pro-United States and Canada is going to be eaten away as the economic situation continues to worsen. All the conditions that cause instability around here are going to worsen.'

164

Carter's policy of military containment combined with diplomatic and political pressure and selective economic assistance failed to please any sector of US opinion. It had neither tackled the causes of unrest nor succeeded in crushing the radical movements. On the right there were increasingly strident calls for a firmer military commitment. On the more liberal side of the spectrum, the Dissent Paper quoted earlier expressed the fears of many: '. . . should President Reagan choose to use military force in El Salvador, historians will be able to show that the setting for such actions had been prepared in the last year of the Carter administration.'

Reagan and the New Right

The election of Ronald Reagan to the presidency heralded a new shift in United States foreign policy. There was speculation as to how extreme the shift would be.

Reagan had the backing of the most right wing sectors of the population: small and medium-size businessmen, independent oil magnates, the defence industry, disaffected labour and the so-called Moral Majority of the New Right. The Republican landslide, which gave the party control of the Senate as well as the White House, enabled it to claim a major swing to the right within the country although it in fact won the votes of only 27% of the electorate, 48% of which abstained. Nevertheless, Jerry Falwell, the Moral Majority's foremost evangelist proclaimed: 'The godless minority of treacherous individuals who have been permitted to formulate national policy, must now realize they do not represent the majority . . . The movement made up of conservative Americans can no longer be ignored and silenced. America's destiny awaits action.'

The New Right had great expectations of Reagan's victory but there was no guarantee that their extreme views would predominate once Reagan was in office. It was noted that in 1968 Nixon, also a candidate of the Republican right, had done an about-turn after defeating Nelson Rockefeller and appointed his opponent's aide, Henry Kissinger, as his national security advisor. Nixon's right wing campaign advisors, such as Richard Allen, suddenly found themselves without influence. The trilateralists of the eastern establishment had already made some effort to come to terms with Reagan and the selection of the 'moderate' Republican George Bush as vice-presidential candidate was considered a victory for these interests. Bush had been a member of the Trilateral Commission since 1977 and reported to be David Rockefeller's personal choice for the presidency.

Whatever the final complexion of the Reagan administration, the

The Right Kind of Investment

The following are extracts from an interview with Peter Johnson, executive director of Caribbean/Central American Action (CCAA), and Alice Booth, director of communications and government affairs for CCAA, published in *Multinational Monitor*:

'MONITOR: Why did the change from the Committee for the Caribbean to Caribbean/Central American Action come about?

JOHNSON: To telescope this thing fairly drastically, we were asked if we would change our name in such a way that the President of the United States could sort of formally and officially bless the whole thing. So we changed the name from Committee for the Caribbean to Caribbean/Central American Action, we made very clear in our new by-laws that we were an apolitical organization, that we were unqualifiedly private sector with respect to funding. Those were the two key ingredients: apolitical in character and unqualifiedly private sector . . . we didn't turn to the White House, they turned to us. It's very clear. They came to us; we didn't go to them. It's very important. They came and sat in our conference room for two hours, and said that is what *we* want.

MONITOR: How much do national security concerns inform the activities of CCAA?

JOHNSON: With respect to the national security thing, CCAA is interested in helping relationships between the United States and these island countries. It would seem to me that that relationship, that political relationship, you can call it national security if you want to, is best served if you've got the kind of societies that we've mentioned — freely functioning and consistently functioning democratic systems, and vigorous private sector, trade and business occurring on a mutually respected basis between those island countries, with what they can produce and manufacture, and this country, with what it can provide.

MONITOR: But what precisely is the national security risk involved?

JOHNSON: Well, I mean, the national security risk, the national security ingredient in all this, would be, if the private sectors cannot perform, and if we can't produce, or for some reason are stifled in the process, then you're not going to have the kind of productivity, the kind of results for the people of these countries that you could best have.

MONITOR: What effect did Cuba have on the formation of the group?

JOHNSON; We're not operating against Cuba. That's never been part of our premise at the CCAA. But if you're engaged in an enterprise where, as I think we are, you're trying to help strengthen the private sector, which will invigorate the democratic process in these countries, then you could say that this is against Cuba, if you want to.

MONITOR: Can we turn to CCAA's business activities? You speak of bringing "the right kind of investment" to the region. What is "the right kind of investment" that you are trying to bring in?
JOHNSON: . . . you got enclaves; you got the agricultural sort of stuff. When I say the right kind, those are the two broadest areas that I'm shooting at.

MONITOR: Could you talk about what sort of companies you're going to, with those sorts of plans?
JOHNSON: We find a major company which is involved in the Caribbean that we can sit down with and say: You know, you're doing well in this area; now there are some real high needs over in that area; why don't you go into that area as well. For profit; I'm not asking you to be a philanthropist about it. Go into whatever the hell you want, you know, you go in and you can make some money at it . . . I would not, because Gulf and Western had a problem or United Brands had a problem in 1955, I would not exclude them. The last thing I would do is to exclude those kinds of companies from the kind of productive role they have to play in this region . . .

I'm aware just like everybody else is about problems Gulf and Western has had in its history in the Dominican Republic. Gulf and Western is a good company . . .
ALICE BOOTH: We're engaging these companies in looking at the region not only out of their own personal self-interest in terms of their immediate profit, but also out of perhaps what they perceive as a broader self-interest, which is the economic growth and stability, political stability, whatever you want to call it, of the region as a whole.

MONITOR: If we could shift the discussion to some of the Central American countries for a moment . . . Advisors to President-elect Reagan are on record favoring the restoration of military aid to Guatemala. You've staked-out aid as an area that you're interested in lobbying on. What does the CCAA think about restoration of arms sales?
JOHNSON: Well, we haven't taken a position, but I'll tell you where I'm coming from. I would think that there's a point where we would go contrary to the US government.

MONITOR: Which US government?
JOHNSON: The current US government. I would like to see some military hardware going into Guatemala. Not lethal stuff, but I'd like to see some of the basic little things go in, like helicopters. Things that would enable the United States government to have a better access to the current Guatemalan government, which has a lot of military people in it.'

Multinational Monitor, *November 1980.*

The Third World Threat

'In order to understand US foreign policy in the period ahead, we must first identify the forces which threaten the *status quo* in ways likely to upset the stability and profitability of the US economy.

As we have already seen, the answer is *not* the Soviet Union, which in fact has become an increasingly valuable customer for US goods and a borrower of US funds in recent years. There have been many changes unfavourable to US capitalism since the Second World War. None has been initiated by the USSR — from China in 1949 to Iran in 1979. It is true that the Soviet Union has helped some (though not all) of these initiatives, but attempting to deal with them by striking at the Soviet Union (which was the central idea of John Foster Dulles' ill-fated doctrine of "massive retaliation") was never feasible and would always have been self-defeating.

The source of these changes — aside from what may have originated in the growing strength of America's advanced capitalist allies, which is an entirely different story — was in every case national liberation movements in the Third World, usually combining nationalistic and social revolutionary elements and in all cases carrying threats to US economic and political interests in the countries affected. All signs are that these movements are active in various parts of the world today, (Southern Africa, Central America and the Caribbean) and are likely to become so in others (South America, the Middle East, Southern Asia) in the not distant future. Deteriorating economic conditions and mass living standards in all but a few Third World countries (OPEC, South Korea, Taiwan, Hong Kong, Singapore) virtually guarantee that what may be called the revolt of the Third World will steadily grow in intensity during the 1980s.

This and not superpower rivalry, is the number one contradiction in the world today and in the foreseeable future, hence also the primary concern of US foreign policy.'

Monthly Review, *April 1980.*

---

last year of the Carter government had shown that a reassessment of United States foreign policy was already under way. The international environment of stability and predictability so sought after by corporate America had eluded it under Carter. The country had failed to recover its global supremacy, the domestic and international economic crisis persisted and Third World liberation movements continued to challenge American interests.

Robert Tucker, by no means a member of the far right, wrote in *Foreign Affairs*, the journal of the Council on Foreign Relations, at the end of 1980: 'Everywhere the signs point to the conclusion that for the third time in the post-World War II period we are in the throes of far-reaching change in the nation's foreign policy. What these signs do not divulge are the eventual scope and magnitude of the change.' For Tucker this debate over foreign policy recalls that of the late 1940s rather than the late 1960s. In the 1980s reconsideration of American security, particularly in such key areas as the Persian Gulf, is accompanied by a growing conviction that the military balance now favours the Soviet Union. United States foreign policy has 'come closer to insolvency' in the past decade, unable to secure its most vital interests. The United States is left with two alternatives:

> . . . either a policy of a resurgent America intent once again on containing wherever possible the expansion of Soviet influence — as well as the expansion of communism generally — or a policy of moderate containment that may prove inadequate to sustain the power and discipline even to protect interests on which our essential security depends. For if the latter is less demanding, it is also considerably less appealing in the promise it holds out: not of a world moving progressively under American leadership toward the eventual triumph of liberal-capitalist values, but of a world in which America would have to abandon expectations that only yesterday she confidently held. We would have to reconcile ourselves to the prospect of a world of which a large, and perhaps increasing, part outside the industrial democracies would resist American influence.

During its first three years in office, the Carter Administsration had pursued stability by apparently adjusting United States behaviour to its diminished status in the world. Now, in Carter's final year, a vociferous body of opinion maintained that by so doing, the country's vital security interests had been put at risk without achieving that stability and the United States must now reassert its influence and recover its military position. For some this means relative recovery, but for the ultra-conservatives it means an absolute recovery. Reagan and his closest allies were particularly influenced by the 'Team B' report commissioned by the CIA in 1976 which reassessed the Soviet Union's intentions and capabilities and concluded that it was aiming not at parity with the United States but at superiority. The implication was that the Soviet Union had rejected peaceful coexistence and now sought world domination. The Republican Party platform called for a strategy of 'peace through strength' aimed at 'overall military and technological superiority over the Soviet Union'.

The right pointed to Mozambique, Angola, Ethiopia, Iran, Afghanistan, Grenada and Nicaragua as examples of renewed Soviet aggression. However, a more sober assessment of Soviet activity carried out in 1980 by the Washington based Center for Defense Information produced very different conclusions:

A comprehensive study of trends of Soviet world influence in 155 countries since World War II does not support perceptions of consistent Soviet advances and devastating US setbacks . . . Soviet foreign involvement has to a large extent been shaped by indigenous conditions, and the Soviets have been unable to command loyalty or obedience . . . Soviet setbacks in China, Indonesia, Egypt, India and Iraq dwarf marginal Soviet advances in lesser countries . . . Temporary Soviet successes in backward countries have proved costly to the Soviet Union. They provide no justification for American alarmism or military intervention. US policies should emphasize our non-military advantages in the competition for world influence.

Indeed, the editors of the New York-based *Monthly Review* suggest that the real concern of the United States is not any direct threat posed by the Soviet Union, but the need to preserve the vast economic stake built up particularly since World War II by American business and finance in various parts of the capitalist world. The greatest threat to the profitability and security of American economic interests, including regular supplies of vital raw materials, lies in the Third World not from the Soviet Union (see box).

The Right and Central America

During Reagan's presidential campaign, a number of right wing think-tanks rose to prominence and Central America became a frequent focus of their attention.

The American Enterprise Institute (AEI) is one of the most important of these think-tanks. It was founded in 1942 and is dedicated to the 'maintenance of the system of free enterprise'. Georgetown University's Center for Strategic and International Studies (CSIS) also became very influential. It was founded in 1962 and its staff and associates include trilateralists at the conservative end of the spectrum such as Henry Kissinger, Ann Armstrong and David Abshire, as well as Reagan's top foreign policy advisor Richard Allen. The Hoover Institute was set up in 1919 'to demonstrate the evils of the doctrines of communism, socialism, economic materialism or atheism'; its three honorary fellows are Friedrich Hayek, Alexander Solzhenitsyn and Ronald Reagan. The Heritage Foundation was founded in 1974 by one of the leading 'financial angels of the New Right', Joseph Coors. A recent study by this institution calls on the Justice Department to reinstitute a witch-hunt of political radicals in the US.

Reagan's foreign policy transition team was largely drawn from these think-tanks. Amongst the individuals most concerned with Central America and the Caribbean were Georgetown University professor, Jeane Kirkpatrick, considered one of the most hardline members of the AEI and the CSIS; James Theberge, one time director of Latin American studies at the CSIS; Roger Fontaine, who succeeded Theberge at the CSIS and had been a Reagan advisor for a number of years; Pedro San Juan, the AEI's director of Western Hemisphere affairs and Cieto Di Giovanni, a former member of the CIA, a member of the Heritage Foundation and advisor to businessmen in El Salvador and Guatemala. Lt-General Daniel Graham, former head of the Defense Intelligence Agency and chairman of the committee which produced the 'Team B' report, became an advisor to Reagan on defence matters and took a particular interest in Central America. Daniel Graham is also chairman of the Coalition for Peace through Strength, a Washington lobby led by retired senior military officers seeking a larger defence budget.

During 1980 this team and their associates produced a considerable number of articles and research papers and regularly leaked their views on the crisis in the Caribbean basin to the press.

All were unanimous in their condemnation of Carter's policies towards the region. He was accused of betraying the country's national security interests: not only did he play down the strategic importance of the 'backyard' he allowed the Soviet Union and Cuba to penetrate it to an unprecedented degree. His human rights policy was vehemently condemned for discriminating against right wing pro-US regimes and allowing left wing governments and movements to flourish. According to this body of opinion, under Carter tolerance of ideological pluralism and encouragement of human rights had replaced resistance to Soviet expansionism as the main priority of foreign policy.

Carter's betrayal coincided with what the transition team interpreted as a period of major expansion of Soviet activity in the Third World in general and in Central America and the Caribbean in particular. The role of Cuba as a supposed Soviet surrogate was attacked with especial virulence. As a result of Soviet-Cuban subversion, they suggest, the United States had lost Nicaragua and Grenada, previously American allies, a pro-US military government in El Salvador had 'been replaced by a center-left government supported by the US embassy', and the pro-US military government in Guatemala was now threatened by Cuban-backed Marxist guerrillas. Not only was Mexico now in danger, according to these authors, but the United States itself.

Although the emphasis was on the role of these external forces in fomenting unrest in the region, the internal causes of instability were not ignored. But the problem was seen as one of order rather than social justice. Jeane Kirkpatrick for instance considers the problem a cultural one: 'the Latin style of politics' which she analyzed with

The Transition Team Speaks

'I disagree . . . with the aid that we have provided for (Nicaragua) because I think that we did it under the illusion that somehow we were helping hold off a truly leftist government, that we had some kind of moderate government there . . . I think we are seeing the application of the domino theory . . . and I think that it's time the people of the United States realize . . . that we're the last domino.'

Ronald Reagan, September 1980.

Extract from an interview with Roger Fontaine, Reagan's top Latin American advisor:

QUESTION: What do you think would be the most significant differences between a Carter administration and a Reagan administration regarding policy toward Latin America?
FONTAINE: Well, I think in one of the broadest aspects a Reagan administration is going to act a good deal more aggressively in preserving what's left of, and preserving what opportunities are left for, democracy, particularly in Central America. This is a personal feeling because it hasn't been spelled out officially, but I would like to see something shape up in the Reagan administration that would be nothing less than a Truman doctrine for the region. You remember the Truman doctrine was designed for Greece back in the late 1940s to help regimes in serious trouble who were friendly to the US but under attack from armed minorities that were aided and abetted by outside, hostile forces, mainly the Soviet Union and Yugoslavia.

A somewhat similar situation is occurring in Central America. Armed minorities supported by principally the Cubans are attempting to destabilise regimes to the point where I think the chances for democracy as we know it are going to be closed out, foreclosed.

I think you have to do something like a Truman doctrine. A Truman doctrine means that you are going to have to give these countries — El Salvador being one, Guatemala another — a good deal more economic aid than they are getting, at least short-term, particularly in the case of El Salvador. It means that they need military advisers. It means that they need military training. Kind of a combination of the kinds of things we did in the early 60's under the Alliance for Progress and what the Truman Doctrine did for Greece and Turkey in the 1940s.

QUESTION: You would think that military advisers are essential, are required?
FONTAINE: Yes. And military assistance. Again, a personal opi-

nion, but I think this controversy between lethal and non-lethal aid is absurd. You don't fight terrorists and guerrillas with non-lethal aid.

Roger Fontaine, interview published in Miami Herald, *24 August 1980.*

Jeane Kirkpatrick, subsequently Reagan's ambassador to the United Nations:

'Our policy has brought us from a situation in which we lived in marvellous security in our own hemisphere to a situation in which we could very well be surrounded by Soviet bases on our southeastern and southern flanks . . . (this) creates a kind of a geopolitical nightmare — one that we have never confronted and one which, if we were to confront, would totally alter our strategic position and problems in the world. . . . The doctrine of social change has been embraced like a religious dogma by the Carter Administration. Now the problem is that progress often turns out to look a lot like Cubans and Russians. What they have been doing, I think, is confusing change with progress. And, equally important, they've been confusing democracy with socialism.

So they end up supporting anything that looks like change, which very frequently turns out to be sponsored by the Cubans and the Soviets.'

Jeane Kirkpatrick, interview in the film Attack on the Americas! *1980.*

'If we are confronted with the choice between offering assistance to a moderately repressive autocratic government which is also friendly to the United States and permitting it to be overrun by a Cuban-trained, Cuban-armed, Cuban-sponsored insurgency, we would assist the moderate autocracy.'

Jeane Kirkpatrick, Washington Post, *28 December 1980.*

'Castro is a self-declared enemy of the United States, allied to the Soviet Union, dedicated to undermining US interests and influence throughout the Caribbean and in the world, and serves as Moscow's proxy or "sub-imperialism" in the Caribbean . . . Moscow and Havana consider that by permitting the survival of the Cuban revolution, which has strengthened Marxist influence in the hemisphere, the United States committed a fundamental "strategic error" for which it is now paying . . .

The deliberate expansion of Cuban and Soviet military capabilities in America's backyard, and their coordinated effort to create a hostile bloc of states, has increased significantly the possibility of a dangerous great power confrontation in the Caribbean in the 1980s. Growing Soviet self-confidence and assertiveness and the perception of American weakness and retreat have improved the likelihood that the Caribbean will become a more active theatre of East-West competition and conflict . . .

It is imperative that the next US Administration bring to an end the Carter Administration's abandonment of this strategically important area to our adversaries who have grown stronger and bolder while we have slept . . .

The United States may find it necessary to enforce a political solution if the alternative is civil war and the capture of a power by another Marxist regime in Central America.'

James Theberge, Commonsense, *Spring 1980.*

'The United States must launch a new positive policy for the greater Caribbean, including Central America. That policy will provide multi-faceted aid for all friendly countries under attack by armed minorities receiving assistance from hostile outside forces. The program will wed the most successful elements of the Truman Doctrine and the Alliance for Progress.

Concurrently, the United States will reaffirm the core principle of the Monroe Doctrine: namely, no hostile foreign power will be allowed bases or military and political allies in the region. A revitalized Monroe Doctrine will be made multilateral . . . a view long held by key Latin American republics. The United States can no longer accept the status of Cuba as a Soviet vassal state. Cuban subversion must be clearly labelled as such and resisted. The price Havana must pay for such activities cannot be a small one. The United States can only restore its credibility by taking immediate action. The first steps must be frankly punitive . . . if propaganda fails, a war of national liberation against Castro must be launched.

The United States is being shoved aside in the Caribbean and Central America by a sophisticated, but brutal, extracontinental super power manipulating client states. Soviet influence has expanded mightily since 1959. The Soviet Union is now ensconced in force in the Western Hemisphere and the United States must remedy the situation.'

A New Inter-American Policy for the Eighties, *1980, prepared by the Committee of Santa Fe, part of the right-wing Council for Inter-American Security, Inc., whose members include Roger Fontaine, retired General Sumner, and David C. Jordan.*

reference to the theories of the seventeenth century English political philosopher, Thomas Hobbes: 'The problem confronting El Salvador is Thomas Hobbes' problem: how to establish order where there is none.' Di Giovanni and Kruger made a similar point in the *Washington Quarterly* in the summer of 1980:

It would be wiser for the Carter Administration to accept the fact that threatened governments must take firm measures to provide public security against militant leftists and, at the same time, to encourage flexible and reasonable members of the private and public sectors to tackle their nation's problems within a non-Marxist framework. Their solutions may not be as progressive as many would like or as might be possible in the future, but communists are on the offensive in Central America, and the first objective is to stop them and restore a sense of order before US interests deteriorate any further.

These ideologues of the right developed the rationalizations for a policy aimed at suppressing movements for change in the region. They had the enthusiastic backing of a number of right-wing businessmen with interests in Central America. The greatest concentration of extreme right-wing opinion in the United States is in the south and south-west of the country — the so-called sunbelt. This area has been a major source of investment in Central America, particularly in Guatemala following the CIA-sponsored overthrow of Arbenz. Close ties were forged in this period between right-wing Guatemalan businessmen and politicians and their counterparts in the sunbelt states. Some prominent figures in the Republican Party had such connections and during Reagan's presidential campaign the ties were considerably strengthened.

Two organizations in Guatemala representing right-wing businessmen and landowners with strong links with the 14,000-strong expatriate American community in Guatemala, helped promote these ties. The *Asociacion de los Amigos del Pais* (Friends of the Country Association) was founded in 1966 and is alleged to have close connections with the government of General Lucas Garcia. It is led by Roberto Alejos Arzu, a wealthy landowner whose ranch was used as a training camp for the Bay of Pigs invasion. Alejos Arzu is also a member of the *Fundacion Guatemalteca por la Libertad* (Guatemalan Freedom Foundation), an organization with particularly close links with former President Arana and reported to be even more right-wing that the *Amigos*. Many prominent members of the *Fundacion* are also members of Guatemala's extreme right-wing party, the Movement of National Liberation (MLN), which has links with paramilitary death squads. Another *Fundacion* member is a Texan lawyer, John Trotter.

Bumping off the Commies

'The State Department opposes the use of violence as a weapon to subdue the leftist oriented groups which seek to depose Guatemala's government . . . There is another point of view that contends that the only feasible way to stop Communism is to destroy it quickly. Argentina and Chile are demonstrated as nations which used this approach with considerable effectiveness and have gone on to become among Latin America's most stable and successful economies.'

Thomas Mooney, President of the American Chamber of Commerce in Guatemala, April 1980.

'Why should we be worried about the death squads? They're bumping off the commies, our enemies. I'd give them more power. Hell, I'd get some cartridges if I could, and everyone else would too . . . Why should we criticize them? The death squad — I'm for it . . . Shit! There's no question, we can't wait 'til Reagan gets in. We hope Carter falls in the ocean real quick . . . We all feel that he (Reagan) is our saviour.'

Fred Sherwood, former President of the American Chamber of Commerce in Guatemala, September 1980.

'What they should do is to declare martial law. Then you catch somebody, they go to a military court, three colonels are sitting there, you're guilty, you're shot. It works very well.'

Keith Parker, Vice-President for Guatemala of the Bank of America, 8 September 1980.

Trotter gained international notoriety when the workers of his Coca-Cola bottling plant in Guatemala tried to form a trade union. An international campaign was launched when a number of workers and union leaders in his factory were murdered by death squads. In 1980 the Coca-Cola parent company was forced to remove his franchise. However, Trotter has retained his links with the country, and has been a key figure in arranging contacts between Guatemalan businessmen and politicians and members of the Republican Party. Trotter was also involved in the American Security Council film *Attack on the Americas* (see box). Trotter himself pointed to these connections in an interview in 1980:

Attack on the Americas!

Attack on the Americas! is a documentary film made for US television and produced and paid for by the American Security Council, one of the most powerful pro-military lobbies in the United States, in which over 1,700 companies from the private sector participate, together with many former high-ranking military officers. Made with a budget of 150,000 dollars, a further five million dollars is being spent to ensure it is shown on some 200 TV stations throughout the United States. The following are extracts from the film commentary:

'For almost twenty years, Cuba was the solitary outpost of Communism in the Western Hemisphere. Today, Fidel Castro is exporting revolution throughout Central America and the Caribbean, waging "wars of national liberation" for his Soviet sponsors. But this time the challenge is not half way around the world in Afghanistan or Southeast Asia, but in our own backyard . . . Castro has helped sponsor unsuccessful revolutionary efforts in many nations in South America, such as Chile, Argentina, Brazil, and Bolivia. But Castro's recent and continuing success in Central America is rapidly advancing the Soviets' goal. Their strategic objective is to separate the United States from Latin America. By dominating the land bridge between the Americas, they will succeed in slashing the Americas in half . . .

What is at stake is more than the freedom of our neighbours to the South, more than the oilfields of Guatemala and Mexico, more than the natural resources of our allies in the Western Hemisphere. Today: El Salvador and Guatemala. Tomorrow: Honduras, Costa Rica, Belize, Venezuela, the Dominican Republic, Mexico . . . the United States . . .'

The Council has budgeted half a million dollars, which is being collected in Guatemala by the Friends, to make a documentary about the situation in the country. The Friends are collecting money and I am working with them. I offered my services to collect the money through contacts with other North American businessmen and I ask them to contribute, just as I have given a cheque for five thousand dollars to the Council during its last visit . . . there is another organization not very different from the Friends, more or less with the same people, called the Guatemalan Foundation for Freedom. I work more with them . . . the Generals (Singlaub and Graham) of the Council had private visits with the President of the country. President Lucas asked them both to go and speak to Reagan. I am sure they supported him. On another occasion, after the visit of the generals, we went to Washington D.C. and we talked to congressmen and their aides. I went with the Foundation. The President had a meeting with the main Guatemalan businessmen, and said to them, 'We have to unite' and they called me and said: 'We are going to try and make contact with special people who we want to see, including your friend John Connally in Houston' and he said to me: 'It would be much appreciated if you could organize a meeting.' This I did and he received us at five in Houston.

In 1979 President Lucas had called together a group of businessmen and landowners to launch a campaign to counteract the negative publicity about the country arising from Carter's human rights policy; he is alleged to have raised half a million dollars in contributions to the campaign at that meeting. The visit of retired generals Daniel Graham and John K. Singlaub to Guatemala on behalf of the American Security Council, referred to by Trotter, took place shortly afterwards, in December 1979. On his return Singlaub called for sympathetic understanding of the death squads. He criticised the Carter administration's unwillingness to back the Lucas regime and stated that under a Reagan administration 'the directive of the ambassador would be to support the President's (Lucas) efforts to solve his problems rather than creating more problems for him'.

Contacts between the Guatemalan and American right continued throughout 1980 and have been documented by Allan Nairn, a research fellow of the Washington-based Council of Hemispheric Affairs. The Congressional aides of such right-wing politicians as Jesse Helms and Jack Kemp have visited Guatemala and in April 1980 the *Fundacion por la Libertad* invited the main representatives of America's New Right to the country. They included Bow Billings of the Moral Majority, Jeffrey Gayner of the Heritage Foundation, Bow Haekman of Young Americans for Freedom, John Laxalt of Citizens for the Republic, Howard Philips of the Conservative Causus, Jack Pierney of the American Conservative Union, and Bryn Benson of the *Conservative Digest*. On their return to Washington they held a press conference. Howard Philips expressed the view of all when he stated: 'Guatemala has a brilliant future, if the policy of the United States does not ruin it'. The State Department under Carter had tried, he claimed, to 'replace anti-communists with moderate Marxists'.

Members of Reagan's advisory team on Central America made frequent trips to Guatemala during 1980. Roger Fontaine made at least two visits and Richard Allen, Reagan's top foreign policy advisor, visited the country and talked with Ayau and Juan Maegli of *Amigos del Pais*. The Guatemalan right also made numerous trips to Washington and elsewhere in the United States. Graham's Coalition for Peace Through Strength organized meetings with Guatemalan and El Salvadorean businessmen in which Ayau and Alejos participated. Reagan himself has met both men. After meeting Ayau in 1979 Reagan described him as 'one of the few people in the high political sphere who understands what is going on down there'.

Both *Amigos del Pais* and the *Fundacion* hired public relations firms in the United States to help improve the country's image. *Amigos del Pais* hired Deaver and Hannaford, a firm with close ties to the Reagan presidential campaign, and are reported to have paid US$150,000 for press contacts and meetings with State Department officials and members of Congress. Michael Deaver subsequently left the firm to become President Reagan's deputy chief of staff in the White House. The *Fundacion* hired the firm of McKenzie and Mc-Cheyne, paying it over US$250,000 to launch a campaign in favour of the Guatemalan government. This firm has acted for Somoza of Nicaragua and Major D'Abuisson, a leading figure of El Salvador's extreme right-wing whose name has been linked with the country's death squads (see Part V).

There have been suggestions that the enthusiasm of Guatemalan businessmen for Reagan and their anxiety to see Carter defeated went beyond verbal expressions of support and included donations to Reagan's campaign fund. Guatemalan businessmen have openly boasted of such contributions which are illegal in the United States and could seriously embarrass Reagan if substantiated (see box). In any case they were delighted with the election result and a number attended the inauguration. Among them were Juan Maegli, Francisco Reyes, Alfonso Castillo, Jorge Serrano and Eduardo Carrete, all prominent members of *Amigos del Pais* as well as former President Arana, and Mario Sandoval Alarcon, leader of the MLN and friend of John Trotter.

According to research carried out by Allan Nairn, the result of these close connections was a tacit understanding between Reagan and the Guatemalans on Reagan's policy towards the country if elected. This included the restoration of arms sales if legal restrictions could be circumvented, and army and police training and an end to US criticism of the death squads. A former high official of the Guatemalan government now in exile has stated that his ex-colleagues have been assured by Reagan's associates that the death squads will be able to operate without adverse pressure from the White House or the State Department. Finally, there is an expectation that Reagan would intervene militarily in the event of a popular uprising, as Jorge Garcia Granados, Lucas's chief of staff has said: 'that's my feeling, because of the kind of person Reagan is.'

There was no guarantee that all such promises or understandings would be translated into policy once Reagan was in power, but the pressures to do so from within his own party and from his closest associates would be strong. The Republican Party platform specifically mentioned Guatemala as an outpost against communism, it also ex-

Blood Money

'Guatemala is important, not just because it's a buffer against revolution but because it is now widely thought to be sitting on enormous reserves of oil. Mr Reagan's own access to advice about what is going on in Guatemala is likely to have been limited. His deputy chief-of-staff, Michael Deaver, was, until taking office two weeks ago, a partner in the public relations firm of Deaver-Hanaford. In November, Deaver-Hanaford promoted a briefing on behalf of a Guatemalan organization called *Amigos del Pais* (Friends of the Country) to which senators and congressmen were duly invited. The *Amigos del Pais* claimed to be businessmen simply interested in promoting a better image for their country. According to (Villagran) Kramer, that is probably true of about a third of them. The rest, he says, are less than reputable, including 10-15 people directly linked, he says, with organized terror. But there is another worrying allegation of which Mr Reagan may not so far be aware.

KRAMER: "I do recall several cases where rather important businessmen in Guatemala told me that they had made contributions to the Republican Party and thereby to Mr Reagan's victory."

INTERVIEWER: "How much money were they talking about?"
KRAMER: "All in all, they went up to 10 million dollars. Now I would say that the Republican Party would not receive money from foreign sources such as the Guatemalans."

INTERVIEWER: "So how would the money have got to the campaign?"
KRAMER: "The only way that I can feel it would get there would be that some North American residing in Guatemala, living in Guatemala, would more or less be requesting money over there or accepting contributions and then transmitting them to his Republican Party as contributions of his own. Later on, he might reveal, in a very intimate form, the names of the Guatemalans that gave him the money."

If what Sr. Kramer says is true, then the implications are very serious indeed.'

Villagran Kramer, ex-Vice President of Guatemala, interviewed on BBC Radio's File on Four*, 4 February 1981.*

pressed its concern about the situation in Central America:

We deplore the Marxist Sandinista takeover of Nicaragua and the Marxist attempts to destabilize El Salvador, Guatemala and Honduras. We do not support United States assistance to any Marxist government in this hemisphere and we oppose the Carter administration aid program for the Government of Nicaragua. However we will support the efforts of the Nicaraguan people to establish a free and independent government.

Reagan in Power

The Reagan administration, formed in January 1981, reflected the shift in the centre of gravity of American politics towards the right. But the right in the United States is not a monolithic body of opinion, and Reagan found himself in charge of a coalition of views and struggle for influence, much as Carter had.

Some analysts divide the administration along a 'far-right to left' spectrum in which the far right is concentrated in the Senate and led by Jesse Helms and other conservative senators who seek absolute US military supremacy and no detente with the Soviet Union whatsoever. Alexander Haig, who became Reagan's Secretary of State, stands on the 'left' of this spectrum. It was Haig who advocated the 1970 invasion of Cambodia (Kampuchea as it is today) and the Christmas 1972 bombing of Hanoi; as he himself exclaimed, 'Imagine my being liberal in any administration!' But Haig, a member of the Council on Foreign Relations, learned realpolitik under Henry Kissinger and is known to adapt his hardline views to changing circumstances: 'The trouble with foreign policy is that it is dirty. To get results you have to compromise, make deals, give a little.'

Others divide the administration into pragmatists and ideologues. One administration insider told Leslie Gelb, the *New York Times* national security correspondent: 'There are no groups. There is a continuum from purists to pragmatic conservatives, with one and the same person falling in different places on different issues. The purists are Manichaean in the medieval sense. They believe that the Soviets are the devil, and that you can't bargain with the devil without losing your soul. The pragmatists take into account the world as it is.'

According to this analysis, Casper Weinberger, the Defense Secretary and member of the Trilateral Commission, falls midway on the continuum with Richard Allen, the National Security Advisor, tending towards the purists and Haig more towards the pragmatists. The situation is further complicated by Haig's ambitions and bid for absolute control over foreign policy and Richard Allen's quieter but no less determined efforts to stop him. Reagan's personal aides in the White House — the powerful triumvirate of Edwin Meese, James Baker and Michael Deaver — are well to the right of centre politically, but seem intent on preserving a certain balance between the various personalities in an effort to promote a team approach to foreign policy.

Reagan himself is strongly influenced by the ultra-conservatives, who provide him with a power base in Congress and a rallying cry for Republican party unity. But while he has not challenged their influence neither has he given into their more extreme demands. It is pragmatists rather than ideologues who hold the most prominent positions in the administration — several of them members of the Trilateral Commission — but many ideologues occupy secondary positions and cannot be ignored. Indeed, reports in the US press suggested that Senator Jesse Helms had effectively been allowed to make these latter appointments. It is difficult in these circumstances for a coherent policy to emerge. The President failed to make a single major foreign policy speech in his first six months in office, and it was still uncertain at the end of that six months where control over foreign policy formulation would eventually come to rest.

The one subject which does unite the administration is the Soviet threat and an obsession with Soviet-backed subversion in the Middle East, Africa and Central America. Clear priority has been given to restoring the military balance between the superpowers. In March 1981 the administration announced what *Time* magazine called the 'most expensive peacetime military build-up in US history'.

The administration would like to increase arms sales and reduce Congressional control over them particularly where it is exercised on human rights grounds. The Republican majority in the Senate may well help it achieve this objective. The administration has also made clear its intention of increasing security assistance at the expense of development assistance.

It has already taken steps to counter liberation movements in the Third World. Haig has broadened the concept of 'terrorism' to include all such liberation struggles and these have replaced human rights violations by right wing governments as the administration's main concern. Such a policy is justified by the subtle distinction drawn by Haig between totalitarian and authoritarian regimes, as he explained to a meeting of the Trilateral Commission:

The totalitarian model unfortunately draws upon the resources of modern technology to impose its will on all aspects of a citizen's behaviour. The totalitarian regimes tend to be intolerant at home and abroad, actively hostile to all we represent and ideologically resistent to political change . . . The authoritarian regime usually stems from a lack of political or economic development and customarily reserves for itself absolute authority in only a few politically sensitive areas.

According to an article by the arms transfers analyst Michael Klare in *Le Monde Diplomatique*, counter-insurgency has never been so much in vogue in the Pentagon since Vietnam. A Joint Special Operations Command (JSOC) at Fort Bragg has been set up to coordinate the activities of the special counter-insurgency units of the three armed forces. The administration also has plans to step up military aid to all regimes facing guerrilla movements. Its own Rapid Deployment Force is aimed at protecting oil supplies in the Middle East, but could also be used in other Third World trouble spots such as Central America and the Caribbean.

Many strategists have been absorbing the lessons of Vietnam rather than rejecting any future American involvement in anti-guerrilla warfare as inevitably leading to defeat. The new emphasis, according to Klare, is on a military war without the civic action programmes and reforms to win people away from the guerrillas which Kennedy encouraged; it is also on 'preventive medicine' and urban counter-insurgency to identify potential activists, and the building up of militarized, anti-terrorist police forces. Where necessary American intervention would be rapid and massive, making use of all the range of weapons available rather than gradually escalating involvement.

The initial rhetoric of the administration matched the belligerence of these strategies. Richard Pipes at the National Security Council declared that Soviet leaders must choose between peacefully changing the communist system in favour of the Western model 'or going to war'. But the action has been far less consistent than the tough talk and seems to have been taken on a rather *ad hoc* basis. The administration could not for instance totally ignore its allies' fears that they were being dragged into a needless confrontation with the Soviet Union and had to agree to negotiate over limiting missiles in Europe. One congressman complained of the contradictory path the administration's foreign policy was taking: 'They've got us on this roller coaster, zigging and zagging every day. Nicaragua is up, Nicaragua is down; El Salvador is up, El Salvador is down; Poland is up, Poland is down. We almost need a valium for the country.'

The Front Yard

The lack of clear foreign policy objectives increased uncertainty about the future. Even if it looked at the end of the first six months of the Reagan administration as if some degree of pragmatism would prevail, there were no guarantees that this would continue to be the case, particularly as the crisis in the Caribbean basin, a region of particular importance to the extreme right, was only just beginning.

The struggle over who would be given responsibility for this region in the new administration was intense. Roger Fontaine became, as expected, Richard Allen's advisor on Latin American affairs at the National Security Council. But the far right failed to install retired General Vernon Walters, former deputy director of the CIA, as Assistant Secretary of State for Inter-American Affairs. That post went to Thomas Enders, who had personally supervised the bombing of Cambodia ten years previously. In a speech before the Council of the Americas in June 1981, shortly after his appointment had been confirmed, Enders named three tasks for the United States in the Western Hemisphere: the first was to improve relations with Mexico and the second to counter Cuban influence in the Caribbean and Central America. Cuba, he claimed, had declared covert war on its neighbours and he promised that the US would 'bring the costs of that war back to Havana'. If this did not satisfy the far right, they had two representatives strategically placed to ensure that there was no relaxation in policy toward the region. General Walters became a special advisor on Latin American affairs to Haig, acting as a roving ambassador, and retired General Sumner, chairman of the right-wing Council for Inter-American Security, became an advisor to Enders with ambassadorial rank.

Changes in US ambassadors also took place. The Reagan transition team had made no secret of its dislike of Carter's choice of ambassadors in the region, referring to them as 'social reformers'. Robert White in El Salvador was given the sack; Lawrence Pezzullo in Nicaragua was asked by Haig to stay, but he resigned in June 1981. White was replaced in El Salvador by Deane Hinton, a career diplomat, expelled from Zaire in 1975 after allegations of involvement in a coup attempt against President Mobutu; he had also headed the USAID mission in Guatemala during the crucial years 1967-69.

There was no doubt that the administration's policy toward the region would be based first and foremost on the view that Cuban-Soviet expansionism in the region had to be stopped. El Salvador became the administration's first test case of this policy (see Part V). Reagan himself declared that El Salvador is located 'in our front yard'. The rhetoric was strong, particularly in the first few months of the new administration. Haig told the House Foreign Affairs Committee that the Soviet Union had drawn up a phased, four-stage plan, starting with the revolution in Nicaragua, that would soon lead to the fall of El Salvador, Honduras and Guatemala unless the United States blocked it: 'I wouldn't necessarily call it a domino theory, I would call it a priority target list — a hit list, if you will — for the ultimate takeover of Central America.'

Hostility towards Cuba, Nicaragua and Grenada was intensified. The administration used evidence, later discredited (see page 242), that Nicaragua and Cuba were responsible for channelling arms to El Salvador to justify its hardline policy. The US$15 million final instalment of the previous administration's US$75 million aid package to Nicaragua was suspended in January 1981, and this was followed by the withdrawal of a US$9.6 million credit for the purchase of essential wheat supplies. There were fears in Managua that the United States was aiming at economic strangulation of the country, that it might block the payment of credits awarded prior to the revolution by USAID and by the Inter-American Development Bank or organize a blockade of Nicaraguan exports, an estimated 22% of which still relied on the United States market. Such threats to the country's economic survival immensely strengthen, as is the intention, those members of the private sector in Nicaragua who seek to halt further moves towards socialism, but who lack any base in the country to mobilize against the government.

But the threat to the Nicaraguan revolution is not just economic. An estimated 5,000 former members of Somoza's National Guard fled to Honduras after the revolution and began preparations for an invasion of the country. They frequently cross into Nicaragua to carry out raids on villages and border posts, killing peasants and teachers involved in the literacy campaign as well as members of the Sandinista militia. In particular, they have tried to take advantage of the mistrust of the revolution felt by the black and Miskito Indian population of the Atlantic coast regions of Nicaragua. This poor and remote area, which comprises 56% of the national territory and only 9% of the total population, was isolated from the revolutionary struggle against Somoza. Most of the population speaks English in this former British settlement and has special problems which the Sandinista government has not always understood. The government now fears that any National Guard invasion of the country would be spearheaded through an uprising provoked in the Atlantic region.

The Guard stepped up its incursions in 1981 and in June of that year the Nicaraguan government issued a booklet documenting the raids and calling upon the Honduran government to control them. They listed 37 attacks, 44 air space violations and 15 infiltrations from Honduras, including actions by the Honduran army. However, Honduras, the United States' most important ally in the region, allowed the raids to continue. In April 1981 two Honduran soldiers were seized inside Nicaragua; they admitted working with Honduran military intelligence and Somoza's National Guard. A powerful right-wing faction of the Honduran army led by Colonel Gustavo Alvarez Martinez would like to crush the growing peasant mobilization in his own country and engage in direct military confrontation with the Nicaraguan government. Indeed, in May 1981 there were three serious border

Beef and Bulls

'The United States is threatening to ban beef imports from Nicaragua, in a move which the ruling junta considers to be politically motivated. Also under threat are imports of a resin used to manufacture polyvinyl chloride (PVC).

According to the US ambassador to Managua, Lawrence Pezzullo, the US import quota for Nicaraguan beef could be cancelled, to protect the domestic market from foot-and-mouth disease. Nicaragua itself has no serious incidence of the disease, but Washington officials argue that this could change as a result of an agreement to import a batch of high-quality breeding bulls from Cuba.

The Cuban bulls are being offered at special prices . . . and the Nicaraguans have seized the opportunity to try to expand and improve their herds, which remain seriously depleted as a result of the 1979 civil war. Before agreeing to go ahead with the deal, the Managua authorities consulted the *Organizacion Panamericana de la Salud* (OPS), the *Centro Panamericano de la Fiebre Aftosa* (Panaftosa), and similar European-based organizations. All confirmed that Cuba had had no recent outbreaks of foot-and-mouth.

Washington, however is basing its position on reports produced by the *Organismo Internacional Regional de Sanidad Agropecuaria* (OIRSA), an El Salvador-based agency which the US helped set up. OIRSA has not inspected the situation in Cuba, so the country does not appear on its list of areas free of foot-and-mouth. This appears to be the sole basis of the US threat . . . Reports that PVC resin exports to the US could also be banned add to the fears that an economic blockade is beginning to shape up. In this case, the US decision is allegedly linked to the possible sale of Nicaragua's surpluses to Cuba.'

Latin America Weekly Report, *15 May 1981*.

clashes between Honduran and Nicaraguan forces and there were fears that war might break out between the two countries. Alvarez Martinez also opposes the elections planned in Honduras for November 1981. President Paz Garcia and his supporters are reported to oppose open war but still support attempts to destabilize Nicaragua. The United States has so far not advocated war and has used its influence to avert such an outcome.

Another military threat to Nicaragua and Cuba is from Nicaraguan and Cuban exiles training together in paramilitary camps in Florida. The existence of such camps has been amply documented. Under Reagan they have become even more open in their activities boasting of their intentions on television. An estimated 2,000 men were being trained in such camps in 1981 (see box, page 188). The response of Haig to complaints by the Nicaraguan government has been to declare that the camps are legal because they are on private property.

Cuba has been under relentless attack since Reagan took office, including threats of a naval blockade. A terrorist group calling itself 'Alpha 66' made up of Cuban exiles in the United States announced in March 1981 that it had carried out thirty sabotage attacks on Cuba in the previous six months. Cuba has also suffered from a succession of apparently natural disasters including blue mould which wiped out the 1980 tobacco crop, rust which seriously affected sugar production, and African swine fever which decimated the pig population. Oil spilt from tankers passing close to the Cuban coast destroyed the island's best lobster farms, and in July 1981 nearly 300,000 people fell sick and 113 died from a tropical disease known as *dengue* transmitted by mosquitoes. Castro called on Washington to 'define its policy of bacteriological war'. While there is no proof that the United States is responsible for these outbreaks, the Cuban's suspicions are quite understandable in view of the CIA's documented past attempts at sabotage and destabilization in Cuba (see page 34).

In June 1981 a right-wing think-tank, the Institute of American Relations, published an outline proposal for measures to prepare US public opinion for 'the direct action necessary against Cuba'. The proposals also suggested that the administration should step up and strengthen the economic isolation of Cuba by tightening up on the US boycott, set up a Radio Free Cuba to broadcast anti-Castro propaganda, increase the US military presence in Florida and Guantanamo, and bring Latin American nations into line with the US against Cuba. Amongst the figures on the Institute's board are such leading British anti-communist crusaders as Brian Crozier and Robert Moss as well as Roger Fontaine and James Buckley, Under-Secretary for Security Affairs.

As if to reinforce the military threat to Grenada, Nicaragua and Cuba a United States and NATO exercise was held in the Caribbean in August 1981 involving 250 ships, 1,000 aircraft and 120,000 troops and including an invasion exercise on the island of Vieques. The exercise involved a ficticious country named Amber (there is a district of that name in Grenada) and its objective was to take power until an election could be called and a pro-American government installed. Rear-Admiral Robert McKenzie of the Caribbean contingency task force said the exercise was aimed at demonstrating the 'US capability to respond in the Caribbean basin' where there is a 'political military' problem. He described Nicaragua, Cuba and Grenada as 'practically one country'.

Florida's Paramilitary Camps

'I could hardly believe my eyes when the two men who came to call for me at the Holiday Inn in Coral Gables, Florida, walked into the lobby wearing US army type camouflage uniforms with bayonets and canteens strapped around their waists. They were there to take me to a nearby military camp where Cuban and Nicaraguan exiles are training and practising to invade their former homelands in a supreme effort to overthrow the leftist regimes that rule them.

Until I encountered my two guides I had no idea of how openly and extensively these displaced Latins are operating throughout southern Florida, including Miami, the Everglades and the Keys. Some of them use code names like Condor and Bombillo (Spanish for light bulb) but most make no attempt to conceal their identities — or their purpose. They are determined to liberate their homelands from the Castro regime in Cuba and the Sandinista junta in Nicaragua — or die in the process.

Right now there are at least ten paramilitary organisations composed of Cuban and Nicaraguan exiles operating in Florida.'

Eddie Adams, Parade Magazine, *15 March 1981.*

'One of the most active training camps is called 'Cuba'. Administered by Jorge Gonzalez, who is called "Bombillo" — (light bulb) . . . Mr Gonzalez explained that most members of the paramilitary group, including Jose Infiesta, a Vietnam veteran who is the top officer, were in a camp in Central America on a mission. A man who said he could be called 'Frank' or 'Ronald' and was wearing a Nicaraguan National Guard insignia on his beret explained that all the Nicaraguans in the camp were former members of the National Guard. The Nicaraguans he said have seven training camps in the United States, Honduras, El Salvador, Costa Rica and South American countries that he declined to name. There are approximately 600 Nicaraguans training in the United States, he said. "We'll fight the Communists with the same means they use — weapons", he said . . .

He explained that the former guardsmen had managed to get out of the country with their weapons and were also obtaining arms from South American countries "which have identified with us". When asked to name these countries, he said he would list only those who had lent moral support: Chile, Uruguay, El Salvador, Guatemala and Honduras. "The hour of our return is approaching", he said "but we can't say when . . ."

> Mr Gonzales said that his would-be guerrillas have had no conversations with the CIA but would accept any help offered. "The principal aid we've received", he said, "has been the declarations of the President. It's not weapons we need but freedom of action".'
>
> *Jo Thomas*, New York Times, *17 March 1981.*

The administration has already launched a diplomatic offensive against Cuba. In March 1981 Colombia broke off diplomatic relations with Cuba. It was later revealed by a leading Colombian newspaper that the government had agreed to make trouble for Cuba and Nicaragua in the OAS and elsewhere in return for US military aid and support for Colombia's longstanding dispute with Nicaragua over some Caribbean islands and cays. In the same month the Panamanian government, for some time under pressure from the US to reduce its links with Cuba, made a strong statement attacking Cuba's presence in Central America and the Caribbean. In May Costa Rica severed diplomatic links with Cuba. Costa Rica was in severe economic difficulties and awaiting IMF assistance. The government was moving to the right with increasing talk of strengthening still further the Civil Guard to deal with internal unrest, something long sought after by the United States.

Similar attempts to isolate Grenada have continued. Only Guyana, St Lucia, Belize, Suriname and Venezuela of the Caribbean states attended the revolution's anniversary celebrations in March 1981. Washington unsuccessfully put pressure on the EEC to refuse financial aid for the new airport under construction on the island and considered essential to the country's economic survival (see box). During the Brussels meeting to discuss the aid application the World Bank circulated a document claiming that the project was not feasible. In May the Grenadan Foreign Minister charged that US pressure was responsible for the blocking of an IMF funding facility although the loans in question had been agreed by the IMF management. The United States representative at the IMF had claimed that Grenada did not qualify for the loan. In June the United States failed to persuade Caribbean governments to exclude Grenada from sharing in a proposed US$4 million 'basic human needs' grant from the United States through the Caribbean Development Bank, despite intense US lobbying. Grenadans continue to believe that these events are part of a CIA-organized destabilization plan.

In contrast to these policies towards its perceived enemies, the

Grenada's Controversial Airport

'In recent weeks . . . we have all seen a series of articles in the European and North American press, all designed to discredit our international airport project. . . . Contrary to reports that our airport consists of several landing strips and is of unusual length, our international airport consists of a *single strip* of 9,000 ft . . . which in practice would be one of the smallest international airports in the Caribbean region. Any independent observer, including the consultants, SOFREAVIA, and the EEC resident representative in Grenada who has visited the site several times, can confirm this as a fact!

I wish to state publicly and unequivocally that the sole purpose and objective of our international airport is the development and expansion of our tourism and export agriculture through air cargo, which presently accounts for approximately half of our foreign exchange earnings. We have no intentions and have never had any intention of using this modest international airport which we are constructing, as a military base.

The argument has been that our airport will be a military base for "Cuba and Russia". If the purpose of this airport was for "a military base for Russia and Cuba" as the propaganda claims, we would like to pose two questions. Firstly, how did the Cubans, according to the International Press Report, transport 20,000 troops to Africa in 1975/76 when Grenada had no international airport? Secondly, if this airport has such military and strategic importance to "Russia and Cuba" do you seriously believe that the "Russians and Cubans" are incapable of providing all the *materials, equipment and finance* amounting to US$30 million, required to complete the airport? Would it indeed be necessary for each single minister of the government of Grenada including the Prime Minister, to spend eight percent of our time travelling throughout the world and spending sleepless nights over the past two years in order to raise that US$30 million?'

Address by Bernard Coard, Vice-Prime Minister of Grenada to Aid Donors Conference — International Airport Project, April 1981.

United States gave considerable assistance to its allies. Military aid has been a major part of this assistance. Jamaica's Edward Seaga, referred to by the State Department as 'America's man in the Caribbean', was offered US$1.5 million in military aid. Seaga intends to improve the capabilities of Jamaica's security forces to deal with the mounting rate of violent crime as well as political dissent. In March 1981 Reagan announced he was seeking a 60% increase in military assistance for

Latin America in Fiscal Year 1982. The Eastern Caribbean and the Dominican Republic would be the main recipients in the Caribbean. El Salvador is the major recipient of US military aid in Latin America, followed by Colombia and Honduras. In addition, the administration announced it was seeking discretionary funds of US$230 million, of which US$130 million could be spent in emergency economic assistance and US$100 million in military supplies.

President Reagan's Security Assistance Request for Latin America
(in millions of US dollars)

FMS: Foreign Military Sales credits
IMET: International Military Education and Training
ESF: Economic Support Fund

Country	FMS	IMET	ESF
Barbados	1.0	0.06	—
Costa Rica	—	0.06	—
Dominica	—	0.06	—
Dominican Republic	7.0	0.6	—
Eastern Caribbean	5.5	—	20
El Salvador	25.0	1.0	40
Guyana	—	0.04	—
Haiti	0.3	0.415	—
Honduras	10.0	0.7	—
Jamaica	1.0	0.075	40
Nicaragua	—	—	20
Panama	5.0	0.5	—
St Lucia	—	0.06	—
St Vincent	—	0.06	—
Canal Zone	—	4.6	—

Source: *Center for International Policy, Washington.*

Honduras has taken the place of Somoza's Nicaragua as the United States' strategic buffer state in Central America. The US$10.7 million in military aid projected for fiscal year 1982 would be more aid in one year than the country received in all the years between 1950 and 1979. The United States is reluctant to use its own forces in the regional conflict and it appears to be using the Honduran military as a proxy army. The Honduran army is playing an important role in the Salvadorean war, cooperating closely with the Salvadorean army. The border between the two countries is a virtual militarized zone. Church sources in Honduras have reported that the town of Marcala fifty kilometers from the Salvadorean border is being used as a centre for Honduran counter-insurgency forces trained by the United States. A new airstrip has been built there and civilian flights over the area are prohibited. In August 1981 a US embassy spokesman in Honduras said that a twenty-one man team of US military advisors, including four Green Berets, which had arrived that month would help with 'technical things such as communciations, aircraft maintenance and detection of smuggled weapons'. A total of fifty such advisors were in the country 'to assess the needs of the Honduran armed forces'.

In May 1981 General Vernon Walters visited Guatemala as part of a trip which also included Honduras and Panama. He was accompanied by Frank Ortiz, ambassador to Guatemala until he was removed by Carter because of his close associations with President Lucas. Guatemala is particularly important to the administration and it made clear its wish to resume military aid to the country. Walters is reported to have concentrated his inquiries on the military situation in the country, maintaining that the guerrilla threat had to be tackled before anything else.

The United States has reason to be worried about the situation in Guatemala. It has the most experienced guerrilla movement in the region, aided by highly suitable terrain. By 1981 the four main guerrilla organizations were moving towards unity and all had grown considerably in strength. Most observers agree that the growth is due to large-scale recruitment from the Indian population.

About half of Guatemala's population is made up of Indians and their participation in the guerrilla movement has been a major turning point in the struggle in that country. The Guatemalan oligarchy has always feared that one day the Indians would rise up against it. Many Indians suspected of opposition to the prevailing social order have been kidnapped, tortured and murdered by death squads. In recent years there have been indiscriminate massacres of large numbers of Indians including women and children in villages suspected of sympathy for the guerrillas (see box, page 196). These massacres, together with the guerrilla movement's own realization of the specific problems and needs of the Indian population, has led increasing numbers of Indians to join the guerrillas. Already the Guatemalan army, 95% of which is conscripted troops of Indian extraction, is having tremendous difficulty in finding recruits and for the first time it has begun recruiting *ladinos* (people of mixed white and Indian blood) whose racial prejudice against the Indians will, it hopes, sustain the war against the guerrillas.

In July 1981 a group of dissident Guatemalan officers claiming to represent the views of 60% of their colleagues gave an interview in the Mexican daily *Unomasuno* in which they estimated the guerrilla forces at about 6,000, compared with a State Department estimate of 2,000. They also admitted that in the first six months of 1981 the Guatemalan army had suffered about 1,000 casualties in engagements with the guerrillas. This is undoubtedly an underestimate, but it is the first time that the real strength of the Guatemalan guerrillas has been publicly acknowledged.

The techniques used by the Guatemalan government to suppress the growing opposition continue to be exceptionally brutal and sadistic. During 1981 death squad killings were reported to be up to 35-40 people a day, most victims showing signs of severe torture. At least 25,000 people have been assassinated in the past fifteen years, and according to one report, 'Military strategists around President Lucas Garcia have estimated that 50,000 "subversives" will have to be eliminated'.

It is only a matter of time before Guatemala becomes the United States' biggest problem in the region with much more at stake than either Nicaragua or El Salvador. Here there are powerful oil interests, both within Guatemala and in neighbouring Mexico, as well as a nucleus of right-wing US businessmen close to Reagan and to the Guatemalan right determined that Guatemala will not be lost to the United States.

The military capacity of the Guatemalan army is evidently insufficient to deal with the guerrillas. The dissident officers already referred to speak of the demoralization within the army and claimed that corruption on the part of senior officers as well as the growth in guerrilla activity, contributed to this. The army is also in need of US military equipment, particularly spare parts for their ageing aircraft much of which date from the counter-insurgency operations in the 1960s. The United States is also concerned that the lapse in military contact during Carter's presidency has reduced its influence over the Guatemalan army, as one military source pointed out: 'US training is good for associating the (Guatemalan) army with US doctrine and way of doing things. From 1977 to the present there has been a vacuum among young army officers and the four-year gap has created problems — there has been no updating among young officers and this has created ill feeling towards the US.'

But the full restoration of military aid and cash sales of arms above US$21 million are still subject to congressional review and human rights restrictions. President Lucas's record in this respect has been a stumbling block for the restoration of the traditionally close ties between the two countries. In June 1981 the administration approved the sale of 100 jeeps and 50 trucks to the regime, and announced its inten-

The Guatemalan Government — A Good Ally

'What should the United States do (in Guatemala)? It should support the responsible right and not polarize it as it did in El Salvador. It should signal to its Andean Pact allies, to the other Central American countries, and to those Guatemalans on both extremes that it has faith in this segment of the right to help resolve the nation's social, economic, political, and security problems. It should be willing to give this segment a reasonable time to do so, and it should stop berating Guatemala's political, military, and business leaders with reminders of their nation's problems and with criticisms of their handling of those problems; the reminders are not necessary, and the criticism is neither informative nor helpful, except to the left.

On balance, Guatemala can solve its problems within a non-Marxist and non-socialist framework, it can be a stabilizing force within Central America, and it can remain a good ally of the United States. Much will depend on the attitude of the US government. Given the growing Cuban and Soviet influence in Nicaragua and the uncertain outcome of the turmoil in El Salvador, the preservation of Guatemala's pro-US orientation is essential.'

C. Di Giovanni and A. Kruger, Washington Quarterly, *Summer 1980.*

'GUATEMALA CITY, MAY 13th — Retired general Vernon Walters, special emissary of Secretary of State Alexander M. Haig Jr., today dismissed most criticism of the human rights situation here.

In terms similar to those used by the Guatemalan government, he said the United States hopes to help that government defend "peace and liberty" and the "constitutional institutions of this country against the ideologies that want to finish off those institutions.' . . .

Walters said, "It is not difficult to see which countries are our friends and which are not."

Walters repeated the position of President Reagan that Washington will "stay by the side of our allies and there will be no more Irans . . . our purpose is to balance once again the military situation with respect to the Soviet Union and to do this we must strengthen our allies." He met with President Romeo Lucas Garcia and other top officials of the military-dominated government in his two-day visit here . . .

Walters, speaking in fluent Spanish at a press conference this morning, said that in his opinion "there will be a human rights problems in the year 3,000 with the governments of Mars and the moon. There are some problems that are never resolved." . . .

Walters, a former deputy director of the CIA, said it is "essential" that the government here "earn the confidence of the people and get rid of the guerrillas, who are against liberty."

Washington Post, *14 May 1981*.

. . . With a Programme of Political Murder

'Nearly 5,000 Guatemalans have been seized without warrant and killed since General Lucas Garcia became President of Guatemala in 1978. The bodies of the victims have been found piled up in ravines, dumped at roadsides or buried in mass graves. Thousands bore the scars of torture, and death had come to most by strangling with a garotte, by being suffocated in rubber hoods or by being shot in the head.

In the same three-year period several hundred other Guatemalans have been assassinated after being denounced as "subversives". At least 615 people who are reported to have been seized by the security services remain unaccounted for.

In spite of these murders and "disappearances" the government of Guatemala has denied making a single political arrest or holding a single political prisoner . . . The government does not deny that people it considers to be "subversives" or "criminals" are seized and murdered daily in Guatemala — but it lays the whole blame on independent anti-communist "death squads" . . . Amnesty International believes that abuses attributed by the government of Guatemala to independent "death squads" are perpetrated by the regular forces of the civil and military services . . . The vast majority of the victims of such violent action by the authorities' forces had little or no social status; they came from the urban poor and the peasantry and their personal political activities were either insignificant or wholly imagined by their captors . . . The evidence compiled and published by Amnesty International in recent years indicates that routine assassinations, secret detentions and summary executions are part of a clearly defined program of government in Guatemala. New information in the possession of Amnesty International bears this out. It shows that the task of coordinating civil and military security operations in the political sphere is carried out by a specialized agency under the direct supervision of President Lucas Garcia.'

Guatemala: A government program of political murder, *Amnesty International Report, 1981*.

Massacre in Guatemala

'Four Indian campesinos were taken prisoner in El Quiche. Soldiers drove stakes into their rectums, their ears, their mouths, their eyes. Then, in front of their horrified families and the rest of the village, they were burned alive.' *Green Revolution*, late Winter, 1981.

The following chronology lists some of the massacres carried out by the security forces over the past six years.

1975 Huehuetenango	35 peasants arrested by the army in Santiago Ixcan, Santo Tomas, and Mayaland. None of them ever seen again.
1977 Quiche	37 peasants kidnapped by the army and never seen again.
May 1978 Alta Verapaz	Over 100 Indians, including 25 women and five children, shot to death by the army in the main square of Panzos, with many others wounded.
September 1978 Chiquimula	23 peasants taken from their homes in Olopa and killed by the army.
31 January 1980 Guatemala City	39 persons burnt to death in the Spanish embassy during a police attack, although the Spanish ambassador had asked the police not to intervene.
3 March 1980 Quiche	11 persons, including six women, killed by the army in Nebaj.
1 May 1980 Guatemala City	31 people shot to death in May 1st demonstration.
13 June 1980	100 persons kidnapped by security forces from the villages of Pinula, Almolonga and Champas Pinula.
14 July 1980 Guatemala City	13 students killed, many more wounded when a group of armed men burst into the campus of San Carlos University.
28 July 1980 Quiche	60 men rounded up in San Juan Cotzal and killed in front of their families and friends.
24 October 1980 Solola	Six Indians kidnapped and 14 women raped by the army in Santiago de Atitlan.

November 1980 Quiche	13 Indians killed by soldiers in Macalajau.
February 1981 Chimaltenango	168 men, women, and children killed during a week's operation by the army in Papa-Chala, Patzaj, and Panimacac.
February 1981 Chimaltenango	90 people killed, some of them after torture and mutilation, by the army in Pachay Las Lomas, and Sacala Las Lomas.
March 1981 Peten	Indiscriminate massacres by the army in the destruction of the villages between Melchor de Menocs and the frontier with Belize.
11 April 1981 Chimaltenango	23 Indian peasants and a five year-old girl killed by the army in Choabajito.
15 April 1981 Quiche	69 villagers from Cocob murdered by the security forces.
April/May 1981 Quiche	12 peasant women assassinated and decapitated in Uspantan.
February to June 1981 Chimaltenango	The following villages were destroyed by the army in this period, apart from the ones mentioned above: Choatalun, Xesuj and El Molino. There are reports from reliable sources that the victims of the army's campaign of repression in this period in Chimaltenango alone reached 1,500. Similar campaigns were also carried out during this period in the following other Departments: El Peten, Solola, San Marcos and Huehuetenango.
31 May 1981 Huchuetenango	The army captured and killed 50 persons in San Mateo Ixtatan and wounded six others.
17-24 June 1981 Peten	The army attacked the cooperative villages of Bonanza, Flor de la Esperanza and El Arbolito and 15 other settlements in the region of the River Usumacinta. They killed at least 60 persons

	torturing some and mutilating others. 4,000 peasants fled to Mexico across the river but all but about 10 families were forced to return to Guatemala by the Mexican govt. There is no news of their fate.
19 July 1981 Huehuetenango	Between 150 and 300 Indians, mostly women, children and the aged were massacred by the army in the village of Coya, San Miguel Acatan.
19 August 1981 Huehuetenango	Unidentified gunmen occupy San Miguel Acatan, force the Mayor to give them a list of all those who had contributed funds for the building of a school, pick out 15 from the list (including three of the Mayor's children) make them dig their own graves and shoot them.
17 August 1981 Quiche	Thirty peasants killed by unidentified assassins in the village of Panasmic.

Washington Office on Latin America, *4 September 1981.*

tion of sending helicopter spare parts. The trucks and jeeps were reclassified as 'regional stability equipment' rather than police equipment which is subject to human rights legislation. In July the administration brought sixteen Guatemalan military officers to the United States for two days of pilot training as part of a FMS cash sale agreement with the Guatemalan government. These actions were questioned by the Human Rights Subcommittee of the Inter-American Affairs Subcommittee. Congressman Bonker stated:

How can the United States address the problem of human rights in Guatemala? I do not have an answer . . . However, it is clear to me that offering military assistance as means of 'leverage' over the Guatemalan government, as some suggest, is not the solution. By selling or giving the Lucas regime helicopter parts, training packages, or jeeps and trucks, we are literally aiding the indiscriminate attacks on innocent peasant villages and households . . . we are sending an unmistakeable signal that such activities have the explicit approval of our government.

The subcommittee went on to threaten to invoke Section 502(b) of the Foreign Assistance Act (see page 109) if the administration entered into any military transactions or agreements with the Guatemalan government without prior consultation with the subcommittee, and to sue the administration for violation of Section 502(b) if further military aid went to Guatemala without proper consultation with Congress.

Elections are scheduled in Guatemala for March 1982 and Lucas Garcia will not be standing. The Reagan administration may well hope that a change of government will give them the opportunity to extend their participation in Guatemala's counter-insurgency effort.

The United States' concern with guerrilla activity in Guatemala and the tensions within the region as a whole have also forced it to consider the situation of Belize. The British have long been anxious to shed this colony but Guatemala has maintained a claim to the country and has threatened to take it by force. The United States also fears that an independent Belize under its left-of-centre Prime Minister George Price could become a base for guerrilla operations. Independence was, however, inevitable and by 1980 the United States had come to accept that fact and tried to persuade Guatemala to withdraw its claim. In July 1981 it was announced that independence would go ahead on 21 September, although negotiations with Guatemala had broken down apparently because Guatemala insisted on the right to build military installations on two Belizean cays in the Caribbean. At the same time it was reported that an American military mission would be stationed in Belize and that Belizean officers would go to the United States for training. The presence of the mission would help persuade Belize that it was not being abandoned to a Guatemalan invasion force and reassure Guatemala that Belize would not harbour its guerrillas. For the United States it provided a foothold in a country which could play an important role in its efforts to contain 'communism' in the region. Nevertheless, Belize remains an emotive issue for the nationalist right in Guatemala and just before independence the Guatemalan government broke all remaining diplomatic and commercial ties with Britain.

Another country of strategic importance in the anti-communist crusade is Haiti. In November 1980 the Duvalier regime had celebrated Reagan's victory by arresting all the country's leading journalists and political dissidents. It clearly looked forward to an end to criticisms of its human rights records and began to terminate the period of relative liberalization which occurred during Carter's presidency.

Reagan, as Jean-Claude Duvalier well knew, was anxious to strengthen his anti-Cuban front in the Caribbean through closer ties

'A Warning Shot Across the Bows'

'A report appearing in the American news magazine *US News and World Report* has caused a minor stir in the opposition press and, more importantly, implicates the US government in what appears to be a deliberate campaign to discredit the government of Belize.

The short item, appearing in the "Washington Whispers" section of the June 1 *US News and World Report*, states as follows:

> "From US intelligence comes a report that Guatemala and Belize have replaced Nicaragua as conduits for secret shipments of Cuban arms to leftist guerrillas in El Salvador, now that Nicaragua has bowed to US pressure to discourage such traffic."

This is not the first time that Belize has been mentioned in connection with the various states of rebellion in Central America (other allusions have appeared in *Business Week* and various right-wing newsletters) but the *USN & WR* story is the first attributed to official US sources . . .

US policy toward Belize, it must be remembered, is formed totally within the context of its overall policy in the region: that is opposition to communism and the establishment and maintenance of governments friendly to the United States of America. Thus whatever things the US does for Belize are not done out of any great love for the Belizean people or genuine desire to see them take control of their own destiny but solely to promote the above US objectives. The US support for Belize in the UN, for example, did not arise from any sudden realization of the justice of the Belizean cause. It happened because the State Department believed that to remain in opposition to Belize's independence after it had become a fait accompli would be to greatly reduce its influence here vis-a-vis that of other nations, particularly those of socialist-oriented states which have consistently backed Belize without reservation. Such are the facts of international politics.

Having now earned the Belize government's friendship (the US Consul General has unhindered access to the Premier), the next step for the US is to make sure that the leftists stay out of power. In Belize that means Assad Shoman and to a lesser extent, Said Musa. Seen in this light the meaning of the planted arms story is clear. It is, as one observer suggested, "a warning shot across the bow", the political equivalent of the message on the gate of the US Consulate which says, "Don't even *think* of parking here". In this case it means: "Don't even *think* of supporting the rebels in Central America".'

Brukdown, *Belize, No.2, 1981.*

with Haiti and possible acquisition of the Mole St Nicholas, 'Haiti's only strategic card in world politics', across the Windward passage from Cuba, as a military base. But the Duvaliers' graft as well as their repressive rule has brought them into such international disrepute that it is difficult for Reagan to associate himself too closely with the regime. Haiti, isolated even within the Caribbean, has been refused admittance to CARICOM because of its appalling human rights record as well as fears that the near starvation wages paid to Haitian workers would result in a flood of cheap goods on the regional market.

The country's state of near bankruptcy adds another factor of instability to the regional situation, while Haiti's desperate boat people continued to leave the country at a rate of 500 a week in 1981, heading when possible for the United States, causing it considerable embarrassment. In August 1981 it was reported that the administration was seeking powers from Congress to instruct the United States coastguard to intercept boats carrying refugees and turn them back. But United States' foreign policy objectives, which could not deny support to an American ally in the Caribbean basin, has reduced its leverage over the Duvaliers. In the spring of 1981 General Walters was despatched to the country to discuss fiscal reforms and the IMF exerted strong pressure on the government to reform its economic management. However, the development of an alliance between Duvalier and Seaga of Jamaica, suggests that the United States has found a way of improving its ties with Haiti via Kingston. Jean-Claude Duvalier called for a 'chain of unity' centred on Haiti and Jamaica as an 'oasis of peace', and the Haitian Foreign Minister has called for a Caribbean front 'against international communist expansion'.

But as Carter discovered, Caribbean countries are less interested in military assistance than in economic aid. This has presented Reagan with a dilemma as he is strongly against foreign aid programmes. Indeed, the Republican Party platform states:

American foreign economic assistance is not a charitable venture, charity is most effectively carried out by private entities. Only by private economic development by the people of the nations involved has poverty ever been overcome. United States foreign economic assistance should have a catalytic effect on indigenous economic development, and should only be extended when it is consistent with America's foreign policy interests. America's foreign assistance programme should be a vehicle for exporting the American idea.

A number of countries in the region have been quick to seize the opportunity to link their political allegiance to the United States to requests for economic assistance. In Puerto Rico leading pro-statehood politicians and government leaders produced a document suggesting that the United States 'has a unique opportunity to actively involve Puerto Rico in the development and implementation of foreign policy towards this region of the hemisphere'. Their preoccupation is not only with statehood but with a proposal by the Reagan administration to make a US$300 million cut in the island's food stamp programme (60% of the population depends on United States food stamps) and a US$350 million reduction in education, health care and employment programmes.

Nevertheless, Puerto Rico has continued to serve as an instrument of Reagan's foreign policy. In February 1981 Romulo Barcelo, the Governor of the island, together with the head of the Puerto Rican National Guard, General Orlando Llenza, and his director of civil defence, Juan Enrique Lopez, went to the Panama Canal Zone to be briefed by United States officials on the situation in Central America and the Caribbean. Genertal Llenza also visited Uruguay, ruled by one of the most right-wing military dictatorships in Latin America, and arranged an exchange programme between the Uruguayan army and the Puerto Rican National Guard. After a visit to France, Barcelo agreed to strengthen Puerto Rico's ties with French territories in the Caribbean as a response, he stated, to Marxist penetration in the region. Puerto Rico is reported to be the most favoured site for the US military School of the Americas when it is forced to leave Panama in 1984.

Seaga also hopes to benefit from his anti-communist stance in the region. He has already received almost US$1 billion in international aid since he took office. But he has not managed to attract the large amount of foreign investment so crucial to the economic model he aims to pursue. A United States Business Committee on Jamaica has been set up under the chairmanship of David Rockefeller. But even Rockefeller has shown few signs of optimism, warning that there were 'real challenges' to be faced in persuading United States multinationals to invest in Jamaica.

The urgent need for a large-scale economic aid programme for the Caribbean basin as a whole, as well as Jamaica, prompted Seaga to call in December 1980 for a regional anti-communist alliance, with United States economic aid for the participants. He made it clear that, unlike his predecessor, he was not interested in a new international economic order nor in a North-South dialogue. Instead, he suggested a 'Marshall Plan for the Caribbean'. The original Marshall Plan had been launched in 1947 by the United States to pump massive amounts of aid into rebuilding war-ravaged Europe; it also pressured recipients to accept President Truman's Cold War doctrine.

The West German Chancellor, Helmut Schmidt, urged the United

States to consider Seaga's idea. The Reagan administration, however, has been reluctant to commit any major funds to economic assistance programmes for the Third World; it already has enough problems balancing promised tax cuts to its citizens with the massive escalation in United States defence expenditure. In any case, aid to the Third World does not accord with the administration's political philosophy.

However, it is increasingly difficult to ignore the deep economic crisis throughout the region. The economies of the Caribbean continue to stagnate, while the Central American region's economy grew by only 1% in 1980 compared to an annual average of 6% in the 1970s. Capital flight from Central America is now so great that one American expert considers there is more Central American capital outside the area than within it. The region's trade deficits and foreign debt have been growing at an alarming rate. Its continued dependence on agricultural exports has made it particularly vulnerable to the world economic crisis.

In June 1981 the idea of a 'mini-Marshall Plan' for the Caribbean Basin was revived when Secretary of State Haig met with the foreign ministers from Mexico, Venezuela and Canada to discuss a joint operation to rescue the Caribbean Basin from economic collapse. But it was clear that the United States sees the exercise primarily in political terms, as 'pacification through development'. It is willing to consider a scheme which will reward its pro-free enterprise allies in the region but exclude Nicaragua and Grenada. Mexico, however, has made it clear that it will not participate in any plan whose main objective is anti-communism.

There are other points of disagreement between the United States and its Latin American partners in the proposed aid programme. The governments of Central America met in Tegucigalpa in August 1981 and called for US$20 billion over the next five years and for higher prices for their commodity exports. The Reagan administration is strongly opposed to both. Myer Rashish, Under Secretary of State for Economic Affairs and mostly responsible for the administration's foreign aid policy, has made clear his philosophy toward Third World development. This, he maintains, 'depends on creating more wealth, not on sharing existing resources . . . We believe in the allocation of resources through free markets. The marketplace has a crucial role to play. There is no free lunch.' He condemned cartel-like agreements to raise the price of commodities produced by Latin American and other Third World countries, and what he called the poor nation's search for an 'economic bargain' from the rich world.

Such a laissez-faire attitude to economic development will not suit even the United States' allies in the Third World. But failure to tackle the severe economic problems of the Caribbean basin will further reduce the policy options open to the United States as social unrest grows in the region. The crisis in El Salvador provides a prime example.

PART 5

El Salvador: The Eagle's Reckoning?

Contents

1979
Oct.   Young officers overthrow General Romero; military-civilian junta formed (Junta I)
Nov.   US sends $205,000 in military aid (anti-riot equipment and military advisers) and approves $300,000 credit from the International Military Education and Training (IMET) fund
Dec.   US sends Defence Survey Team
1980
Jan.   Civilian members of government resign; Christian Democrats join new government (Junta II)
Feb.   Robert White appointed US ambassador
Mar.   Napoleon Duarte joins junta following more civilian resignations (Junta III); State of Seige and US-backed agrarian reform announced; Archbishop Romero assassinated
Apr.   US Congress approves US$5.7 millions in 'non-lethal' Foreign Military Sales (FMS) credits
Nov.   Internal 'Dissent Paper' criticises US policy towards El Salvador
Dec.   American missionaries murdered by security forces — US suspends economic and military aid; Majano ousted from junta and Duarte named President (Junta IV)
1981
Jan.   US restores military aid as guerrillas launch major offensive; US$5 million shipment of small arms, grenades and ammunition rushed through without Congressional approval using emergency clause (Section 506(a)) of the Foreign Assistance Act;

	twenty military advisers sent to El Salvador; Robert White sacked as ambassador
Feb.	State Department White Paper alleges Cuban intervention in El Salvador
Mar.	A further US$25 millions of military aid announced for the purchase of helicopters, vehicles, radar, small arms, communications and surveillance equipment; extra military advisors sent making a total of 56 in the country; mass demonstrations in Washington against US involvement in El Salvador
Jun.	US White Paper discredited
Aug.	Four extra helicopters approved
Sept.	France and Mexico recognize the FMLN as a 'representative political force'; US Congress approves economic and military aid package to El Salvador conditional on six monthly human rights reports and assurances that the Salvadorean regime is willing to negotiate a political solution to the civil war; 31 US military advisors to remain in El Salvador

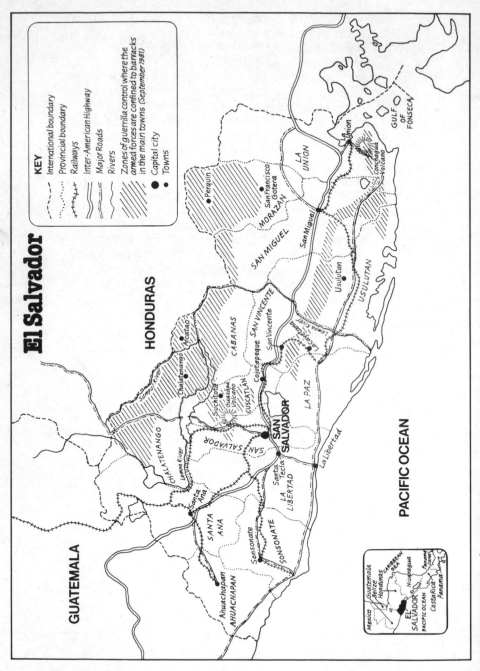

El Salvador

KEY

- – – – International boundary
- ······· Provincial boundary
- ⌗⌗⌗⌗ Railways
- ╌╌╌ Inter-American Highway
- ═══ Major Roads
- ～～～ Rivers
- ▨▨▨ Zones of guerrilla control where the armed forces are confined to barracks in the main towns (September 1981)
- ● Capital city
- ○ Towns

GUATEMALA

HONDURAS

PACIFIC OCEAN

GULF OF FONSECA

La Union

LA UNION

San Francisco Gotera

Perquin

MORAZAN

Conchagua Volcano

San Miguel

SAN MIGUEL

Usulutan

USULUTAN

Loma Larga River

SAN VICENTE

San Vicente

Acajutla

CABANAS

Cojutepeque

Ilopango

LA PAZ

Arcatao

Chalatenango

CHALATENANGO

Suchitoto

CUSCATLAN

Guazapa Volcano

SAN SALVADOR

San Salvador

Santa Tecla

LA LIBERTAD

La Libertad

Sumpul River

Lempa River

Santa Ana

SANTA ANA

Sonsonate

SONSONATE

Ahuachapan

AHUACHAPAN

Mexico
Guatemala
Belize
Honduras
CARIBBEAN SEA
Nicaragua
Panama Canal
EL SALVADOR
PACIFIC OCEAN
Costa Rica
Panama

The Politics of Land

In February 1980 the Department of State had three special working groups. One was for Afghanistan, one for Iran and one for El Salvador.

The United States awoke to the crisis in El Salvador only once it was about to erupt into full scale civil war. But its roots date back over a hundred years to the international coffee boom of the late nineteenth century. In 1881 the government abolished all communal forms of land tenure, paving the way for the expulsion of Indians from their land and the consolidation of vast estates in the hands of the coffee magnates.

Many of the Indians who lost their communal lands received a tiny subsistence plot from the plantation owner in return for work on his land and sometimes a share of the peasant's crop. They became known as *colonos*. But during the twentieth century wage labour and rental arrangements for land gradually replaced traditional relations between landowner and peasant. This process was accelerated in the 1960s and 1970s as the plantations were modernized and more land was needed by the large landowners to make way for new cash crops such as cotton and sugar cane. The number of *colono* plots fell from 55,000 in 1961 to 17,000 in 1971. The land available for rent was usually of poor quality, unsuitable for cash crops. In addition, El Salvador is highly overpopulated in relation to the land available for rent and the number of tenant farms smaller than one hectare increased from 107,000 in 1961 to 132,000 in 1971; dispossessed *colonos* frequently found themselves on tiny infertile plots, which would not sustain them or their families.

Even more dramatic has been the increase in landlessness. In 1961 the number of landless peasants was only 12% of the rural population. By 1971 this had risen to 30%, by 1975 it was 41% and in 1980 the figure has been estimated at 65%.

The problem of landlessness and the inability of the small rented plots to support a family is made even more acute by the fact that there are few sources of employment in El Salvador. The coffee and cotton plantations mostly require temporary, seasonal labour and mechanization has reduced even this. Between February and October under-employment in the countryside affects over 50% of the rural population and sometimes as much as 80%. In 1975 the number of permanently unemployed in the rural sector was estimated to be over 45%.

Until 1969 Honduras acted as a safety valve for the pressures from the rural poor. Many crossed the border in search of a living, but after the 1969 war between the two countries most were forced to return to

El Salvador and the border was closed. The war was to have important consequences: it both intensified the tensions in the rural sector of El Salvador and strengthened the Salvadorean army which emerged victorious from the five-day conflict.

Nor did the process of industrialization which took place in the 1960s and 1970s open up sufficient new sources of employment. Between 1961 and 1971 the manufacturing sector grew by 24% but the number of people employed in the capital-intensified export industries grew by only 6%. Although there was an increase in the number of industrial workers in the early 1970s (they came to represent a not inconsiderable 27% of all those economically active in the urban sector) this went nowhere near absorbing the thousands of peasants forced off the land. Many of these migrated to the city in search of work but found themselves condemned to a precarious existence of semi-employment as street vendors, servants, shoe-shiners and prostitutes living in the squalid slums around San Salvador.

Sixty percent of the population of El Salvador lives in rural areas, most in conditions of absolute poverty. An estimated 84% of the rural population receives an annual income of less than US$225 per capita. Sixty percent of rural families earn less than the minimum required to buy sufficient basic food for a healthy diet. On the other hand, 2% of the population (about 200 families) owns 60% of the land and receives one-third of the country's income. This oligarchy, which once comprised a mere fourteen families (see box), dominates key sectors of the economy — such as coffee production and banking — with some of its branches moving into industry in the 1960s. Such a concentration of economic wealth and power has precluded the emergence of an independent industrialist class strong enough or willing to challenge the country's rigid social structure.

The oligarchy has had to maintain its dominance through force. The peasant uprising of 1932, in which an estimated 30,000 peasants were massacred by the army, engraved itself on the oligarchy's memory and ever since it has been resolutely determined to prevent any further attempts by the rural population to organize in defence of its interests. Since that rebellion the oligarchy has ruled through the military who have usually controlled the Presidency and the Ministries of Defence, Interior and Labour, while the oligarchy's representatives have kept charge of economic policy.

Together the oligarchy and the military have institutionalized repression and brutality. In addition to the army itself, commanded by graduates of the Salvadorean military academy, many of them trained by the United States, there are a number of police bodies. The National Guard has been given a free hand to fight 'communism' and has garrisons throughout the country often described as independent

The Fourteen Families

There are fourteen of them. Their names are emblazoned outside the air-conditioned office blocks, the banks, the trading firms and the insurance companies of San Salvador. They play golf. They give parties by their swimming pools. They join exclusive clubs. They own vast coffee *fincas* (farms) in Libertad and cotton fields around Sonsonate. These fourteen heads of families have a close grip on the whole political and economic life of El Salvador. You find them, their sons-in-law, their nephews or their cousins, running every business, and most of all the coffee industry, which is Salvador's greatest wealth. They control cotton, cocoa, sugar, palm oil, phosphates and livestock; they control cement works, transport, the sales of Coca-Cola, mineral drinks, beer and American cars. Without themselves taking any direct part, they have created or destroyed almost all the governments that have held office since independence. A study of El Salvador's Business Yearbook tells you everything you could possibly want to know about all the political intrigues of a country barely larger than Wales. The Duenas, the Regalados, the Hills, the Meza Ayaus, the De Solas, the Sol Millets, the Guirolas, the Alvarez, the Melendez, the Menendez Castros, the Deiningers, the Quinonez, the Garcia Prietos, and the Vilanovas: this oligarchy runs the lives of three million *mestizos*.

Marcel Niedergang, The Twenty Latin Americas, *Pelican Latin American Library, 1971.*

fiefdoms. The National Police is a smaller organization mostly working in the urban areas but also active in some rural areas. The Treasury Police has a particular reputation for violence and corruption. These security units have often acted independently of any central command structure and frequently serve as a personal police force for local landowners, responsible for terrorizing the peasants. Members of these units and the army itself became the backbone of the right wing death squads formed in the mid-1970s to eliminate the growing opposition.

Industrialization brought the first challenge to the power of the oligarchy since 1932. The growth of the urban working class and middle class led to the emergence of trade unions and new political parties. In 1962 a group of professionals founded the Christian Democrat Party (PDC). It was headed by Jose Napoleon Duarte, who became mayor of San Salvador in 1964. In 1968 the social democrat National Revolutionary Movement (MNR) was formed and the National Democratic Union (UDN), reflecting the politics of the banned Communist Party, emerged in 1969. All these parties centred their activities on the electoral process.

The PDC, together with the Catholic Church and various labour unions, also began to encourage rural workers' associations and the Federation of Christian Peasants (FECCAS) was set up in the late 1960s. At the same time the government established ORDEN, a rural vigilante organization, officially linked to the Ministry of Defence and controlled by the army, made up mostly of peasants granted certain privileges such as credit facilities, hospital beds, school places, in return for their services in identifying and eliminating 'subversives'. By the early 1970s there was a network of these informers in most villages. There were an estimated 10,000 armed members of the militia and up to 100,000 collaborators.

The political parties had their moment of greatest influence in 1972 when together they formed a coalition, UNO, to fight the elections. El Salvador's elections have always been fraudulent and this was no exception. UNO won the election but were deprived of victory. Nevertheless, its member parties still clung to the electoral strategy, only to find themselves gradually losing support as others reached the conclusion that social justice in El Salvador could only be achieved through extra-parliamentary struggle. Unlike in neighbouring Nicaragua where sectors of the business class had joined the movement against Somoza, in El Salvador the struggle would eventually take the form of a more clearly defined class war.

The guerrilla organizations formed in the early 1970s were set up by disillusioned members of the political parties. The Popular Liberation Forces (FPL) was formed from members of the Communist Party and the People's Revolutionary Army (ERP) by members of the Christian Democrats. In 1975 the Armed Forces of National Resistance (FARN) split from the ERP.

In the mid-1970s, mass 'popular' organizations emerged as an alternative vehicle for change to the political parties, which they dismissed as 'reformist'. These organizations won considerable support among the urban working class, slum dwellers and the peasantry, as well as teachers and students. Their growth was phenomenal and by 1979 their combined membership numbered tens of thousands of people. Their activities, based on mass mobilization, included the non-violent invasion of land in the countryside, and the peaceful occupation of public buildings and factories in the cities.

Early in their development they began to form links with the guerrilla organizations, thus combining political organization with military struggle. The Popular Revolutionary Bloc (BPR) became linked to the FPL, the United Popular Action Front (FAPU) to the FARN, and in 1977 the Popular Leagues of 28 February (LP-28) was set up with links to the ERP. These organizations emerged, in the words of one of their members, 'not from the will of political leaders but from the desperate need of the people to defend themselves, both politically and, finally, when all peaceful means were exhausted, militarily.'

In the early 1970s the Church became increasingly involved in the movement for social change in El Salvador. Between 1974 and 1976 El Salvador's seven bishops either individually or collectively issued a series of pastoral letters protesting the violation of human rights and the injustice of the country's economic system. This strong stand played an important role in undermining the government's legitimacy, particularly abroad. Signs of an impending confrontation between the Church and the government could be seen in 1974 when President Molina addressed the Bishops' Conference. He divided national organizations into two camps: those in favour of democracy and those seeking to impose communist totalitarianism; he identified the 'Theology of Liberation' as the ideology of the 'subversive' camp. In February 1977 Oscar Arnulfo Romero (no relation to General Romero who had been voted President of El Salvador in fraudulent elections but two days earlier) became Archbishop of San Salvador and emerged as an outspoken critic of government repression and a key figure in the struggle for social justice.

The Church, as well as peasants, students and trade unionists, became one of the selected targets of right wing death squads which began to appear in the mid-1970s in response to the growth of the opposition. In 1975 the Armed Forces of Liberation-War of Elimination (FALANGE) appeared promising to exterminate all 'communists' and their allies, including bishops and priests. In 1977 others appeared, such as the White Warriors Union (UGB) and the Organization for the Liberation from Communism (OLC). These organizations are widely believed to be financed by the most right-wing sectors of the oligarchy.

El Salvador and the Eagle

The United States has not figured as prominently in El Salvador's history as in that of other Central American republics. The fruit companies, for instance, did not penetrate the country's economy at the beginning of the twentieth century. In 1932 the United States did offer the government help in suppressing the peasant movement, but El Salvador's oligarchy proved very efficient at putting down peasant unrest through its own military establishment.

United States economic interests in the country have never been very important. Investment rose with the creation of the Central American Common Market from around US$19 million in 1950 to US$104 million in 1975. It was mostly concentrated in the more dynamic branches of industry, such as food processing, pharmaceuticals, paper products and petroleum, and usually took the form of joint ventures with local businessmen. But the United States' principal concern with the country remained strategic rather than economic.

In October 1960 a group of democratic young officers allied to middle-class reformers overthrew the corrupt government of Colonel Jose Maria Lemus, and announced their commitment to free elections and a literacy programme. In hearings before a US House subcommittee in June 1976, Dr Fabio Castillo, former president of the National University of El Salvador, recalled the role of the US military mission in El Salvador in encouraging a conspiracy to overthrow the new government. The military counter-coup occurred in January 1961: 'The participation of US diplomatic and military representatives was at that time evident and open'. The repressive pro-US government of Colonel Julio Rivera which followed had direct US support: 'Governments of the civil-military type of El Salvador are the most effective in containing communist penetration in Latin America', said President Kennedy.

Rivera was committed to the modernization and counter-insurgency strategies of the Alliance for Progress. But, for the oligarchy, any attempt to include agrarian reform in the former was totally unacceptable and once again it was repression, not reform, which characterized the period. As the US ambassador at the time, Murat Williams, explained: 'There was a time when the Republic of El Salvador made great social progress back in the early 1960s, but fearful of Castroism, the United States government, under pressure from the Department of Defense, began to build up the Salvadorean security forces.'

From 1963 to 1970 General 'Chele' Medrano was the closest collaborator of the US military agencies in El Salvador and the main liaison with the CIA. He had a record of extreme brutality and had been responsible for torturing political prisoners and common criminals. In 1967 he became head of the National Guard. It was Medrano, with CIA help, who founded ORDEN in 1968. A US Office of Public Safety (OPS) programme was started in El Salvador in 1967 and an OPS investigations advisor was involved in working with Medrano to establish a special intelligence unit in the National Guard and, to work with it, what was described as a 30,000 man informant network — this organization was to become known as ORDEN.

Repression in the countryside was only one part of the US strategy of rural pacification; the other was co-option of peasant leaders. In

US Involvement with Salvador's Security Forces

From the turn of the century until immediately after World War II, Chilean officers directed military training and operations for the Salvadorean Armed Forces. Chileans founded the first War College, later renamed the Command and General Staff School, and directed its activities until 1957. US training and doctrine became increasingly important following World War II, when El Salvador received its first US grants under the Military Assistance Program, as well as the first US military mission.

Security assistance from the United States to El Salvador between Fiscal Year 1950 and Fiscal Year 1979 has totalled $4.97 million in Military Assistance Program grants, $3.479 million in Foreign Military Sales Agreements, $2.454 million in Excess Defense Articles, and $5.814 million in International Military Education and Training Program grants, all for a total of $16.72 million. The United States has trained a total of 1,971 Salvadorean officers, including at least 17 in Urban Counterinsurgency, 14 in Military Intelligence, 108 in Basic Combat and Counterinsurgency, and 124 in Basic Officer Preparation. According to the Pentagon in 1977, ". . . our security assistance program facilitates our overall relations with the government of El Salvador and fosters useful professional contacts with key members of the Salvadorean armed forces."

Arms sales
Until the mid-1970s, the Salvadorean Armed Forces were equipped primarily with surplus US equipment, largely from World War II stocks. In 1975 the Israeli and Salvadorean governments concluded a package deal to re-equip the Salvadorean Air Force: Israeli sales of 18 refurbished French fighter bombers and trainers were the first jet aircraft operated by the Salvadorean Air Force. Since the Israeli sales in 1975, France has sold several more trainers, as well as light tanks, and the state-owned Brazilian firm EMBRAER has concluded a sale of 12 patrol aircraft, which use US-designed engines and radar.

Arms sales by private US firms, which must be licensed by the State Department's Office of Munitions Control, have totalled $2.0 million since Fiscal Year 1971. Increasingly, US companies have been selling to private guard services in El Salvador, as well as to traditional security forces.'

Frente Democratico Revolucionario, El Salvador: Struggle for Democracy, *August 1980.*

1962 USAID signed an agreement with the Ministry of Labour and AIFLD as part of the Alliance for Progress programme. During the 1960s AIFLD, sometimes in conjunction with the PDC, held training seminars for peasant leaders. In 1968 the Salvadorean Communal Union (UCS) peasant organization was formed with AIFLD support and clearly aimed at counteracting the influence of 'communist' unions. The main victims of ORDEN, set up in the same year as the UCS, were the members of FECCAS and the independent Farmworkers Union (UTC) with which it joined forces in 1975. These organizations had grown considerably in size and militancy in the early 1970s. There are cases of entire villages, suspected of supporting FECCAS-UTC, being sacked and burned by ORDEN members. FECCAS-UTC joined the BPR and was eventually forced underground.

The next major example of United States involvement in the Salvadorean political process was in 1972. Following the fraudulent election of that year a number of officers who supported a return to constitutional rule had staged a coup to try to install Duarte as President. Dr Fabio Castillo has recounted subsequent events:

At about 8 o'clock in the morning, the headquarters of the insurgents agreed to receive the US military attache who arrived in order to intervene on behalf of the military faction of (the) overthrown government which, at that moment, was at the international airport, ready to flee the country. At 11 am unmarked planes flying in from unknown bases started to bomb the civilian population and the positions held by the insurgents. The bombardments were intense and bloody and lasted until 5 pm. During the raid rockets and missiles were used of a type not available to the army of El Salvador. While this happened Guatemalan troops penetrated into Salvadorean territory after crossing the eastern border, and units from Nicaragua appeared in San Miguel in the east of the country . . . A few days after the Constitutionalists' insurrection had been smashed, officers of that movement declared that they had been able to observe the participation of US personnel using the US Embassy's communications facilities for the purpose of coordinating the operations of the armies of Guatemala, Nicaragua and Honduras across the so-called *Consejo Centroamericano de Defensa,* CONDECA (Central American Defence Council).

The United States then provided the new President, Colonel Arturo Armando Molina, at the time travelling in Taiwan, with a US air force jet to rush him back to El Salvador.

The United States' action in 1972 was to prove disastrous to its long-term interests. On the one hand the army felt no restraint in launching a bloody wave of repression against the opposition, and on the other, the 1972 electoral fraud signalled the gradual demise of the reformist centre and the rise of the militant mass organizations demanding structural socio-economic change.

The Americans backed Molina because they believed he would carry out a minimal reform programme, a strategy defined by two

Salvadorean social scientists, Oscar Menjivar and Santiago Ruiz, as 'structural capitalist modernization within the framework of national security'. Molina revitalized ORDEN and the army stepped up its repression against peasants, students and trade unionists in order to provide the 'security' needed to carry out any reforms (see box). Military officers occupied higher government positions than in previous governments, and a programme of 'National Transformation' was declared. This included generous incentives to foreign capital (the San Bartolo tax-free trade zone was set up under Molina) and a USAID-funded agrarian reform. The reform was announced in 1976. It would have affected a mere 4% of the country's land and about 12,000 peasants. It was to be administered by a new body, the Salvadorean Institute of Agrarian Transformation (ISTA).

The reform would hardly have affected the oligarchy's power. One of its objectives was to encourage the oligarchy to diversify its investment into other areas of the economy through the compensation paid for any expropriations, at the same time as alleviating some of the social tensions in the rural areas. But the only basis of support for the reform was from the handful of modernizing industrialists and a sector of the oligarchy, including the De Sola family, which had broadened its economic interests and was closely tied to US capital through joint industrial ventures.

Rural Terror

On 29 November 1974 more than 60 soldiers and members of ORDEN armed with automatic weapons, mortars, hand grenades and tear gas entered the hamlet of La Cayetana in San Vicente province. The villagers had for some time been involved in a land dispute with a neighbouring estate owner.

> '. . . I saw the plaza covered with people's hair. The National Guard had cut off their hair with machetes, taking part of the skin with it . . . The National Guard arrived in Cayetana with 60 machine guns, tear gas, a cannon . . . When the farmers came, they grabbed their machine guns and sprayed the workers with gunfire . . . (A) wife was able to reach her husband, grabbing him by the leg. The bullet hit him and she was bathed in blood . . . Those they killed, they cut their faces in pieces and chopped up the bodies with machetes. If you like, I will show you where they buried the brains.'

Report from a Salvadorean priest, 1974. NACLA, El Salvador — A Revolution Brews, *July-August 1980.*

However, the most reactionary sector of the oligarchy — the large landowning dynasties still primarily involved in the production and export of coffee, cotton and sugar cane — remained intransigently opposed to the reform. Their suspicions of US activities had become apparent in 1973 when they had had AIFLD expelled from the country. Now they mobilized all their influence through their powerful lobby, the National Association for Private Enterprise (ANEP), and the newly formed Eastern Region Farmers' Front (FARO) representing those landowners affected by the reform. These groups had the support of the right wing of the army which brought pressure to bear on Molina. He was forced to capitulate and the reform was shelved. Instrumental in his defeat was his own Minister of Defence and Public Security, General Carlos Humberto Romero, who was associated with the hardliners in the army and was head of ORDEN. In February 1977 General Romero replaced Molina as President of El Salvador in fraudulent elections characterized by mounting political violence by the army and security forces.

Romero did not actually take power until July 1977. During the transition period repression escalated and, in particular, a systematic persecution of the Church was launched. The first open attacks on the Church had begun after the agrarian reform was announced. During 1976 five bombs exploded in the Catholic University in San Salvador which is run by Jesuits. Then in January 1977 a Colombian priest was expelled from the country. In the following four months a further six foreign priests were deported, seven were refused entry to the country, two were murdered, three tortured or beaten by government forces, and several were threatened by death squads.

These attacks on the Church focused considerable international attention on El Salvador and the United States government began to pay greater attention to the human rights situation in the country. Relations between the two countries reached their lowest point for many years. The publication of a State Department investigation of the human rights situation in the country in March 1977 led El Salvador to reject all future US military or security aid. In June the White Warriors Union death squad (UGB) accused the Salvadorean Church of promoting communism and threatened to kill all the Jesuits in the country. A leaflet distributed by the UGB urged, 'Be a patriot, kill a priest.'

The United States reacted strongly making it clear to the Salvadorean government that a US$90 million loan from the Inter-American Development Bank was being held up because of the government's human rights record. Romero was forced to give into United States pressure. He gave the Jesuits government protection, lifted the state of siege in force for the last months of Colonel

Molina's government, and made a number of public statements condemning all forms of violence. The United States apparently believed the situation would improve and that the most severe human rights violations would be restricted to the brief period between Romero's election and his inauguration. Richard Arellano, Deputy Assistant Secretary of state for Inter-American Affairs, said in a testimony before Congress in July 1977: 'We are anxious to work with the Salvadorean government to prevent the trend of an anomalous, unsettled period becoming a continuing part of normal Salvadorean life.' The United States then lifted its veto on the US$90 million loan.

But this 'carrot and stick' approach proved totally inadequate. At the end of November, one month after the loan had been approved, Romero introduced a draconian Law for the Defence and Guarantee of Public Order which made active, written and even verbal opposition to the government a crime. Romero had been encouraged by statements from Terence Todman, Assistant Secretary of State for Inter-American Affairs, in which he accepted that the Salvadorean government faced 'a cruel dilemma between a government's responsibility to combat terrorism, anarchy and violence, and its' obligation to avoid applying any means which violate human rights.' In a letter to the Salvadoren Women's Front, the female branch of FARO, in November 1977, Todman wrote: 'Let me assure you that your government can continue to count on our active collaboration and support in promoting economic and social development while combating the cruel and unforgiveable challenge of terrorism within the framework of our shared standards for the protection of human rights.' It must also have been noted by the Romero government that in an address to the American Chamber of Commerce in El Salvador on 25 November, the day the Law for the Defence and Guarantee of Public Order was passed, the new US ambassador, Frank J. Devine, made no direct reference to the law but stated that the United States government believed that every government had the complete right and duty to employ all legal measures at its disposal to combat terrorism.

Towards the end of 1978 the United States embassy in El Salvador attempted to promote a dialogue between the 'moderate' opposition forces — i.e. the PDC, the MNR, and the Church — and the government and ANEP to 'improve the climate' for the 1980 municipal and legislative elections. But the moderate parties did not trust the government while the security forces continued to torture and murder. Nor did the oligarchy trust Romero's ability to withstand American pressure to introduce reforms. According to Philip Wheaton of the Washington-based EPICA Task Force, they began to organize an army within the army as early as January 1979. It was known as ANSESAL and it coordinated a double command within the armed forces with control over the intelligence services and power to make high level decisions behind the backs of the supreme command. It also controlled the right wing terror groups — ORDEN, the White Warriors Union and FALANGE — many of whose members came from the army itself as well as other branches of the security forces.

It was the Nicaraguan revolution which forced the United States to develop a more coherent strategy towards the country in order to forestall a second revolution in the region. An indication that it was about to tackle the crisis was the memorandum of understanding which the United States signed with the Salvadorean government in June 1979 which allowed AIFLD back into the country. Shortly afterwards US Assistant Secretary of State for Inter-American Affairs Viron Vaky, followed by William Bowdler, Washington's roving ambassador to Central America, visited El Salvador to wrest a commitment to reforms from Romero. Apart from government officials, Vaky's only other talks were with the Christian Democrat Party. Romero offered very little, agreeing to allow the OAS to attend the 1980 elections and exiles to return. But the United States expressed optimism. If Vaky's statements before a US House subcommittee in September 1979 are to be believed, the United States was still prepared to work through Romero who in mid-August had announced 'a series of significant electoral measures, which if they can be effectively implemented, hopefully would go far to end the spiralling violence, frustration and polarization'.

Nevertheless, the United States cannot have been displeased when a group of young, apparently progressive, army officers overthrew Romero on 15 October, 1979.

Junta I

Although the United States was not directly involved in the coup, it suited Washington very well. Not only did it remove the obstinate Romero, it confused and divided the left.

The proclamation issued by the young officers at the time of the coup spoke of agrarian reform, and the nationalization of foreign trade and the banks. The officers behind the coup had formed a Permanent Council of the Armed Forces (COPEFA) and chose Colonel Adolfo Majano as their representative on the junta. Their second choice was Colonel Guerra y Guerra, but according to one of the officers participating in the coup who subsequently spoke to Carolyn Forche, an American journalist: 'The United States opposed the naming of Guerra y Guerra and instead proposed to us two names: Colonel Jose Garcia and Colonel Jaime Abdul Gutierrez. We needed

American support, and we agreed to this. Gutierrez became the second military man on the junta. Garcia became Minister of Defence. Guerra y Guerra accepted a lesser post as Under Secretary of the Interior.'

Both Garcia and Gutierrez had been associated with ANTEL, El Salvador's state telecommunications agency, Garcia as president and Gutierrez as a manager. Colonel Nicolas Carranza, Garcia's second in command, had been a technical manager with the company. Control of ANTEL is highly prized by the Salvadorean military as it is the centre of military intelligence. Garcia and Carranza were also accused of corrupt dealings with the US multinational ITT during their tenure at ANTEL. Another figure, Mario Antonio Andino, who was named as representative of private enterprise groups on the junta, had been associated with an electrical installations firm, Conelca, a subsidiary of Phelps-Dodge Corporation and a major supplier of cable to ANTEL.

Garcia and Gutierrez were both hardline officers with close ties to General Medrano, the founder of ORDEN. Despite the reformist declarations of the younger officers who carried out the coup, the hardliners never lost power. Once the coup was accomplished the institutional order within the military was restored. Garcia took charge and remains there. Medrano's nephew, Colonel Marenco, swiftly reorganized COPEFA, as one of the younger officers told Forche: 'Eighty percent of its membership changed, all of them loyal to Garcia. Garcia is not one of us. What you hear about the repression is true, and it comes from Garcia's group.' In the next few months five of the progressive officers involved in the coup had to flee the country and only two garrisons reportedly remained loyal to the group.

But the initial promises in the young officers' proclamation encouraged reform-minded politicians to accept invitations to join the new government. Roman Mayorga, rector of the Catholic university, and Guillermo Ungo, leader of the MNR, became members of the junta, and representatives of the Communist Party, the left wing of the PDC and the MNR were appointed to cabinet and under secretary positions and to major posts in government institutions.

The mass organizations and guerrillas were unprepared for the coup. Their immediate reaction was to reject it as a manoeuvre by Washington, but when the junta announced its platform of reforms within days of the coup, their responses varied. However, the escalation of repression — the civilian death toll in the first two weeks of the junta exceeded the number in the first nine and a half months of Romero's government — soon brought all these organizations together in united opposition against the junta.

The oligarchy was also on the offensive, attacking the reformist members of the junta and reorganizing the terror squads. Major Roberto D'Abuisson, who had directed torture activities in the National Guard for nine years, has close links with the White Warriors Union death squad, and has been called by ex-United States ambassador Robert White 'a pathological killer', founded the National Broad Front (FAN). Retired General Medrano re-established ORDEN, banned by the junta, under the name of the National Democratic Front (FDN). These organizations, dedicated to the physical elimination of the opposition, were backed by the extreme right of the oligarchy and the military. According to Forche, wealthy landowners also began bribing the military; an estimated US$10 million had been handed over by the end of 1979.

In a statement before a US House subcommittee in March 1981, Leonel Gomez, chief advisor to the agrarian reform institute ISTA during 1980, threw light on the relationship between the oligarchy and the military in El Salvador. Gomez claimed first of all that the Salvadorean army, rather than the oligarchy's right-wing terror squads, was responsible for most of the repression in El Salvador. His assertion is important because the United States has always claimed that the violence in the country, which escalated after October 1979, is caused by the extreme right and left, not by the army in power, which it backs.

Gomez also maintained that the Salvadorean army had come to believe it could run the country without the oligarchy. It had been shaken by the Sandinista victory in Nicaragua and the subsequent dissolution of the National Guard, and also believed that it alone had the technical expertise capable of modernizing the economy. But its primary motivation, which Gomez emphasizes above all others, it is greed and corruption and the wish, in common with the oligarchy, to exclude the poor majority of the population from all access to wealth and power. The army is as determined as the oligarchy to crush the opposition forces but, unlike the oligarchy, mostly accepted that minimum reforms were required to ensure United States backing (see box page 224).

The United States showed its approval of the October coup almost immediately. In November 1979 it sent US$205,000 in riot equipment and a six-man training team to advise the local military in the use of the equipment. In December it sent a Defence Survey Team without informing junta members Mayorga or Ungo; in the same month it proposed US$300,000 in IMET credits. According to the American journalist Tommy Sue Montgomery, at the time United States representatives were having private conversations with the Salvadorean military in which they stressed law and order and the need to restore authority. The military took this as a green light to escalate the repression; this rather than reform was the military's priority.

In November the BPR gave the junta thirty days to prove its sincerity. By the end of that month little had been accomplished. No human rights abuses were investigated and the whereabouts of 300 'disappeared' people had not been discovered. No reforms had been introduced; two cabinet members with close ties to the oligarchy, Dr Luis Nelson Segovia, Minister of Justice, and Manuel Enrique Hinds, Minister of the Economy, in collusion with ANEP, blocked all proposals for reform.

The civilian members of the government genuinely committed to reforms found they were unable to push them through or to control the excesses of the army and security forces. In late December the majority of cabinet ministers issued an ultimatum that the armed forces, and in particular Minister of Defence Garcia, submit themselves to the authority of the junta and accept dialogue with the mass organizations. Their failure to secure these demands led to the resignation during the first three days of January 1980 of the entire cabinet, except Garcia, other civilian members of the government, and finally Mayorga and Ungo themselves.

Junta II

At the end of December right-wing members of the Christian Democrat party had begun talks with the American embassy and the military. The United States had never trusted the civilians in the first junta who had demanded structural reforms and the involvement of the mass organizations in the political process. The conservative old guard of the Christian Democrat party would be far more acceptable and would give the military a moderate civilian facade. On 5 January a Christian Democrat-military government was formed, including Hector Dada, Morales Erlich and an independent civilian, Dr Jose Avalos; no other parties would join.

In mid-January the mass organizations and the UDN formed the Coordinating Council of the Masses (CRM); the polarization of forces was evident to most observers but the United States continued to insist it supported a middle ground. On 22 January a peaceful demonstration organized by the mass organizations rallied over 200,000 people in San Salvador; 22 people were killed when the army opened fire. A total of 309 people were killed in January 1980 by the army, the National Guard and the National Police; the Carter administration remained silent.

'A Vast Network of Corruption'

'My name is Leonel Gomez. I am the owner of a 40 hectare coffee farm in El Salvador. During most of 1980, I was chief advisor to the President of the Institute of Agrarian Transformation (ISTA). I left El Salvador on January 14, 1981, ten days after Rodolfo Viera (President of ISTA) had been assassinated and a death squad came to get me . . .

What is the nature of the Salvadorean army and by the army I mean the 500 or so officers who lead the Salvadorean army, the National Guard, the National Police and the Treasury Police? Your left says they are an instrument of the oligarchs. The State Department says they are people willing to learn, who want to do what is best for the country. Your right wing says they are anti-communist and pro-American.

While you will find individual Salvadorean army officers who fit one or another of those descriptions, the Salvadorean army, in essence, is none of those things. Traditionally, and still today, men join the army in order to get rich.

Young men enter the officer corps to acquire the power and the spoils military service provides. Over 90 percent of the officers have attended the El Salvador military school; very few officers come up through the ranks. By law, graduates from this school may remain in the army for thirty years. Each officer comes from a graduating class, called a *tanda*, and each *tanda* has a president.

Loyalty to the *tanda* is generally greater and more commanding than loyalty to the institution in which they serve. During their thirty-year careers, the officers of a *tanda* seek contacts, form alliances with other *tandas* and otherwise prepare for their goal of political power.

Every five years, in the past, elections were held. No matter which party had the most ballots, the army won. The winning President had been chosen by the previous President. Together they assembled a coalition of officers from one major *tanda* and several allied *tandas* which were to enjoy the spoils of the next five years . . .

The Salvadorean army is not held together by an ideology of anti-communism. It is held together by a vast network of corruption . . . The factors that bind officers together from different services, especially the *tandas*, are greater than those which separate them. In summary, there is an integrated officer corps. If its leadership truly wanted to eliminate substantially the abuses now occurring it could. But remember it doesn't. The army is bent on a war to exterminate all possible challenges to its power.

In each military region, the army commander is responsible for the activities of the army. Through the chain of command and the informal ties, he knows which forces are doing what and which soldiers are a part of formal or informal death squads. I have no doubt that many people in the cities have been killed by death squads, who owe their allegiance to the oligarchs, now residing in Miami or Guatemala. But those kinds of killings are very few.

The vast majority of killings are made in sweeps in the countryside by the armed forces engaging in indiscriminate killings or by death squads that operate under the formal or informal direction of the regional or local army commanders. Let me be clear. I am talking about the majority of the army officers now in charge. There are some, especially younger officers, who are revolted and shocked by what is going on.

If these types of killings were to be brought under control, there would still be scores of death squad killings, ordered by the radical right in the oligarchy. But, there would not be over 5,000 innocent deaths at the hands of the army, as there were last year in my country.

The fundamental problem in my country is the army, an army which presides over a military dictatorship.'

Prepared Statement of Leonel Gomez before the Sub-Committee on Inter-American Affairs, March 11, 1981.

The United States hoped that this offensive against the left would encourage the oligarchy to accept its reform programme. Since October the American embassy had been trying to persuade it to cooperate. The United States' basic commitment to the private sector and that sector's absolute refusal to accept reforms placed the Americans in a considerable dilemma. There was no social base for the United States' project for the country, yet without reforms the conflict would escalate leaving only a military solution to the crisis and a massacre of the left which could well exceed the *matanza* of 1932. This, however, was the scenario favoured by the majority of the oligarchy. Anxious to avoid alienating it the United States was equivocal in the messages it gave the oligarchy. Bowdler was reported to have told ANEP in January that the most important objective was to restore law and order at the same time as he was telling Archbishop Romero that the United States supported reform. At the end of February the United States exerted its influence to prevent a right-wing coup, which the oligarchy had apparently believed the United States would support.

The United States was now more deeply involved in El Salvador's internal politics than ever before. The junta was extremely vulnerable.

The Christian Democrats had little support in the country, even from the Church. The government was threatened by a coup from the extreme right, an insurrection from the left, and the fact that it had to maintain a moderate facade while its own members were themselves directly involved in the repression. Robert White, who became US ambassador to the country in March 1980, later said: 'When I went down to El Salvador one year ago, there was not one intelligence analyst in Washington who said there was a prayer of the present government lasting more than a month or two.'

At the beginning of March the Christian Democrat Party split over its involvement in the junta. On 3 March Hector Dada resigned. In his letter of resignation he said: 'We have not been able to stop the repression and those committing acts of repression . . . go unpunished; the promised dialogue with the popular organizations fails to materialize; the chances for producing reforms with the support of the people are receding beyond reach.' Dada was replaced by Jose Napoleon Duarte.

Junta III

The United States urgently needed a major initiative to bolster the junta which it, almost alone, supported. The urgency is vividly illustrated by the story that in late February, shortly after the attempted right-wing coup, two State Department representatives had rushed to a hospital in Houston, Texas where Colonel Gutierrez was recovering from an operation. They told him he had to return to El Salvador immediately to implement an agrarian reform.

On 6 March the Basic Agrarian Reform Law, Decree 153, was announced. A state of siege was declared at the same time, as reform could only be carried out in what was described as 'a climate of order'. Shortly afterwards the junta announced the nationalization of the banks and foreign trade. At the same time, Robert White, known for his commitment to Carter's human rights policies, presented his credentials as the new United States ambassador to El Salvador.

The Legal Aid Service of the Archdiocese of San Salvador (*Socorro Juridico*) has carried out a detailed analysis of the repression during 1980. It concluded that it was no longer merely a question of the systematic violation of human rights but a policy of the deliberate extermination of a wide sector of the Salvadorean people (see box, page 228).

The number of political assassinations by members of the army and security forces and the paramilitary death squads had begun to increase in January 1980 following the demise of the first junta. But the situation changed dramatically with the declaration of the state of siege in March. The repression escalated to an unprecedented level. In

March alone the number of victims almost equalled the figure for the previous two months combined. New forms of repression were introduced. Mutilated and tortured corpses began to appear daily throughout the country. Kidnapped victims who survived were later killed in the health centres where they were recuperating; a number of health service employees were also assassinated in this period. One of the victims of this repression was Archbishop Romero, who was shot by a hired assassin while taking mass on 23 March 1980.

Persecution of the Church in El Salvador had not abated since it began in 1977. A total of six priests were killed between 1977 and 1980, five were kidnapped and tortured, nine fled the country after threats had been made on their lives, and twelve were expelled from the country. In February 1980 D'Abuisson and members of FAN went on television and publicly threatened the Archbishop.

Monsignor Romero had been a thorn in the flesh of successive Salvadorean governments ever since he became archbishop in February 1977. Every Sunday he gave homilies during mass in his cathedral which were broadcast nationally by the Church's radio station. In these homilies he would speak of the kidnappings and murders which had taken place the previous week, describing the circumstances in which they took place and calling upon the authorities to release the victims or tell the relatives what had happened to them. Each of the cases he referred to in these homilies was submitted beforehand to legal verification and documentation by the *Socorro Juridico*. This organization had been founded in 1975 by a small group of Catholic lawyers for the purpose of representing the poor of San Salvador in the country's law courts. In June 1977 Archbishop Romero officially recognized the *Socorro Juridico* as the archiepiscopal institution responsible for defending the human rights of the Salvadorean people.

But Archbishop Romero was not only concerned with the immediate issue of the repression. He also took a strong stand on the question of socio-economic injustice and supported the right of the people to resist oppression. On 18 February 1980 he gave a homily in which he said: 'For our Church, the political aspect of faith finds its boundaries in the world of the poor . . . Depending on how the poor people are faring, the Church will support this or that political project from its specific position as a Church.' In a press interview on 7 March 1980 not long before his death, he stated: '. . . given the present situation in the country, I believe more than ever in the popular organizations. I believe in the true necessity for the Salvadorean people to organize themselves because I believe they are the social forces which are going to advance, which are going to pressure, which are going to achieve a society with genuine social justice and freedom.'

A Policy of Extermination

'The violation of human rights in our country already has its history. In the years 1977-79 alone, four inquiries were conducted by international observers, in which repeated violations were proved and recommendations were made to the Salvadorean Government that it should guarantee respect for and observance of these rights.

We can also recall that at the beginning of 1979, the Organization of American States (OAS) had as a point on the agenda of its General Assembly, the possibility of applying sanctions against the regime in El Salvador for its constant violation of those human rights listed in the American Convention of Rights (San Jose, 1969). The point was never discussed in the Ordinary General Assembly because of the events in El Salvador on 15 October 1979.

Since that date the violation of human rights has increased at an exponential rate of growth, despite all the statements of the Armed Forces to the contrary, and against all the hopes of the Salvadorean people and the international community.

We can no longer speak of the mere violation of human rights in El Salvador. The statistics prove that in quantitative and qualitative terms, a policy of systematic extermination is being carried out against a wide sector of the Salvadorean people, and to achieve this, an apparatus of extermination has been designed and is constantly up-dated . . .

Assassinations have been carried out against a very specific group of the population of El Salvador. In terms of profession or occupation, the bulk of the victims have been campesinos, workers and students. These three groups account for 58.9% of all assassinations in 1980. In terms of those victims whose occupation is known, campesinos represent 68.3% of the victims, workers 13.5% and students 13.5% . . .

What do all these people have in common? Obviously, neither ethnic, racial nor religious characteristics. It is far more plausible that what they shared in common was their organized and militant (real or supposed) opposition to the regime. The vast majority of the workers assassinated were either trade union leaders or trade union members. The vast majority of teachers assassinated were members of the Teachers' Association *(Andes 21 de Junio)*. It is public knowledge that this association is affiliated to the *Bloque Popular Revolucionario*, one of the popular organizations in El Salvador. Many of the victims were killed while taking part in political demonstrations to protest publicly against the policies of the present Junta, demonstrations that were attacked and dispersed on setting out.

A large number of the *campesino* victims were killed while taking part in occupations of haciendas to demand better wages. To end these occupations, the Army and Security Forces mounted military operations resulting in bloodshed. To these operations must be added full-scale "combing" of large areas under the name of "clean-up operations", supposedly carried out against guerrilla groups. More recently, artillery and aircraft have been introduced in indiscriminate bombing attacks against vast areas of the countryside in a campaign that increasingly takes on characteristics of sophisticated and merciless counter-insurgency activity.

. . . The USA shares responsibility not only for the initial conception of the plan of "reforms" with genocide, but also for the technical and political assistance needed to put the plan into operation. Responsibility for the extermination falls on the shoulders of the Salvadorean Armed Forces and their paramilitary groups. It is the Salvadorean Christian Democrat Party and its main leaders, Napoleon Duarte and Jose Antonio Morales Ehrlich, that must bear the responsibility for legitimizing and justifying the plan.'

Socorro Juridico: El Salvador: Del Genocidio de la Junta Militar a la Esperanza de la Lucha Insurreccional, *English translation by Commission of the Churches on International Affairs 1981.*

On 17 February Archbishop Romero had sent a letter to President Carter appealing to him not to send arms to the country (see box). On 1 April, shortly after his assassination and despite a growing body of evidence of army involvement in the repression, the Carter administration's request for US$5.7 million in military assistance to El Salvador was passed by Congress. Following the death of Romero the number of assassinations was to increase still further for the rest of the year. The growing number of deaths also coincided with the implementation of the Agrarian Reform.

An agrarian reform had been planned since the fall of General Romero. Large numbers of AIFLD employees had entered the country at the time, taking over two floors of the Sheraton Hotel in San Salvador. AIFLD became the main instrument for channelling United States government recommenations on agrarian policy to the Salvadorean military. An AIFLD consultant, Roy Prosterman, arrived in the country in February to advise on the reform which was largely drawn up by and financed by the United States.

The announcement of the reform took a number of people by surprise. It had been drawn up in secret and even the technical personnel of the Ministry of Agriculture had not been consulted. Nor had the Church, the universities or the peasant organizations (except for the AIFLD-backed UCS). Only top ministerial officials, the military

229

Archbishop Romero's Letter to President Carter

'Dear Mr President:

A recent news item in the press has concerned me very much. According to the article, your administration is studying the possibility of backing the present government junta and giving it economic and military aid.

Because you are a Christian and have said that you want to defend human rights, I take the liberty of expressing my pastoral point of view on this matter and of making a specific request.

I am deeply disturbed over the news that the United States government is studying a way to accelerate El Salvador's arms race by sending military teams and advisors to "instruct three of El Salvador's batallions in logistics, communications and intelligence techniques". If this information is true, the contribution of your administration, instead of favoring greater justice and peace in El Salvador will almost surely intensify the injustice and repression of the common people who are organized to struggle for respect for their most basic human rights.

Unfortunately the present government junta, and especially the armed forces and security forces have not demonstrated any ability to solve structurally or in political practice our serious national problems. In general, they have only resorted to repressive violence and this has resulted in a much greater toll of dead and wounded than in previous military regimes whose systematic violation of human rights was denounced by the Inter-American Commission on Human Rights.

The brutal way in which security forces recently evicted and assassinated persons who occupied the Christian Democratic Party headquarters, in spite of the fact that the government junta and the Party — it seems — did not authorize said operation, is evidence that the junta and the Christian Democrats do not govern the country. Rather, political power is in the hands of unscrupulous military personnel who only know how to repress the people and favor the interests of the Salvadoran oligarchy.

There is a report that last November "a team of six North Americans was in El Salvador . . . They gave out some $200,000 worth of gas masks and bulletproof vests. They also gave instructions on how to use them in riot control." You should be informed that there is evidence to show that beginning then the security forces, with greater personal protection and efficiency, have repressed the people even more violently, using deadly weapons.

Therefore, since I as a Salvadorean and archbishop of the San Salvador archdiocese have the obligation to work for the reign of faith and justice in my country, I urge you, if you really want to de-

fend human rights
- To prohibit the giving of military assistance to the Salvadoran government.
- To guarantee that your government will not intervene directly or indirectly with military, economic, diplomatic or other pressure to determine the fate of the Salvadoran people.

We are going through a serious economic and political crisis in our country, but without doubt the people are more conscientized and organized and thereby are becoming agents responsible for the future of El Salvador and are the only ones capable of ending the crisis.

It would be deplorable and unjust if by the intervention of foreign powers the Salvadoran people should be frustrated, repressed and hindered from deciding autonomously the economic and political course our country should follow.

It would mean violating a right that we Latin American bishops meeting in Puebla publicly acknowledged — "Legitimate self-determination for our peoples. This will permit them to organize their lives in accordance with their own genius and history and to cooperate in a new international order" (Puebla, 505).

I hope your religious sentiments and your sensitivity for the defense of human rights will move you to accept my request and thereby avoid greater bloodshed in this long-suffering country.

Sincerely, Oscar A. Romero, archbishop, February 17, 1980.

Translated by Latinamerica Press, 6 March, 1980.

---

supreme command and the United States participated in designing a reform which struck experts immediately by the lack of planning and preparation which had gone into it.

The reform was divided into three phases. The first involved the expropriation of estates of 500 hectares or more. This size of estate is mostly geared to the cultivation of cotton, sugar cane and cattle raising and accounts for 15% of the country's arable land. Compensation would be paid in bonds, the objective being to encourage landowners to invest this in industry and commerce. They would also be entitled to retain up to 150 hectares of their property if they carried out improvements. The reform would be implemented by the resurrected agrarian reform institute ISTA, although it lacked both experienced staff and technical expertise.

Phase II of the reform would effect land holdings of 150-500 hectares. This would be the heart of the reform as these lands account for the production of over 60% of El Salvador's most profitable export crop — coffee, and are the basis of the oligarchy's power. Compensation and the right to retain 150 hectares also applied here.

The third phase was announced on 28 April 1980: Decree 207. It was called 'Land to the Tiller' and affected rented lands. The tenant would become owner of the land, receiving formal title after thirty years, once he had paid for the plot.

In spite of the apparently sweeping scope of the proposed agrarian reform, it offered nothing to the 65% of the population who are landless.

Phase I was launched immediately. As many of the large landowners are absentee, often living in Miami, the army and about 500 agricultural technicians were able to expropriate thirty estates on the same day the reform was announced. The oligarchy was quick to mobilize its defence. A Devolution of Lands Committee was set up and officers bribed to secure the return of the lands or their exemption from expropriation. Others managed illegally to remove machinery and livestock. An estimated 25-40% of the nation's farm machinery was removed and 30% of the cattle slaughtered by their owners to sabotage the reform. Although ways to circumvent the reform were found, over 200 estates were expropriated.

But the other side of Phase I of the reform was the escalation of repression which accompanied it. The state of siege gave the army complete freedom to intimidate and murder the peasantry. The toll of murders rose dramatically with the introduction of the agrarian reform: from 240 in February to 490 in March, 480 in April, 610 in May and 770 in June. ORDEN was used by the army to identify peasants who supported the mass organizations, and while expropriating a farm the army would also eliminate the radical peasants.

On 26 March, less than three weeks after the reform had been announced, Jorge Villacorta, under secretary at the Ministry of Agriculture resigned. In his letter of resignation he stated:

The agrarian reform had, as a basic political objective, the intention to pacify the country and to channel development within a model of participatory democracy . . . I resigned from my position on 26 March 1980 because I believed that it was useless to continue in a government not only incapable of putting an end to violence, but a government which itself is generating the political violence through repression . . . In reality, from the first moment that the implementation of the agrarian reform began, what we saw was a sharp increase in official violence against the very peasants who were the supposed 'beneficiaries' of the process . . . To cite one case, five directors and two presidents of the new peasant management organization were killed.

The peasants' reaction to the reform was one of fear, as they associated the arrival of the army to expropriate the estates with repression. The main beneficiaries of the reform have been the former owners' administrative employees, who remain loyal to their old employer and, unlike the *colono* workers, have the skills to run the estate. Many of the workers came to believe that the reform merely meant a change of boss.

Phase II of the agrarian reform should have affected 23% of El Salvador's farm land but it has been postponed indefinitely. Phase III came as a complete surprise, even to the agencies charged with carrying it out, when it was announced at the end of April. According to the Minister of Agriculture: 'Decree 207 . . . was completely unplanned for and unexpected'. The reform was to affect rented plots, over 80% of which are under two hectares. Although tiny, these plots provide 50% of the corn, beans and sorghum grown for local consumption, but the majority of them do not provide sufficient income to support a family. Such plots are the predominant form of land tenure in the northern provinces of Chalatenango, Morazan, Cabanas and Cuscatlan. These are also strongholds of the guerrilla movement.

The analysis by Stephens and Simons, the authors of an OXFAM-America study of the agrarian reform, shows how the Land to the Tiller programme failed to take into account the real nature of agricultural practice in El Salvador. Because of the poor quality of the soil, tenants rotate their plots. Land to the Tiller would require the tenant to remain on the same plot for thirty years which would lead to serious soil erosion and reduced yields. Nor was attention given to the question of the farmers' credit needs or to the tremendous administrative problem of working out plot boundaries and legal titles.

The problem was that Land to the Tiller had first been developed for Vietnam by the same Roy Prosterman who now tried to apply it to

---

'A Political Move'

'A sizeable number of people in ISTA (Salvadorean Institute of Agrarian Transformation) and MAG (Ministry of Agriculture) are suspicious of Decree 207 because it was designed virtually in its entirety by Americans and slipped into legislation without their being consulted. This fact is known and resented. It is widely believed that "land-to-the-tiller" is a political move on the part of the US Embassy and the State Department. Many believe it is a "symbolic" and "cosmetic" measure which was proposed because it would look good to certain American politicians and not necessarily because it would be beneficial or significant in the Salvadorean context.'

AID memorandum quoted in L. Simon and J. Stephens, El Salvador Land Reform, Impact Audit, *1981.*

El Salvador with neither knowledge nor experience of the country. As the programme had primarily political aims this problem had not concerned its authors. In Vietnam, Land to the Tiller had been part of a rural pacification programme known as Operation Phoenix. Prosterman believed that this kind of land reform, which basically rewarded loyal peasants with small plots while others were often terrorized and murdered (Prosterman denies being involved in the repression), would pave the way for a non-Marxist road to social change. As one US official commented on Land to the Tiller: 'There is no one more conservative than a small farmer. We're going to breed capitalists like rabbits.' A US government memorandum quotes Prosterman's own justification for the programme: 'A key AIFLD consultant, University of Washington Law Professor Roy Prosterman, and his associate Mary Temple, urge us to look on the program — if not already too late — as a last chance to save El Salvador from a take-over by "a far left so extreme the comparison with Pol Pot's reign in Cambodia would not be far-fetched".'

By April 1981, a year after Decree 207 had been announced, only 1,000 provisional titles had been handed out and officials privately admitted that few more would be distributed, certainly nowhere near the 150,000 envisaged. Many of its potential beneficiaries had in fact become victims of the repression. The head of ISTA publicly de-

---

Protection Racket

The weeds are high, the fence falling down, the administration building badly needs painting and repair and oxen lug carts with solid wooden wheels over the dusty road. But, if the former owners neglected this Pacific coast farm in the western corner of El Salvador, the army has not.

In July, soldiers hauled the president and seven other members of the cooperative that now owns the plantation to the beach and shot them. Now, according to co-op officers, El Penon pays the local military commander $50 a month ostensibly for maintenance of army vehicles, and $180 for the salaries of soldiers who "guard" the ranch.

According to an employee of El Salvador's Institute for Agrarian Transformation, more than 80 cooperatives are being forced to pay such protection money. More than 200 peasant cooperative leaders and five institute employees have been killed since the land reform program began in March. Salvadorans and foreign diplomats blame Government security forces and right wing death squads.'

New York Times, *11 January 1981.*

---

nounced the number of peasants killed 'with the 207 decree in their hands'. The number of refugees began to increase in May, and according to Catholic Relief Services the majority came from rural areas designated for the Land to the Tiller programme. On 13 and 14 May 1980 an estimated 600 refugees near the El Salvador-Honduras border in the province of Chalatenango, were massacred. According to Amnesty International, 'the peasants allegedly tried to cross the river Sumpul and take refuge in Honduras to escape from an attack by National Guardsmen, soldiers and members of the paramilitary group ORDEN. They were reportedly sent back by Honduran troops only to be shot by Salvadorean troops on their return to Salvadorean territory.'

The story illustrates the increasingly close cooperation between the Salvadorean and Honduran armies. Honduras's rugged border with El Salvador had become an important refuge for the guerrillas and the United States encouraged Honduran cooperation in flushing them out. The Guatemalan army was also known to have helped the Salvadorean army and many feared that the United States might use the neighbouring armies as a surrogate invasion force if the need arose.

Meanwhile, the extreme right was still plotting to overthrow the government. In April 1980 Major D'Abuisson went to the United States, hosted by the American Security Council, and had meetings with a number of conservative senators and congressmen. On his return he tried to launch a coup but was thwarted by troops loyal to Majano and arrested. His arrest was formally welcomed by the Christian Democrat Party who also threatened to leave the government if he was not tried and punished. But eight out of fourteen garrisons demanded his release and about 100 members of FAN demonstrated outside the US ambassador's residence chanting 'White is Red', 'Viva Reagan' and 'Viva Jesse Helms'. The Christian Democrats did not resign when D'Abuisson was released without charge on 13 May. In June he made a second, illegal visit to the United States apparently to test support for a government led by him to be installed after a coup. He claimed he had talked to several US senators who had told him 'to hold on until November and that with the new government . . . our luck will change'.

The release of D'Abuisson also signalled the demise of Majano. On 10 May Colonel Garcia announced that the future command of the armed forces, previously shared by Majano and Gutierrez, would go exclusively to the latter. Majano's demotion was the end of the only progressive military influence remaining in the junta. It also led to a new stage in the repression.

According to the *Socorro Juridico*, during the period beginning with Gutierrez's appointment as sole head of the armed forces to the end of June 1980 the junta's policy of extermination against the Salvadorean people became clear. In the fifty days which comprised this period, more than 2,500 Salvadoreans were tortured, assassinated or massacred:

In qualitative terms, the reign of terror would appear to be the most distinctive characteristic of this period. The cruelty of the tortures practised against the victims of the repression had no precedent in the previous stages. The corpses appeared scalped, be-headed, with throats cut and dismembered. The heads of the decapitated began to appear hung from trees or impaled on fences. In addition to the paramilitary-based repression, large-scale military operations were mounted in the north and central-east regions of the country. Massacres included that of women and children fleeing from the country to seek refuge in Honduras. In the towns members of the teaching profession and students, health employees and the Church were the victims of repression without mercy at the hands of the armed forces. Educational centres were constantly searched; the two principal universities were victim to repeated armed intervention; convents, Catholic schools and health centres were constantly checked. In the month of May alone, twenty-one teachers were assassinated.

'You just gas 'em'

'The Salvadorean army, with 30 years of US training behind it, was said to be more "professional" than the security forces — meaning less prone to "excess" in controlling the opposition. New equipment would be channelled to the Army, while the National Guard and Police would be trained to use less barbaric methods. "The idea is that if a guy is standing with a protest sign, you don't have to cut him down with a machine gun", a US official explained. "You just gas 'em".'

NACLA, El Salvador — A Revolution Brews, *July-August 1980.*

The escalation of the repression also corresponded to the increasing unity and strength of the opposition. In April the opposition political parties and the mass organizations formed the Democratic Revolutionary Front (FDR). In May the guerrilla organizations united to form the Unified Revolutionary Directorate (DRU). In late June the CRM organized large-scale strike action which was followed by a wave of repression against trade unionists, a clamp-down on the media and an attack on the offices of the *Socorro Juridico.* Increasingly large-scale operations were mounted in the countryside. In

236

September the air force began to be used in counter-insurgency operations. There were reports of indiscriminate bombing attacks on villages and the use of heavy artillery and helicopter gunships. Some 5,000 troops were deployed in an operation against a guerrilla stronghold in Morazan; an estimated 3,000 civilians were reported to have died in that operation. In October the guerrilla organizations moved towards a higher degree of military unity when the Farabundo Marti Liberation Front (FMLN) was formed.

In November the 'Dissent Paper', purporting to come from individuals within the United States government who were critical of the administration's policy toward El Salvador and the rest of the region, appeared. It called on the US government to recognize the FDR/DRU as a legitimate political force in El Salvador and to reduce military support for the junta. It also drew attention to the deliberate misinformation about the situation in El Salvador both in the media and before Congress:

The articulation of US policy for public and congressional audiences has misrepresented the situation in El Salvador emphasizing the viability of the current regime, downplaying its responsibility for the excesses being committed by security and paramilitary forces, exaggerating the positive impact of current reforms and portraying opposition forces as terrorists unsuitable for and unwilling to engage in constructive dialogue. These misleading rationalizations of our policies have played upon domestic frustrations resulting from perceived setbacks in other theatres, and have legitimized grossly inadequate arguments in favor of military intervention. Our actions and our words have narrowed down our policy options to a single path of gradual escalation of direct military involvement in a region vital to our national interests and within a political context that gives the use of force few chances to achieve a satisfactory outcome.

But the carnage continued. By November there were an estimated 70,000 refugees. That month six political leaders of the FDR were kidnapped in San Salvador by the security forces — their mutilated bodies were found later. The death toll for 1980 reached at least 13,000 by December, with most observers agreeing that the majority of the murders were carried out by the army and the security forces and that most of the victims were ordinary peasants.

The murder of three American nuns and a Catholic lay worker in December signalled another crisis for the junta and American policy toward El Salvador. It was difficult for the Carter administration to ignore the assassination of US citizens especially when all the evidence pointed once again to the Salvadorean security forces. Economic and military aid to the junta was suspended and William Bowdler and former Assistant Secretary of State William Rogers went on a special mission to the country. On 13 December Majano was finally ousted from the junta and a reshuffled government team was announced with Duarte as President, and the United States restored economic aid. But the continued presence of Garcia and the mere redeployment of his deputy, Carranza, to the apparently innocuous post of head of the state telecommunications centre, ANTEL (i.e. head of intelligence), failed to convince anyone that any real change had taken place. In January 1981 two American AIFLD technicians and Roberto Viera, the head of ISTA, who not long before had gone on television to denounce army corruption, were assassinated by a right-wing death squad.

Junta IV

On 10 January 1981 the guerrillas launched a major offensive. Their objective was to establish a position of strength before Reagan took office and force him to negotiate.

On 14 January the Carter administration resumed military aid (US$5 million in FMS credits, US$420,000 in training and the lease of two Bell helicopters), claiming that the guerrillas were receiving weapons from abroad: '. . . We must support the Salvadorean government in its struggle against left-wing terrorists supported covertly with arms, ammunition, training and political and military advice by Cuba and other communist nations.' On 16 January the administration authorized a new US$5 million emergency package of lethal aid to be sent immediately: it included grenade launchers, M-16 rifles and ammunition together with four more helicopters. The aid was released under Section 506(a) of the Foreign Assistance Act which allows the President to grant military assistance without congressional approval in an unforeseen emergency requiring immediate military aid.

In addition to the increase in military assistance, the number of US advisors in El Salvador was growing. A 'headquarters counter-insurgency operational planning and assistance team' of five or six military personnel had gone to the country prior to the resumption of military aid on 14 January. According to ambassador White, on the eve of Reagan's inauguration he was presented with a proposal to increase massively the number of advisors:

The chief of the (US) military group (in El Salvador) came to me on the 19th of January with a five or six page telegram which gave a rationale and a request for putting something like 75 military advisors into El Salvador. Thus, one component of the United States mission presented the ambassador with a full-blown telegram, drafted in final form, without any discussion with the country team. I said, 'Colonel, what possessed you to do this?' He said, 'I'm under instructions to do this from the Pentagon and from Southcom (The United States joint military command in Panama). I said, 'Well, you obviously know that this telegram would totally change United States foreign policy'. This was a straight power play by the Pentagon to have on the desk of the new administration a request for so many military advisors.

The telegram was not sent.

Thus, by the time Reagan took office the United States was already deeply involved militarily and politically in El Salvador. Carter himself was said to be hesitant and equivocal about the growing military involvement and he insisted on linking aid to reforms. Carter's ambassador Robert White opposed any further military commitment, although that was the direction in which the Carter administration's policies seemed inexorably to be leading.

Reagan, it was widely assumed, would not have the same qualms as his predecessor. Reagan advisors Fontaine, Di Giovanni and Kruger had no illusions about the political centre in El Salvador: 'The centre in El Salvador has disappeared, and the current junta is supported more by the US embassy than by anyone else', they wrote in the *Washington Quarterly* in the autumn of 1980. In a previous article in the same journal, di Giovanni and Kruger had argued: 'In El Salvador, the private sector must either be incorporated into the existing government to provide the junta with better balance, broader support, and more competent policies and procedures, or else the private sector and other reasonable elements must be given US backing in forming a new non-communist government.'

But there were still strong political reasons for preserving the myth of the centre. Internationally the FDR had won considerable support, especially from Mexico and the Socialist International, which influenced a number of European governments. Panama, whose most prominent political figure, General Torrijos, was a close friend of Majano, did not give the FMLN the support he had given the Sandinistas, but neither did he back the United States' military role in the region. The junta, on the other hand, had the direct support of the Venezuelan government and the international Christian Democrat movement. If Duarte was ousted by a right-wing coup this support would go with him and the credibility of US policies before its European allies would sink further. Apart from the question of international respectability, there was a widespread feeling that a right-wing coup would serve the interests of the left rather than leading to their defeat, escalating the struggle still further and drawing the United States into more direct military involvement.

The guerrillas had neither won nor lost their offensive in January.

They had failed to convince Reagan that he should negotiate with them and they had not scored any notable military victory but they had shown their strength in certain key rural areas, particularly in the northern provinces of Morazan and Chalatenango. It was clear that a protracted war was emerging which the army would find difficult to win.

It was Reagan's turn to go on the offensive. His administration announced its intention to 'draw the line' at communist subversion in El Salvador. El Salvador would prove the new government's resolve to halt Soviet aggression, distinguishing it clearly from the vacillation of the previous administration and showing that, unlike Carter, Reagan would defend the 'backyard'.

In late February 1981 the State Department published a White Paper entitled 'Communist Interference in El Salvador'. It argued that 'the insurgency in El Salvador had been progressively transformed into a textbook case of indirect armed aggression by Communist power'. To support the White Paper a number of documents were published which the State Department claimed had been captured from the guerrillas by the security forces. These documents were supposed to prove that Cuba was channelling arms to the guerrillas from Ethiopia, Vietnam, the USSR and East Germany, and various Arab nations, with Nicaraguan assistance. Not only did the documents present a very weak case, but in June they were shown by leading US journalists to contain 'factual errors, misleading statements and unresolved ambiguities' (see box). Most people were in any case aware that the guerrillas bought their arms on the open market, frequently from American dealers.

Nevertheless, before their authenticity was decisively refuted, the administration put the documents to good use. The objective was similar to that used in Vietnam when, in 1965, a document had been published entitled 'Aggression from the North: The Record of North Vietnam's Campaign to Conquer South Vietnam' which aimed to prove that the struggle in Vietnam was caused by external aggression, hence justifying American military involvement. The administration used the documents first to launch an international diplomatic offensive to convince their allies to support a tough line on El Salvador. In February 1981 two Reagan emissaries, General Vernon Walters and Lawrence Eagleburger, were despatched respectively to Latin America and Europe. Eagleburger met a lukewarm response; few governments were convinced by the documents. The French and the British showed the highest degree of acceptance, but not even the British, who are most closely identified with Reagan's policies, would give unequivocal backing to his stance on El Salvador. Most European leaders feared an escalation of American military involvement and urged a political settlement. Indeed, American efforts to stop the European Common Market sending US$900,000 of humanitarian aid to El Salvador, on the pretext that it was reaching the guerrillas, also failed.

The documents were also used to justify a considerable increase in military aid. At the beginning of March 1981 the US government announced it would send twenty more military advisors and four more helicopters into El Salvador and an additional US$25 million in military aid, US$20 million of which was provided under Section 506(a) of the Foreign Assistance Act, as Congress at this time was by no means united on the need to send military assistance to the country. The advisors would be used to train Salvadorean personnel in communications, intelligence, logistics and other skills but would not, it was claimed, take part in combat. By March there were an estimated fifty-four to fifty-seven US military advisors and personnel in El Salvador. Duarte himself warned: 'Washington should not send too many military advisors here. Otherwise this will soon be seen as America's war.' The spectre of Vietnam was once again raised in people's minds. Representative Clarence Long said: 'I think we made a great mistake going in for a Vietnam approach and sending a lot of weapons and advisors. The advisors are going to get hurt, and when they get hurt the American people are going to get excited. Then we would face massive intervention or humiliating withdrawal.' References to Vietnam became so common that Secretary of State Alexander Haig appeared before the House Foreign Affairs Committee early in March and assured them that the administration's action would not lead the Americans into a military entanglement as in Vietnam.

The administration's rhetoric and actions gave new confidence to the Salvadorean military. In February the State Department had said that because US support was 'of vital necessity' US aid would no longer be conditional on Salvadorean help in investigating the murder of the American missionaries. According to Robert White, dismissed from his post as ambassador by the new administration, 'there never was and there never has been a serious investigation of the deaths'. In March Reagan refused to rule out a continuation of military aid in the event of the military taking complete control of the government.

These statements were made as reports of murder, torture and massacres became increasingly frequent. 7,700 people were killed in the first four months of 1981. 'The chief killer of Salvadoreans', White informed a congressional hearing, 'is the government security forces'.

On 15 March the Salvadorean military accompanied by members of ORDEN surrounded nine guerrilla-controlled towns in the province of Cabanas. About 10,000 civilians were in the area when the army at-

Tarnished Report? Apparent Errors Cloud US 'White Paper' on Reds in El Salvador; State Department Aide Says Parts May Be Misleading But Defends Conclusions

Washington — The State Department's now-famous white paper 'Communist Interference in El Salvador', which was issued on Feb. 23, has served the Reagan administration well as the launching pad for its anti-Soviet foreign policy.

The anonymous authors of the eight-page document displayed no false modesty in declaring in its preamble: 'This special report presents definitive evidence of the clandestine military support given by the Soviet Union, Cuba and their Communist allies to Marxist-Leninist guerrillas now fighting to overthrow the established government of El Salvador.'

Bearing copies of the report, State Department emissaries visited the principal capitals of Western Europe and elicited statements of support from most of them. Domestically, too, the white paper, said to be based on 19 captured guerrilla documents, was accepted as fact by most of the nation's press, and there were numerous follow-up stories quoting administration spokesmen on their plans for countering the allegedly growing military power of the Salvadoran guerrillas. Within days, the National Security Council announced it had approved plans to provide the tiny country with $25 million of additional military aid and $40 million of economic assistance.

Admissions of 'Mistakes'

With this kind of track record for the white paper, it is surprising, therefore, to hear John D. Glassman, who is given the major credit for its existence, describe parts of it as possibly 'misleading' and 'over-embellished'. In a three-hour interview in his new office just one floor below Secretary Alexander Haig's at State Department headquarters, policy planner Glassman freely acknowledges that there were 'mistakes' and 'guessing' by the government's intelligence analysts who translated and explained the guerrilla documents, which were written in Spanish with code names.

The white paper says that the 19 documents prove El Salvador is a 'textbook case of indirect armed aggression by Communist powers'. But a close examination of the documents the State Department has brought forward indicates that, if anything, Mr Glassman may be understating the case in his concession that the white paper contains mistakes and guessing.

Several of the most important documents, it's obvious, were attributed to guerrilla leaders who didn't write them. And it's unknown who did. Statistics of armament shipments into El Salvador, supposedly drawn directly from the documents, were extrapolated, Mr Glassman concedes. And in questionable ways, it seems. Much information in the white paper can't be found in the documents at all. This information now is attributed by the State Department to other, still-secret sources . . .

'A close reading of the white paper indicates . . . that its authors probably were making a determined effort to create a "selling" document, no matter how slim the background material.'

Wall Street Journal, *June 8, 1981.*

Romero's Murderers

'Robert White, the former US ambassador to El Salvador told a Congressional committee last week that there was "compelling if not 100 percent conclusive evidence" that one-time military intelligence officer Robert D'Abuisson and his followers were implicated in the murder of Archbishop Oscar Arnulfo Romero. The "hit" was dubbed Operation Pina, and its details were contained in a document submitted by White to the Senate Foreign Relations Committee.

The 45-page document, said to have been captured from D'Abuisson after his arrest last May and subsequently handed over to White by Colonel Adolfo Majano, contains lists of supplies, arms and right-wing informants. Operations plans are also included, along with the names of more than 100 people said by White to have been involved in right-wing terrorist activities as "active conspirators against the government". Those listed include exiles in Miami and Guatemala City, and military officers in El Salvador.

White said that he had passed the document on to the State Department some time ago; he regretted that it had not been used in the recent White Paper, implying that its evidence had been deliberately ignored. He also testified that he had given it to three leading political analysts, who had concluded that the evidence was compelling regarding the assassination of Archbishop Romero.

The purchases of such equipment as night vision devices, silencers, pistols, rifles, shotguns and sub-machine guns are listed, along with pay-offs for informants, drivers and security guards. The calendar of activities runs from January to March 1980, when Romero was murdered.

The notebook also mentions US$120,000 in contributions to Nicaraguan exiles in Miami.'

'White blows whistle on death squad', Latin America Weekly Report, *17 April 1981.*

US and Multilateral Aid to El Salvador
(in millions of US dollars)

AID: US Agency for International Development
CCC: US Commodity Credit Corporation export credit sales program
Exim: US Export-Import Bank total authorizations
HIG: US Housing investment guaranty program
IBRD: International Bank for Reconstruction and Development (World Bank)
IDB: Inter-American Development Bank
IMF: International Monetary Fund
OPIC: US Overseas Private Investment Corporation-insured investments
PL-480: Public Law 480 US Food for Peace program

US fiscal year	1979	1980	1981	1982 (proposed)
AID	6.9	52.3	76.8	75.0
PL-480	2.9	5.5	30.9	16.2
Peace Corps	1.6	0.5	—	—
Military aid	—	5.9	35.4	26.0
Eximbank	6.4	0.7	0.7	—
OPIC	8.5	—	—	—
CCC	—	4.0	30.0	—
HIG	—	9.5	10.0	—
IBRD	23.5	—	77.0*	—
IDB	29.5	48.5	101.6*	—
IMF	—	57.0	160.6**	—
Total	79.3	183.9	523.0	—

* Total costed projects.
** Center for International Policy projection.
Source: *Center for International Policy, Aid Memo, April 1981.*

tacked. The guerrillas managed to break through the military encirclement and organized the evacuation of some 8,000 women, children and elderly people. As these refugees tried to cross the Rio Lempa into Honduras two Salvadorean jet fighters and a US-supplied helicopter bombed them while Salvadorean and Honduran troops shot at them from both sides of the river.

During a talk to representatives of US Church organizations concerned with El Salvador, Deane Hinton, the new US ambassador, commented about the violence in the country: 'That's the way it has always been: it's in the culture.'

Non-US Donors' Share of El Salvador Aid
(in US fiscal year 1981 or beyond; millions of US dollars)

Country	Amount
Argentina	12.5
Belgium	5.6
Brazil	13.5
Canada	11.1
Denmark	1.9
Finland	1.7
France	12.8
Germany, Federal Republic of	13.9
Great Britain	19.2
Italy	7.7
Japan	11.8
Mexico	9.6
Netherlands	4.0
Norway	1.8
Sweden	2.8
119 other countries, excluding United States	110.3
Total	240.2

Note. Amounts shown are each country's share of international financial assistance to El Salvador by virtue of their overall contributions to the World Bank, Inter-American Development Bank and the IMF. On 10 December 1980 West Germany, Denmark and other countries voted against or abstained on a US$45 million Inter-American Bank loan to support land reform in El Salvador. The loan went through because the United States contributes 62 percent of the total to the particular bank account from which it was made. But donors other than the United States have between 66 and 80 percent of the votes for the remaining loans to El Salvador from the Inter-American Development Bank, the World Bank and the International Monetary Fund (IMF). West Germany and other donors are likely to object to the payment of projected loans to El Salvador in 1981.

Source: *Center for International Policy,* Aid Memo, *April 1981.*

The Circus Owner and the Clowns

Reagan still refused to accept political negotiations despite offers to mediate from the Socialist International and the West German government. The FDR insisted at first that it would only talk to the

Huey Helicopters

'In a single week in March, 798 people were killed in El Salvador, according to the Legal Aid Office of San Salvador's Archbishopric. Of these, 681 were peasants killed in bombings during assaults by government planes and helicopter gunships. There were no "general offensives" by the FLMN that week, not even one major battle. These were just the weekly victims of the Army's search and destroy missions, rendered more efficient by the arrival of ten Huey helicopters mounted with machine guns.

The choppers have been leased to the junta at no cost by the US government. According to the *Miami Herald*, such arrangements are not routine; the no-cost procedure was used "in order to bypass time-consuming military procurement procedures that are required for sales or grants". US advisors are currently busy training pilots and mechanics to keep the choppers aloft. One has already been downed by the FMLN.

"The North Americans know that the Army can't enter our zones with infantry", says an FMLN Commander, "so they're trying to get in by air." The main task of the choppers is to airlift the Atlacatl Brigade — the US trained strike force of 2,000 men — into the guerrilla's zones of control.

To be entirely thorough, the US government has leased ten Huey choppers to Honduras, also at no cost, to improve surveillance of the common border area. As a result, thousands of refugees have been caught in the pincer tactics of two armies.'

NACLA, Central America: No Road Back, *May-June 1981.*

United States; in the words of Guillermo Ungo, leader of the FDR: 'There's no point in talking to the clowns if you can talk to the owner of the circus'.

The phrase aptly describes how many viewed the Duarte government. His credibility was extremely low as the military were very evidently in control. In March 1981 threats of a right-wing coup were renewed. D'Abuisson visited the United States again and on his return announced that Washington would support a coup; this, he claimed, was the conclusion of his conversations with Roger Fontaine. D'Abuisson certainly has friends in Washington; Senator Jesse Helms, for instance, has called Duarte's government the 'socialist junta'. His support within the army, sectors of which could be persuaded to abandon reforms without much difficulty, also appeared to be growing and observers noted the ease with which he moved in and out of the country. But Washington denied his story and Garcia declared:

'The armed forces do not support any coup d'etat because this is not the moment to be thinking about those things . . . the armed forces want everything to be done through the present government and they will not heed provocations from any sector.'

By March the country's economic situation was very serious. Since the beginning of 1980 an estimated US$1.5 billion of private capital had left the country. Investment had fallen by a third and GDP by 10% in 1980. Only 50% of the country's industrial capacity was in operation and agricultural production was constantly disrupted. Low world prices and lack of internal and international credit have also badly affected coffee, cotton and sugar production. One of the guerrillas' tactics was to burn crops and destroy power stations in order to interrupt production. In March Duarte put in a request for US$300 million in economic aid in addition to the US$63 million the United States had already provided.

Suddenly, in March 1981, an administration official announced that the US press was giving too much attention to El Salvador. This surprised many journalists as they had merely responded to the administration's own attempt to create a crisis atmosphere by relating the Salvadorean problem to the East-West conflict. Another official explained the dilemma: 'The administration wanted to focus attention on certain parts of the problem. But once they did that, they found that they couldn't keep it selective — that there was no way to control it and keep it from growing as a subject of press interest.'

There appear to be several reasons why the administration decided to reduce El Salvador's high profile in its foreign policy statements. One is that its policy was not enjoying public support. In March the *Washington Post* reported that White House mail on El Salvador was running ten to one against the administration's emphasis on military aid and advisors. A Gallup Poll showed that only two percent of the public thought that the United States should send troops to help the government. The Churches in the United States were playing a particularly active role in mobilizing support against the government's policies. On 3 May an estimated 100,000 people demonstrated in Washington, the largest rally on a foreign policy issue since the days of Vietnam. Shortly afterwards not only the House Foreign Affairs Committee but also the Republican-controlled Senate Foreign Relations Committee voted in favour of restrictions on US military aid to El Salvador. Reagan was required to certify not only that the junta was respecting human rights but that it was willing to negotiate a political settlement with the opposition.

Reagan chose to ignore the last commitment, but it was clearly necessary to restore some credibility to the junta on the human rights question. Garcia announced that six members of the security forces had been arrested under suspicion of murdering the American women missionaries. White claimed that their names had been known for some time by both the Salvadorean government and the FBI. A few months later, on 20 August, US ambassador Deane Hinton told the *Washington Post* that if the six members of the Salvadorean National Guard accused of slaying the missionaries are found not guilty 'and they are released because the jury or the judge finds them innocent or for some other reason, I will regret that but clearly it has to be accepted'.

But another reason why the administration wished to avert some of the attention from El Salvador was that its policy toward the country was clearly failing. Militarily the guerrillas had not been defeated. Indeed, by June 1981 they could claim control over one-third of the country, establishing 'semi-liberated' zones where army patrols could not easily penetrate. Army offensives in Morazan, Chalatenango, Cuscatlan and Cabanas have all failed to dislodge the guerrillas. The army has resorted to bombing villages suspected of harbouring guerrillas. The guerrillas' undoubted strength is their support amongst the population which gives them considerable freedom of manoeuvre denied the armed forces. The FMLN has at times carried out attacks in San Salvador, but in general the army has remained in control of the urban centres. Only a massive escalation of American military involvement could decisively defeat the guerrillas.

Politically the junta remains isolated and vulnerable. International pressure for a negotiated settlement has been strong, with the election of President Mitterrand in France, an important figure in the Socialist International, adding to it. Mexico and the Socialist International have consistently backed the FDR in El Salvador. Even the junta's allies, such as Venezuela, favour a negotiated settlement. Until the death of Torrijos in July 1981, a considerable blow to the opposition, Panama also played a major role in trying to promote a negotiated solution (see pages 145-152).

The United States has received most international support outside the region from the Trudeau government in Canada and the Thatcher government in Britain. While these countries do not wish to see a further escalation of US military involvement, they have expressed sympathy with the American's objectives in El Salvador. For example, Nicholas Ridley, then Minister of State at the British Foreign Office, wrote to a fellow Tory member of parliament in May 1981, following the visit of Reagan's emissary Lawrence Eagleburger:

The evidence provided by the US Government clearly demonstrates that large quantities of arms and equipment have been reaching the Salvadorean insurgents from communist sources . . . it is understandable that the US

Government feel the need to resume military assistance in addition to their very substantial economic aid to the Government of El Salvador. Their interest in countering Soviet and Cuban subversion in Central America is one which we share.

The United States began to stress that it favours a political settlement to the conflict but it rejects negotiations with the opposition. Its political solution centres instead around elections which have been called for March 1982. According to a key speech by Assistant Secretary of State for Inter-American Affairs Thomas Enders in July 1981, United States military aid is now intended to sustain the present military stalemate 'to ensure a climate in which a political solution can take place'.

But to most observers the idea of holding elections in the present state of civil war is absurd. Guillermo Ungo expressed the views of many when he stated 'Elections will have to be held in graveyards'.

In June 1981 Robert White wrote: 'The poverty of this administration's policy towards El Salvador becomes clearer every day. The government of El Salvador is going nowhere. The violence continues. The reforms have stopped. The economy is foundering. The extremes are gathering strength.' In an interview shortly afterwards he added: 'The far right has a stranglehold on the economy . . . They have a deliberate policy of ceasing economic activity until they get their price — and that price is the exit of the Christian Democrats.'

But the United States showed itself to be as ready as ever to step up military assistance to the country at any sign that the guerrillas might be increasing their activity. At the end of August the guerrillas were again on the offensive. San Salvador, the capital city, was without power on 17 August after guerrillas blew up over 100 electricity pylons including those which link the two largest hydroelectric dams to the national grid. Heavy fighting was also reported in Morazan and Guazapa. The guerrillas claimed to have extended their control over large areas of the north and east.

At the same time there were reports that units of the armed forces of Honduras, Guatemala and El Salvador carried out joint operations against the Salvadorean guerrillas. The operation was code named *Operacion Aguilar*. It was also reported that in the same month Honduran troops crossed the border on two different occasions to assist the Salvadorean army. Promises of support also came from the military dictatorships of the southern cone of Latin America. In an interview in the Argentine paper *Siete Dias* at the beginning of September 1981, the Argentine army commander, General Leopoldo Galtieri, confirmed that the Argentine government had offered to send troops to fight alongside the Salvadorean armed forces. It is widely believed that Argentine urban counter-insurgency experts are already advising the Salvadorean security forces.

The United States announced it was stepping up its shipment of military helicopters to the country. Four were sent, accompanied by six US military advisors. These were the first helicopters to be sent to El Salvador since the ten provided in January and March 1981. At the same time Haig gave an interview to the *Christian Science Monitor*: 'I don't want to over-dramatize this', he said, 'but it is clear that Cuba hasn't terminated or modified substantially its level of support for the insurgency in El Salvador'; and Thomas Enders told the Nicaraguan Minister of Foreign Affairs, Miguel D'Escoto: 'The United States is not going to allow a military triumph of the guerrillas; it has the means and the desire to do so, irrespective of the political cost.'

PART 6
Conclusion

Today, Central America is in political and economic turmoil and the Caribbean islands are sinking deeper into economic stagnation and political crisis. United States intervention in the region, which has always been designed first and foremost to pre. erve its own economic and security interests, must bear much of the responsibility for the present situation. United States policy towards the Caribbean basin has failed even in terms of its own objectives. The United States' minimum aim has been to preserve stability in its backyard, but even this has eluded it.

The potential for serious unrest in the Caribbean remains very high. Only a minority of the population has sufficient wealth and power to cushion it during periods of crisis, while the vast majority lacks jobs, decent housing and many other basic needs. Solutions based on implants of foreign aid and capital which are grafted onto the present inequitable social and economic structures — both nationally and internationally — are unlikely to improve the lot of the Caribbean's poor.

But the most immediate challenge to United States domination in the Caribbean basin is in Central America. Here the persistent refusal of the United States to allow the people of the region the right to self-determination has, in practice, left it with only one option for preserving its influence: increasing military involvement.

The risks of such involvement are apparent to many. At the end of August 1981 Claude Cheysson, the French Foreign Minister, visited Mexico and told the Mexicans that he believed Central America could become as explosive a region as the Middle East, with the same danger of superpower conflict. He persuaded the Mexicans to agree to a major initiative aimed at forcing the United States to consider a negotiated solution which would include the opposition forces. At the beginning of September the Mexican and French governments recognized the Salvadorean guerrillas as a 'representative political force'.

Immediately after the French-Mexican initiative nine Latin American nations including Venezuela, the Dominican Republic, Colombia and Argentina accused the two countries of 'intervention'. Venezuela recalled its ambassadors from Mexico and France for consultation and pledged US$98.5 million in economic aid to the junta.

However, Panama refused to criticize the initiative and instead denounced US aid to the junta. Costa Rica reiterated its support for President Duarte but refused to sign the nine nation declaration. The West German government, while it is unlikely to join the French and the Mexicans, will continue to object to further loans from multilateral agencies in which it participates. This may well affect an important US$120 million one year stand-by credit which the Salvadorean government is seeking from the International Monetary

Fund.

The French-Mexican initiative remains, therefore, a serious diplomatic reverse for the United States. It is also a recognition of the strength of the guerrilla movement. But the administration still appears to believe that time is on its side, that with sufficient US military assistance the guerrillas will be eliminated or sufficiently weakened by March 1982 for elections to take place.

But such a scenario is unlikely. Time is not on the United States' side. Not only do the Salvadorean guerrillas remain undefeated, but before long the guerrilla movement in Guatemala will be strong enough to launch a major offensive. Guatemala is topographically different to El Salvador and much more suited to guerrilla activity. The guerrillas enjoy the increasing support of the population and the army is under growing pressure. The guerrilla organizations now claim to be active in nineteen of Guatemala's twenty-two provinces. Columns of the two strongest organizations, ORPA and the Guerrilla Army of the Poor (EGP) coordinated a number of successful attacks on government forces on 19 July. The Indian town of Chichicastenango — a major tourist attraction — was briefly occupied by 500 guerrillas on the same day in an action to celebrate the anniversary of the Nicaraguan revolution. Guatemala is the key to the region. Events there will have a decisive influence not only on the struggle in El Salvador but throughout the Caribbean basin.

In these circumstances the possibility of direct US military intervention cannot be ruled out. Any action by the Soviet Union in Poland could lead to retaliatory action against Cuba and intervention elsewhere in the region, with serious implications for world peace. But direct intervention is an enormous risk internationally which the United States would be very reluctant to take; it also would by no means guarantee a victory in a country like Guatemala where spectres of 'another Vietnam' really do raise themselves.

The only other option, in theory, would be a negotiated compromise with the 'moderate' elements in the opposition involving a complete reversal of Reagan's policies to date and an abandonment of the administration's allies in the local oligarchy. Such a scenario would be difficult to envisage in the present polarized climate of the region, and in any case no government which resulted from such a compromise would survive for long without the support of the guerrilla movement.

One of the most rational spokesmen of the right in the United States, Robert Tucker, has spelt out the implications of these options. Direct intervention he maintains could succeed, though at a price:

Moreover this price cannot be trimmed by halfway measures, that is, by an op-

Under the Eagle

'Over a century ago a Guatemalan foreign minister said prophetical-
ly: "It would be strange if the remedy should come from the United
States, the same place which brings us the disease." Now that the
Alliance for Progress is dead and buried the Imperium proposes,
more in panic than in generosity, to solve Latin America's problems
by eliminating Latin Americans; Washington has reason to suspect
that the poor peoples don't *prefer* to be poor. But it is impossible to
desire the end without desiring the means. Those who deny liberation
to Latin America also deny our only possible rebirth, and incidental-
ly absolve the existing structures from blame. Our youth multiplies,
rises, listens: what does the voice of the system offer? The system
speaks a surrealist language. In lands that are empty it proposes to
avoid births; in countries where capital is plentiful but wasted it suggests that capital is lacking; it describes as "aid" the deforming or-
thopedics of loans and the draining of wealth that results from
foreign investment; it calls upon big landowners to carry out agrarian
reforms and upon the oligarchy to practice social justice. The class
struggle only exists, we are told, because foreign agents stir it up; but
social classes to exist and the oppression of one by the other is known
as the Western way of life. The Marines undertake their criminal ex-
peditions only to restore order and social peace; the dictatorships
linked to Washington lay foundations in their jails for the law-
abiding state, and ban strikes and smash trade unions to protect the
freedom to work.

Is everything forbidden us except to fold our arms? Poverty is not
written in the stars; underdevelopment is not one of God's
mysterious designs.'

Eduardo Galeano, Open Veins of Latin America, *Monthly Review
Press, 1973.*

---

position to radical movements that still fails to prevent their taking power, or,
more important, that fails to remove them should they achieve power. The expected result of such halfway measures will only be to create the conditions for
another Cuba. Radical movements or radical regimes must be defeated. Yet,
even if we pay the necessary price for defeating them, we cannot be sure how
long our success will endure. Success is likely to prove precarious not only
because the defeated may well continue to enjoy broad support, but because
the victors will have to do what has to date been impossible for them to do —
enlist the support of centrist elements. Unfortunately, these elements no
longer exist in Central American states. Right-wing governments will have to
be given steady outside support, even, if necessary, by sending in American
forces.

But then, Tucker asks, does the United States really need to go to such extremes? He dismisses the suggestion that weakness in its 'backyard' would cast doubt on American strength elsewhere.

The eagle that kills the deer in Central America will not frighten the bear in the Middle East. It is not need that would prompt this course but want — a want, moreover, which the Soviet Union would not only accept but probably endorse since it would be seen to help legitimize much of its own behaviour. The only other coherent policy is to observe a hands-off position toward the events now occurring in Central America, a position that implies stopping military aid to El Salvador. Should further radical regimes come to power, we would accept the outcome. More, we would give them reason to maintain a normal relationship with the Soviet Union, rather than to following the footsteps of Cuba . . . What we cannot view with equanimity is that the states of Central America enter into a relationship with the Soviet Union that resembles the relationship with Cuba. Geographical proximity has not lost its significance. At issue, then, is not whether Central America continues to form a part of this nation's sphere of influence. Instead, it is the nature of the influence we should seek to exercise within our sphere and how best such influence may be preserved. It is between those who define our sphere of influence to include the internal order of states and those who do not that there is a clear difference in principle. That difference ought not to be confused with the pre-eminently practical judgement on the policy best suited to prevent the kind of intrusion by an outside power we should clearly aim to prevent. In the Central American case, our claims are rooted in geography and history. If these claims ought not to extend to the internal order of states here, there is still less reason for extending them elsewhere in the Third World.

The suggestion that the United States could accommodate to radical but non-aligned Third World regimes is certainly plausible. United States business interests have proved themselves to be remarkably flexible and pragmatic in their pursuit of profit. American multinationals already have considerable economic interests in the Eastern bloc and have adapted to working with communist governments almost as easily as with the South African regime.

Many apparently radical Third World governments have felt compelled by the dependence and vulnerability of their economies to modify their objectives in accordance with their need to attract foreign aid and investment. Only governments which totally reject incorporation into the present world economic system and who refuse to allow their economic and social development to be determined by the needs of international big business would be completely incompatible with the United States' interests.

The Reagan administration has not yet shown signs of appreciating these subtle distinctions. However, even if it were to do so and permit the opposition forces in El Salvador and elsewhere in the region to

come to power — either through negotiations or a military victory —
it would never tolerate the latter type of government, which, it could
be argued, would be the only kind to allow the possibility of a truly
democratic society with social justice for all.

Update, March 1982

Since the first edition of *Under the Eagle* was completed in September 1981, the Caribbean basin, and in particular El Salvador, has hardly been out of the world's headlines. The Reagan administration has been under mounting pressure to change its policies on El Salvador and support a negotiated settlement with the FMLN/FDR. But it has remained committed to a military solution to the conflict in that country, while its policies toward the region as a whole have continued to be shaped by Cold War sentiments.

Reagan had assumed the presidency in January 1981 believing that victory over the guerrillas in El Salvador would rapidly be accomplished once the Salvadorean army had been supplied with a few more US weapons, helicopters and military advisors. 'We thought it would be easy', a US official told *Newsweek* in March 1982. 'The place was so little and we were so big.' But during the next nine months the guerrillas extended their control over at least one-third of the country and showed signs of increasing military capacity. In mid-October they blew up El Salvador's most heavily guarded and strategically crucial road bridge, the Puente de Oro, which links the eastern and western parts of the country. At the beginning of November, Haig was forced to admit in an interview with *Newsweek* that there was a military stalemate in El Salvador which 'could ultimately be fatal'.

For a while the administration's policy towards the region seemed in disarray. It was leaked to the press that Haig was urging the Pentagon to study military options for action in El Salvador and against Cuba and Nicaragua. At the same time, Defence Secretary, Caspar Weinberger, told journalists that he was opposed to the use of American troops in Central America and the Caribbean. However, as two articles in the *Washington Post* on 14 February and 10 March 1982 have since revealed, in mid-November President Reagan authorized a comprehensive programme of action in an attempt to stem the unrest in the Caribbean basin.

The main elements of these proposals were:
— additional economic support for Central American and Caribbean countries;
— additional military assistance to El Salvador and Honduras from a special emergency fund available to the President;
— US training for Salvadorean military forces in the United States and in El Salvador;

— increased US intelligence activity in the region;
— improvement of the US military posture in the Caribbean to demonstrate US concern and willingness to act, including a new command communications network, military exercises and expanded military intelligence;
— an increased public information programme in the United States to build national support for administration policy;
— tightened economic sanctions against Cuba.

The *Washington Post* gave particular emphasis to a CIA plan to destabilize Nicaragua. This had been presented to a National Security Council subcommittee in November 1981, and later formally approved by President Reagan. The plan called for 'support and conduct of political and para-military operations against the Cuban presence and Cuban-Sandinista support structures in Nicaragua and elsewhere in Central America'.

The covert operations outlined in the proposal aim to 'build popular support in Central America and Nicaragua for an opposition front that would be nationalistic, anti-Cuban and anti-Sandinista'. It would 'support the opposition front through formation and training of action teams to collect intelligence and engage in para-military and political operations in Nicaragua and elsewhere', and to 'work primarily through non-Americans' to achieve these objectives, but in some cases 'take unilateral para-military action — possibly using US personnel — against special Cuban targets'. The initial request was for US $19 million to build up a para-military force of 500 Latin Americans to operate out of commando camps along the Honduran-Nicaraguan border, to be increased in size if necessary.

While these schemes contain economic as well as political and military options, it is the administration's commitment to a military defeat of the guerrillas in El Salvador which has continued to determine US policy toward the region. 'We can't afford to have Ronald Reagan be the President who let Central America go communist', a close Reagan aide told *Newsweek* at the beginning of March 1982.

The Military Options

Three military options have been considered by the Reagan administration with respect to El Salvador. They are not independent or mutually exclusive of each other.

a) Increasing military support for El Salvador's armed forces and a prolonged war

On 15 December 1981, the administration announced that 1,000

US Military Assistance to the Caribbean Basin
(in millions of US dollars)

Country	1981 FMS				1982 FMS				1983 FMS		
	IMET	Credit	Grant	Total	IMET	Credit	Grant	Total	IMET	Credit	Total
Bahamas						1.00		1.00	0.06		0.06
Belize					0.03			0.03	0.10		0.10
Costa Rica	0.04			0.04	0.05			0.05	0.15		0.15
Eastern Caribbean	0.10			0.10	0.24	4.60	1.00	5.84	0.28	5.50	5.78
Dominican Republic	0.43	3.00		3.43	0.45	4.00	1.00	5.45	0.75	9.50	10.25
El Salvador	0.49	10.00	25.00	35.49	1.00	16.50	63.50	81.00	1.30	60.00	61.30
Guatemala									0.25		0.25
Guyana	0.02			0.02	0.04			0.04	0.05		0.05
Haiti	0.12	0.30		0.42	0.25	0.30		0.55	0.42	0.30	0.72
Honduras	0.54	8.40		8.94	0.65	9.00	1.00	10.65	0.80	14.50	15.30
Jamaica	0.07	1.59		1.66	0.08	1.00	1.00	2.08	0.20	6.50	6.70
Nicaragua											
Panama	0.38			0.38	0.40	5.00		5.40	0.50	5.00	5.50
Suriname	0.03			0.03	0.06			0.06	0.08		0.08
Sub Total	2.22	23.29	25.00	50.51	3.24	41.40	67.50	112.14	4.93	101.30	106.25
Supplemental							60.00	60.00			
Annual Total				50.51				182.13			106.25

Note: All figures have been rounded up and therefore totals do not necessarily add up perfectly.
 See page 191 for abbreviations.
Source: US State Department.

Salvadorean soldiers and 500 junior officers would receive training in the United States. This is the largest training programme of foreign troops on US soil ever undertaken, and behind it is the administration's growing awareness of the incapacity of the Salvadorean armed forces to defeat the guerrillas.

US military experts estimate that ten soldiers are needed to defeat one guerrilla. This would require the Salvadorean army to double its numbers from its present strength of 22,000. Such an increase seems almost impossible, since the most recent recruits into the army are fifteen-year-old boys who are press-ganged into service and lack the training or commitment to fight the guerrillas.

The armed forces also lack the capacity to absorb vast amounts of US military aid. Colonel Domingo Monterrosa, the commander of the US-trained Atlacatl Brigade, told the *Washington Post* at the beginning of March that he needed a minimum of 15 helicopters to airlift one of his seven companies. However, there are only 14 helicopters in the whole country (all supplied by the US), and US diplomats estimate that the army lacks the pilots or maintenance facilities to handle even ten more.

The military strategy of the Salvadorean army has also come under considerable criticism. A foreign military officer told *This Week* in February 1982:

General Guillermo Garcia, whose prior battlefield experience was nil, is trying to fight set-piece battles, marshalling regimental-strength units against a mobile enemy that evaporates into the hills. His offensives take such elaborate preparation that the guerrillas know where the units are heading three days before they start out. When the full panoply is on the road, with planes flying cover, a few sharp fights take place, with the exposed soldiers generally taking the worst of it. The army combs the area for guerrillas, claims to have cleared the zone, then returns in triumph to San Salvador. But nothing has really happened.

From January to March 1982 the story was of continued guerrilla successes, beginning with the destruction in the last week of January of 28 planes and helicopters in a guerrilla raid against the key air base at Ilopango. In March yet another army offensive against the guerrilla stronghold on the Guazapa volcano failed.

The United States responded with increased military assistance. In January 1982 it sent US $55million from the Pentagon's own internal budget to replace the aircraft blown up by the guerrillas. US $25 million of this was for 12 Huey helicopters (six had been destroyed at Ilopango), eight A-37 STOL fighter planes, three or four C-123 cargo planes and four O-2 spotter aircraft. This is the first time the United States has supplied the Salvadorean army with military aeroplanes. At the same time Lieutenant-General James Ahmand testified to Congress that the 49 US advisors in El Salvador would be increased by personnel involved in transferring the equipment.

Given the doubts that even this increase in military assistance, or the newly trained army personnel, will give the Salvadorean armed forces the decisive advantage over the guerrillas they seek, the United States has been forced to examine other options.

b) Pan-American intervention

The formation of an inter-American intervention force was discussed at a meeting in Washington at the beginning of November by military commanders and intelligence officers from 20 Latin American countries. These are regular bi-annual meetings, from which Nicaragua was excluded for the first time. Former Colonel, now General Garcia and Caspar Weinberger gave the keynote addresses. According to the *Washington Post,* 'Weinberger's speech said the United States was stressing the need for solidarity among the attending governments against the perceived threat of Cuban and Nicaraguan influence and insurgency in Central America and the Caribbean'. The idea of reviving the 1947 Rio Treaty emerged during this meeting. The treaty (see page 51) states that an attack against any American state 'shall be considered as an attack against all American states and . . . each one . . . undertakes to assist in meeting the attack'. Haig referred again to the Rio Treaty in his speech to the OAS conference in St Lucia in December 1981.

Argentina has frequently been cited as the country most likely to lead any inter-American intervention force, although opposition to such action does exist within some sectors of the Argentine armed forces. There have been persistent reports that an estimated 20 to 30 Argentine advisors are already working with the Salvadorean army. In early 1982 a retired Argentine general, Alberto Valin, who until December 1981 was head of Argentine intelligence, was appointed ambassador to Panama. He has been accused of playing an active role in the United States destabilization plans in the region.

At the end of February 1982, Colonel Flores Lima, chief of staff of the Salvadorean armed forces, went to Argentina to discuss Argentine military assistance. As a result of this trip, Argentina's chief of staff, General Jose Vaquero, announced that his country would give all possible aid to the Salvadorean junta and plans were announced to sell ground attack aircraft and other weapons to El Salvador. Subsequently, at the beginning of March, Thomas Enders visited the country and stated that he expected Argentina to be 'active in whatever action is taken in Central America by other Latin American powers' and that 'the notion of collective action is there' for Argentina and other countries in the region and 'it is a possibility we should all be aware of'.

Honduras is another country which figures prominently in United States strategies for regional co-operation. The Liberal Party won the elections which took place with United States encouragement in November 1981. Roberto Suazo Cordova was sworn in as President on 27 January 1982. But real power has remained with the armed forces. They had secured a commitment prior to the elections that there would be no investigation of military corruption and that the Armed Forces Council would clear all cabinet appointments. The appointment of the hardline officer, Colonel Gustavo Alvarez, as commander-in-chief of the armed forces has helped consolidate the power of the most reactionary faction of the Honduran military. These are the officers who are most likely to support continued co-operation with the Guatemalan and Salvadorean armed forces and with ex-members of Somoza's National Guard in confrontations with the Nicaraguan government. Alvarez stated just after his appointment at the beginning of February that Honduras would be the next target of communism should El Salvador fall.

One of the most recent examples of co-operation between the Salvadorean and Honduran armed forces is the relocation of Salvadorean refugees from camps along the border between the two countries. Alvarez has stated publicly that he believes the refugees are subversives and that Honduras has the right to intern them. In February many of the 30,000 refugees in the border area were moved to a military controlled camp called Mesa Grande, described by a German church delegation to the area as 'an inhuman concentration camp'. There is now a growing body of evidence which suggests that this relocation is part of a Honduran-Salvadorean plan, with assistance from United States military advisors, to create a free-fire zone along the 93 miles of common border. This could be used to mount an offensive against the guerrilla strongholds in the northern and eastern part of El Salvador, an offensive which would involve Honduran as well as Salvadorean soldiers.

c) Direct United States military intervention

Increased United States intelligence and military activities in the Caribbean basin has led to speculation that the United States would, if all else failed, send its own combat troops into El Salvador. CIA stations throughout Central America were reported to have been strengthened in January and February 1982. At the end of February Pentagon sources admitted that the United States navy had stationed a destroyer equipped with electronic surveillance gear off the coast of El Salvador.

On 1 December 1981 a United States Forces Caribbean Command

was established by the Pentagon at Key West, Florida, to streamline the military structure by giving responsibility for the area to a single headquarters. At the same time the Pentagon began to consider re-opening sections of the naval air station in Key West as part of an expansion of the Caribbean Command's activity.

At the beginning of March 1982, the Pentagon disclosed that it was asking for US $21 million in the 1983 fiscal year military construction budget for 'airfield improvements in the western Caribbean area'. This turned out to be Columbia and Honduras. Caspar Weinberger confirmed in testimony before Congress that the administration was seeking such bases: 'We have discussions under way basically of a classified nature that would enable us to add a number of facilities that we see in the future we may need'. When Dean Fischer, a State Department spokesman, was asked if such facilities may be used by the Rapid Deployment Force, which is being developed primarily for the Middle East, he replied: 'We do not envisage the use of such facilities for Rapid Deployment Forces, but I can't anticipate all future contingencies'. At the same time Admiral Thomas B. Hayward, chief of naval operations, told a House armed services sub-committee that the Pentagon was studying options for using navy and marine forces to protect US interests in Central America and the Caribbean. 'The Joint Chiefs of Staff have been examining anew the numerous options considered feasible in support of our continued interest in Central America and the Caribbean. Our commitments require us to present increasingly a counterweight to Castro's expanding support of Central America and Caribbean insurgents, as well as his continued appetite for opportunism in Africa.'

The increasing number of US military exercises in the region have contributed to fears that the US has not ruled out direct military intervention. Between 7 and 9 October 1981, the United States and Honduran governments carried out Operation Halcon Vista, which consisted of joint manoeuvres off the Atlantic coast of Nicaragua. Further manoeuvres were carried out at the end of November in the Caribbean area involving 41 navy ships, including two aircraft carriers. Between 9 and 18 March the first major NATO naval exercise in the Gulf of Mexico and the Straits of Florida took place, involving 30 NATO warships, including a British nuclear submarine. According to Caspar Weinberger, the exercise, code-named 'Safe Pass 82', was necessary because of the threat Cuba posed to NATO supply lines in the event of a crisis in Europe. 'In peacetime', said Weinberger, '44 per cent of all foreign trade tonnage and 45 per cent of the crude oil imports into the United States pass through the Caribbean. In wartime, half of NATO's supplies would transit by sea from Gulf ports through the Florida straits and onwards to Europe.'

Such manoeuvres may well be designed primarily to intimidate Cuba, Nicaragua and Grenada, but they come at a time when the administration has repeatedly refused to rule out the use of American troops in the region in the event of a potential guerrilla victory in El Salvador.

Destabilization and Propaganda Warfare

The Reagan administration's hostility to Cuba, Grenada and Nicaragua has not abated. In particular there has been a rising crescendo of accusations linking Nicaragua with the war in El Salvador. The emphasis of these accusations has recently shifted. At first Nicaragua was accused of being a channel for arms destined for El Salvador. In December 1981, however, Thomas Enders stated that Nicaragua was a 'platform for Cuban-Soviet intervention throughout Central America'. Then in March 1982, this shifted still further and the CIA director, William Casey, claimed 'this whole El Salvador insurgency is run out of Managua by professionals experienced in directing guerrilla wars'.

The administration has in fact failed to produce any convincing evidence either that Nicaragua is channelling arms to the Salvadorean

---

'The United States is not in the habit of engaging in sinister plots'

Edward Meese, Reagan's presidential counsellor, 16 March 1982.

● In February 1982 a photograph appeared in *Le Figaro,* the conservative Paris daily, which illustrated charred corpses in a Nicaraguan street, and claimed that these were the result of a Sandinista massacre of Miskito Indians. Haig referred to this in his testimony to Congress, and got backing from the State Department to pursue allegations of Sandinista repression, which the Nicaraguan government has consistently denied. Yet Haig had failed to check his sources. The photograph in *Le Figaro* proved to be one taken in 1979 during the Sandinistas' struggle against Somoza. It actually depicted bodies being incinerated by the Red Cross as an health measure after an attack by Somoza's National guard. *Le Figaro* later admitted that the caption was incorrect.
● The United States also alleged that extensions of Nicaragua's airports were clear evidence of a massive military build-up by the San-

---

dinistas. Subsequently it was revealed that the extensions had been recommended by the US to the Somoza government in 1975. Richard Miller of USAID confirmed that his agency had financed a study of Nicaragua's transport system which advocated the extensions. The CIA could have saved the huge costs of its spy flights by strolling down to the Washington office of Wilbur Smith and Associates for their airport studies.

● William Casey, director of the CIA, asserted in an interview in March 1982 that representatives of the Palestine Liberation Organisation were providing Managua with weapons. However, when reporters questioned Casey's deputy, Admiral Robert Inman, about the PLO's presence, he replied that: 'I do not consider these reports confirmed with real certainty. There are only a limited number of reports to the best of my recollection and they are not recent — they are several months old.'

● The US adminstration gave a briefing to members of the House and Senate intelligence committees concerning the supply of arms to the Salvadorcan guerrillas by Nicaragua. *Time* magazine described the reaction of one senator, who called William Cascy's briefing 'a farce'.

● In March 1982 the State Department arranged a press conference at which a young Nicaraguan — apparently trained in Cuba and Ethiopia for guerrilla action in El Salvador — would provide proof of Nicaragua's involvement. Instead, Orlando Jose Tardencillas Espinosa, 19, recanted confessions which he claimed to have made while being tortured by the Salvadorean army in 1981. At the same time he denounced the 'criminal and fascist' Salvadorean junta. An embarrassed Washington hastily deported him to Managua.

● At a further press conference in March, the CIA revealed surveillance photographs of Nicaragua, with the aim of showing that the Nicaraguans were assembling military forces for use against their neighbours. It was pointed out that there were 49 'battalion-sized barracks' (36 of which had recently been built by the Cubans) and a total of up to 70,000 military personnel. This analysis puzzled many reporters eager to understand how the Nicaraguans could house so many men in just 49 barracks. Since each barrack could only house between 500 and 700 men, there would either be gross overcrowding or 35-45,000 men without beds! The troops themselves were equipped with 25 Soviet T-54 tanks and 12 BTR-60 armoured personnel carriers. Harold Jackson, reporting for *The Guardian* (London), stated: 'Given the capacity of the BTR-60, Nicaraguan military planners would need to allow for 60 round trips for each vehicle to get one-eighth of their force into a neighbouring country. Once there, given the range of the T-54, they would have to ensure that they did not penetrate more than fifty miles if they wanted to keep their armoured support.'

guerrillas or that it is engaged in anything but a defensive internal military build-up. Even the declassified surveillance photographs taken over Nicaragua by American aircraft and presented to the media in March as conclusive evidence of Nicaragua's aggressive intentions in the region, failed to convince most journalists present (see box). Nevertheless, the administration's allegations have been used to justify its own aggression against Nicaragua in the form of the CIA destabilization plan approved in November 1981.

The administration opted for this plan after it had concluded that direct military action against the Sandinista government was not possible. In part the plan aimed to disrupt the country's economy by forcing it to channel money into defence and in part to give support to those sectors within Nicaragua which oppose the Sandinista government. In January 1982, the Nicaraguan government uncovered a plot to sabotage the country's largest oil refinery and a cement plant. Venezuelan, Honduran, Salvadorean and Argentinian officials were involved in the plot. At the beginning of February, the Nicaraguan foreign minister revealed evidence that the Argentine ambassador in Panama, Alberto Velin, had paid US $50,000 in cash to armed Nicaraguan opposition groups operating near the Honduran border. He accused Argentina, together with Venezuela, Guatemala and Honduras of trying to create an 'international incident' to justify more direct intervention in the country.

Many of the attempts to destabilize Nicaragua have been based on promoting discontent amongst the Miskito Indian population on the Atlantic coast (see page 185). Some 5,000 Miskitos have gone to Honduras, encouraged by Steadman Fagoth Muller, leader of Misurasata, the indigenous movement promoting Miskito culture. Fagoth is known to be in close contact with members of Somoza's National Guard living in Honduras and together they have organized a number of border raids against Nicaragua. Sixty Nicaraguan civilians and Sandinista soldiers were killed as a result of these raids in November and December 1981. Fagoth has mounted a propaganda campaign accusing the Sandinistas of genocide against the Miskitos. This campaign began in December 1981 when rumours were circulated by Honduran officials that 200 Miskitos had been massacred by the Sandinistas. Although the UN High Commissioner for Refugees said it had no knowledge of such a massacre, it was some days before the rumour was shown to be false and by that time it had been widely publicized in the US press.

In the past few months the Sandinista government has begun to move some 8,500 Miskitos away from the conflictive border region to settlements inland. Once more a massive propaganda campaign was launched in the United States claiming that the Nicaraguan government was carrying out a violent campaign against the Miskito population. Jeane Kirkpatrick even claimed that 'Nicaragua probably stands in the first place as a human rights violator in the region'. The attempts to discredit the Nicaraguan government have, however, frequently misfired badly and the US government now faces a growing credibility problem (see box).

Political and Economic Initiatives

It is increasingly difficult for the administration to confine its policies toward the region to military strategies. Growing internal and international opposition has forced it to consider more acceptable political and economic initiatives. However, these alternatives must be assessed in the context of the priority still being given by the administration to the military defeat of the Salvadorean guerrillas.

a) The elections in El Salvador

The elections in El Salvador for a 60-person constituent assembly became part of the US strategy in July 1981, and are due to take place on 28 March 1982. The United States clearly hoped to score a major propaganda victory with its support for elections in El Salvador. It was widely assumed that a victory by Jose Napoleon Duarte's Christian Democrat party would legitimize US support for his government and continued military assistance to the country's armed forces.

But few have been convinced that the elections will solve anything either for El Salvador or the United States. The opposition has refused to participate. They point out that it is impossible to hold free elections in the present climate of civil war, with the Salvadorean armed forces and security forces responsible for the murder of between 200 and 400 people a week. There is no press freedom or freedom of association for the opposition; to publish a slate of candidates would amount to providing the right-wing death squads with a hit list. There will be no electoral register and the fact that the Christian Democrats control the electoral tribunal has led many to suspect a potential fraud. Voting will be compulsory and on polling day slips of paper will be given to those who vote. It has already been claimed that the military has issued dire warnings to anyone who lacks this receipt after the elections. Voters will be allowed to cast their ballot on presentation of their identity cards at any of 5,000 polling stations. The government maintains this will enable the estimated 500,000 refugees to vote, but others point out that few of the refugees have the necessary card.

The six parties that will contest the elections with the Christian

Democrats are all on the far right of the political spectrum. Speculation has grown that it will be one of these parties rather than the Christian Democrats which will win the vote. If the Christian Democrats fail to win a majority, a coalition of two right-wing parties, such as the Party of National Conciliation, the traditional ruling party, and the Nationalist Republican Alliance led by Major Roberto D'Abuisson may form a coalition. D'Abuisson's party platform calls for treason trials for Duarte and members of his government. The party's secretary general Mario Redaelli has stated: 'We don't believe the army needs controlling. We are fighting a war, and civilians will be killed. They always have been. It's got to be that way'. There have already been rumours that such a coalition would call upon a pan-American 'Army of Peace' led by Argentina, to push the guerrillas northwards where they would be crushed with the help of the Honduran army.

The United States sent out 60 invitations to carefully chosen countries, inviting them to send observers to the elections. Only Costa Rica, Uruguay, Egypt, Colombia and Britain have agreed to do so. A West German spokesman summed up the views of most European governments when he said: 'Such elections are themselves a matter of dispute among groups within El Salvador. By sending observers, we would be appearing to take a position'. In March 1982, the European Parliament said that the elections in El Salvador could not be regarded as free.

b) The Central American Democratic Community

It was partly to legitimize the Salvadorean elections that the United States encouraged the formation of the Central American Democratic Community in January 1982. This includes Honduras and Costa Rica as well as El Salvador, both of which have elected governments. But the alliance, which deliberately excludes Nicaragua, also has military aims through a clause in the agreement in which members agree to provide mutual aid and solidarity in the case of any external aggression. Such aid would be governed by the norms of existing regional defence pacts, widely assumed to refer to the Rio Treaty. The agreement also commits its members to co-ordinate action to stimulate the development of the private sector in each country.

c) The Caribbean Basin Initiative

On 24 February 1982, President Reagan finally announced an economic plan for the Caribbean area. The Caribbean Basin Initiative (CBI) however, falls far short of Jamaican Prime Minister Edward Seaga's original proposal for a mini-Marshall plan. Reagan made clear in his presentation of the package that the Initiative is part of his administration's strategy to prevent revolutionary change in the region. 'If we do not act promptly and decisively in defence of freedom, new Cubas will arise from the ruins of today's conflict'. He attacked 'the expansion of Soviet-backed Cuban-managed support for violent revolution in Central America' and the 'tightening grip of the totalitarian left in Grenada and Nicaragua'. In addition to the economic proposals in the plan, it allows for US $60 million in security assistance, of which US $35 million is intended for El Salvador.

The main economic proposals in the plan are 12-year period of free trade for Caribbean products exported to the US, tax incentives for investment, emergency aid of US $350 millions, of which US $100 million is earmarked for El Salvador, US $100 million for Costa Rica, US $100 million for Jamaica, US $40 million for the Dominican Republic and US $10 million for Belize. The money is to be largely 'concentrated in the private sector'. The Eastern Caribbean was included in the package at the last minute and a figure of US $50 to US $60 million will be made available.

The aid component of the plan is minimal. This reflects the basic philosophy behind the proposals which emphasizes, in the words of President Reagan, the 'magic of the market place': 'It is an integrated program that helps our neighbours help themselves, under which creativity and private entrepreneurship and self-help can flourish.' Eighty-seven per cent of the US $10 billion worth of imports from the region already enter the United States duty-free. The extension of a one-way free trade area to most of the remaining exports is intended to encourage US businessmen to invest in the region, knowing that they will receive duty-free treatment during the early period of their investment. Textiles and garments, which make up four to five per cent of the region's exports, are not included in the tax exemptions. Only an additional eight per cent of exports from the region will therefore benefit from Reagan's proposals. But even this is likely to provoke opposition within the United States from the protectionist lobby once the detailed proposals are revealed to Congress — for instance, from the sugar growing states of the south which would face increased competition from duty free sugar imports. In an case, it is unlikely that the programme will be implemented before November 1982.

The CBI is thus based on the same development model as has been promoted since Operation Bootstrap began in Puerto Rico in the 1950's: that is, economic growth through incentives to private foreign investment. Such a model has manifestly failed to bring either sustained growth to the region or socio-economic justice for the people who live there. President Reagan made clear in his speech announcing the CBI that no assistance would be granted to nations that 'had turned from their American heritage and their neighbours', but 'let them return to the traditions and common values of this hemisphere and we will welcome them. The choice is theirs'. In other words, no country which pursues an alternative model of development can expect United States' assistance. The specific mention of Grenada in Reagan's speech is an indication of the administration's continued and uncompromising hostility toward all those countries which attempt to reduce their dependence on the United States.

Few observers feel that the proposals will be able to rescue even the United States' allies from the acute economic crisis facing the region. The countries of Central America have stated that they need US $5 billion in emergency aid and US $15 billion in long-term development aid by 1990. Even the president of the Council of the Americas, which had worked closely with the Reagan administration to draw up the plan, told *Time* magazine in March 1982 that it was no panacea: 'The main problem in the Caribbean is the lack of any infrastructure of airports and transportation facilities to support new industries. And there is the question of security. Until that is resolved I feel there will be little foreign investment in this region.' Indeed, far from increased foreign investment, what increasingly characterizes the region is capital flight, particularly from Central America, where an estimated US $500 million is leaving the region a year. A Costa Rican official summed up the plan as 'ten years too late'.

Opposition Grows

The Reagan administration has faced increased opposition, both internal and international, towards its policies in the region.

Within the United States, the biggest popular mobilization against United States foreign policy since Vietnam is emerging. Indeed, the memory of Vietnam has had a powerful effect on public opinion and many see parallels between the gradual escalation of US military involvement in that country and the administration's policies toward El Salvador. A *Newsweek* poll at the end of February found that 54 per cent of Americans who are aware of the situation feel that the United States should stay completely out of El Salvador. This compares with 47 per cent in March 1981. Sixty-two per cent of the sample favoured sending economic aid to the Duarte government but 89 per cent opposed sending US troops. Seventy-four per cent of the sample thought it likely that United States involvement in El Salvador would escalate into another Vietnam.

The opposition to the administration's policy on El Salvador has additional significance as disillusionment with its economic policies also grows. Even Reagan supporters baulk at the US $91.5 billion deficit projected in the 1982 budget. As the recession continues unemployment nears nine per cent and interest rates remain above 16 per cent. In the circumstances even staunch conservatives have begun to question the proposed 18 per cent increase in defence spending. The Republicans also have an anxious eye on the mid-term elections scheduled for November 1982.

The lack of public support for the administration's policies toward El Salvador is also reflected in growing congressional opposition. In December 1981, Congress voted to attach special conditions to the US $26 million in military assistance and US $40 million in economic assistance scheduled for El Salvador during 1982. These required Reagan to certify that the Duarte government was making a 'concerted, significant effort' to improve the human rights climate and that the Salvadoreans were achieving 'continued progress in implementing political and economic reforms'. Reagan signed the certification at the end of January claiming that 'despite formidable obstacles', the Duarte government had made such an effort to deal with the 'complex political, social and human rights problem it is confronting'. That very week journalists produced reliable reports that the United States trained Atlacatl Brigade had been responsible for the massacre of between 700 and 1,000 civilians during a December search-and-destroy operation in Morazan province.

Persistent reports of such atrocities have continued to embarrass the government. In March 1982 Amnesty International issued a report stating:

The security forces in El Salvador have been carrying out a systematic and widespread programme of torture, 'disappearances' and individual and mass killings of men, women and children. The victims have included not only people suspected of opposition to the authorities, but thousands who were simply in areas targeted for security operations, whose death or mutilation seems to have been completely arbitrary. Testimonies received daily by AI implicate all branches of the Salvadorean security services in such violations of human rights — both military and police units as well as para-military squads acting with their explicit or implicit warrant — and the violations have occurred on such a scale that there can be no question that they constitute a gross and consistent pattern of human rights abuse.

At the beginning of March, 100 members of Congress signed a letter urging President Reagan to change his policy and support negotiations between the Salvadorean government and the guerrilla movement. The letter stated: 'The escalating crises in El Salvador, Guatemala and Nicaragua are reaching a critical juncture and run the risk of involving the United States in a major regional conflagration'. Subsequently, the House of Representatives voted by 393 votes to 3 to press for unconditional discussions 'among the major political factions in El Salvador to guarantee a safe and stable environment for free and open democratic elections'. In the next few months congressional opposition to the administration's request for further military aid to El Salvador is expected to increase considerably.

The Reagan administration has also failed to convince international opinion. The Franco-Mexican initiative of September 1981 has been endorsed by Norway, Austria, Ireland, the Netherlands, Yugoslavia, Algeria, SPD party leader Willy Brandt and ex-Venezuelan president Carlos Andres Perez. A UN General Assembly resolution in December called on the Salvadorean government to negotiate with the opposition before the elections. France and Mexico have been taking the lead in pressing the United States to support a negotiated settlement.

In October 1981, FDR/FMLN proposals for talks with the junta were put forward by the Nicaraguan representative at the UN. The FMLN refused to lay down its arms before talks began, requested direct negotiations witnessed by representatives from other governments and insisted that any talks must cover the fundamental aspects of the conflict.

Numerous attempts were subsequently made to persuade the United States to support negotiations. At the end of February President Lopez Portillo of Mexico presented a three-point proposal for peace in the region while addressing a rally in Managua. He offered Mexico's services as a mediator, not only in the Salvadorean conflict, but also to promote dialogue between Washington and Nicaragua and Cuba. On Nicaragua he proposed that the United States should renounce the use of force against Nicaragua and that the anti-Sandinista forces training in Honduras and Florida with tacit or direct United States support should be disbanded. For its part the Nicaraguan government should simultaneously halt its acquisition of arms, reduce the size of its army, and conclude a series of non-aggression pacts with its immediate neighbours and the United States.

In March, Haig held meetings with Jorge Castaneda, the Mexican foreign minister, to discuss the Mexican initiative. Subsequently, the United States showed some willingness to enter into direct negotiations with Nicaragua. Meanwhile, on 15 March, the Nicaraguan government declared a state of emergency following continued incidents along the country's border with Honduras. 'The difficulty is that the United States is playing two roles at the same time,' Miguel d'Escoto, the Nicaraguan foreign minister, told journalists; 'it is talking about negotiations but has not stopped pursuing the option of intervention.'

The administration is awaiting the outcome of the Salvadorean elections before clarifying its policy towards El Salvador. But whatever the result of the elections the United States has few options left. The Salvadorean army has shown itself incapable of defeating guerrillas and there is no guarantee that an inter-American intervention force could win a decisive victory over them without considerable US involvement. The United States has so far failed to convince national and international opinion that an external threat exists to the region which would justify an inter-American intervention under the terms of the Rio Treaty. Such a move would also alienate some powerful Latin American nations such as Brazil and Mexico which oppose any outside intervention in the region.

The political cost of a direct intervention is very high. Even within the Reagan administration itself there are clear differences on the subject. Weinberger has made clear his fears that, apart from the military difficulties involved, the public outcry against such a step could jeopardize congressional support for his US $1.5 trillion defence budget. The budget is essential, he argues, to protect United States interests in other areas of the world, particularly the Middle East, which he considers more important to the United States than the Caribbean basin. Haig, however, according to private notes leaked to the *Washington Post* in February, appears to believe that Central America is an area 'where we can be tough'. The differences between these two key figures of the present United States foreign policy-making establishment on this and a number of other important issues have further increased the incoherence in United States' policy.

Yet the adminstration, like the Salvadorean army, considers negotiations with the guerrillas tantamount to a guerrilla victory. *Time* magazine summed up this attitude following an interview with Thomas Enders:

Given the stakes, Enders favours US strategic interests over the passion for morality. Some kinds of peace are, of course, not worth the price, and US officials must be asking themselves how important it is just to end the violence. One price Enders believes El Salvador should not pay is a negotiated settlement that would guarantee the rebels a place in a coalition government without having to compete in elections. Enders considers battlefield superiority a prerequisite for peace. One side must have enough 'political and military momentum' to become and remain a dominant partner.

Nevertheless, if direct or indirect intervention prove politically impossible, the Reagan administration may be forced to consider some kind of negotiated settlement. Its objective, however, would still be to exclude the guerrillas and to preserve as much of the existing order as possible. In their anxiety to promote a peaceful settlement the Mexicans and Europeans may be tempted to support such a move and forget the basic structural causes which lie behind the deaths of over 30,000 people in two years in the struggle for social justice in El Salvador. No settlement which maintained existing economic and political structures, even if 'reformed', could pave the way for the radical transformation in El Salvador required to build a just and truly democratic society. In any case, a settlement which did not include the guerrillas would have little chance of survival and would merely prolong the war indefinitely. Meanwhile, the escalation of the struggle in Guatemala is adding a new dimension to the Central American crisis.

Guatemala — the Crisis Deepens

At the beginning of March 1982, Haig spoke to the *Los Angeles Times* about the situation in El Salvador. During the interview he stated: 'It's a matter of weeks or months before you see — perhaps even more consequential in terms of potential damage to United States interests — a similar situation developing in Guatemala. It is a clear, self-influencing sequence of events which could sweep all of Central America into a Cuba-dominated region and put a very fundamental threat on Mexico in the very predictable future . . .' This is the first time that the United States has publicly acknowledged the growing strength of the guerrilla movement in Guatemala.

During 1981 the Guatemalan army made a determined effort, reportedly with considerable assistance from the Argentine, Chilean and Israeli armed forces, to improve its intelligence network. In January 1982 General Benedicto Lucas Garcia, the army chief of staff, acknowledged that the technical modernization of the Guatemalan army had been achieved 'thanks to the advice and transfer of technology from Israel'. In December 1981 the army launched a major offensive against the guerrilla movement when it sent 5,000 troops into Chimaltenango province; this was followed in January by an operation in Quiche province involving 15,000 of the army's 22,000 soldiers. However, far from being defeated the guerrillas have steadily increased their level of activity. The response of the Guatemalan army has been to continue its policy of massacre and slaughter (see box). The massacres usually occur in areas where there has recently been a successful guerrilla operation. For instance, on 15 November 1981 a guerrilla unit attacked an army camp in Chupol, Quiche. On 30 November the village was attacked by the army and an estimated 700 people were machine-gunned to death.

On 7 February the four main guerrilla organizations announced the formation of a united front, the National Revolutionary Unity of

Massacre in Guatemala
(This updates the table on page 196)

28 September 1981 **Baja Verapaz**	31 peasants massacred by the army in Rabinal.
28 September 1981 **Baja Verapaz**	During the Festival of San Miguel, the army fired indiscriminately into the crowd in San Miguel Chicoj. 31 peasants were killed and 80 wounded.
6 November 1981 **Chimaltenango**	7 peasants killed by the army in the villages of Paquixic and Comalapa.
7 November 1981 **Chimaltenango**	16 peasants killed by the army in the villages of Buenos Aires and Buena Vista.
13 November 1981 **Quiche**	23 peasants killed by the army in the village of Joyabaj.
28 November 1981 **Alta Verapaz**	18 peasants machine gunned by the army in the village of Cpula.
30 November 1981 **Quiche**	The village of Chupol was surrounded by the army. The inhabitants were machine gunned, the village was bombed and crops burnt. An estimated 700 people were killed.
2 January 1982 **San Marcos**	During an army offensive, the military massacred 66 peasants in the village of San Francisco El Tablero.
3 January 1982 **San Marcos**	The army killed 33 men and 3 women and dropped their bodies around the village of Saduchun Dolores.
17 February 1982 **Quiche**	53 people including 11 children and 14 women (5 of them pregnant) were hacked to death in the village of Calante.
6 March 1982 **Quiche**	200 men, women and children butchered by having their throats cut in the villages of San Jose and San Antonio Sinanche.

Sources: Church and press reports.

Guatemala (URNG). This was followed on 17 February by the establishment of the Guatemalan Committee of Patriotic Unity (CGUP) which includes the 31 January Popular Front (FP31) and the Democratic Front Against Repression (FDCR) the country's two most important opposition political movements representing the principal peasant, worker and student organizations in Guatemala and in exile, as well as a number of prominent Guatemalan intellectuals and public figures who have been forced to live outside the country. The aim is to combine the URNG and CGUP into a single national opposition movement along the lines of the FDR/FMLN in El Salvador.

The Reagan administration is anxious to give military aid to the Guatemalan armed forces to enable them to respond to the growth of the guerrilla movement. But General Lucas Garcia's government refused to succumb to United States pressure to improve its human rights record so that the administration could win congressional approval for such aid. On 7 March elections were held in Guatemala which the United States hoped might result in a government more open to its influence.

Elections in Guatemala are notoriously fraudulent. Popular disillusionment with the electoral process is reflected in the percentage of registered voters who abstain. This rose from 31 per cent in 1951 to 64 per cent in 1978, although voting is compulsory and there are stiff penalties for abstention.

Four candidates contested the elections, representing parties of the right and extreme right. General Anibal Guevara Rodriguez, the official government candidate and Lucas Garcia's own chosen successor, was declared the winner. All three losing candidates and most independent observers denounced the result as a fraud.

On 23 March there was a coup in Guatemala. It was reported to have been carried out by junior officers who annulled the election results and promised to end corruption and introduce democratic reforms. It is known that young officers in the Guatemalan army have for some time harboured resentment towards their superiors who have exploited their positions of power for personal financial gain (see p193). However, such resentment is more likely to be based on their desire to have access to these benefits themselves rather than on high moral principles. In the event, though, the three-man junta which emerged was made up of senior military men with the junior officers relegated to an advisory council. The junta was headed by General Efrain Rios Montt, presidential candidate in the 1974 elections when he too had been deprived of victory by fraud; the other two members were General Horacio Maldonado and Colonel Francisco Gordillo. The junta pledged to call new elections within six months and to 'change Guatemala's image as regards its foreign relations, especially with the United States'.

Civilian support for the junta seems to have come from the defrauded parties in the election with the extreme right-wing Movement for National Liberation (MNL) playing the most prominent role in the prior planning of the coup. There are many sectors of the oligarchy who also resented the greed and corruption of President Lucas Garcia

276

and his supporters. This was enhanced by the serious deterioration in the economy in 1981 when GNP grew by only one per cent compared to some eight per cent in 1977. Foreign exchange reserves have fallen steadily and there is a serious shortage of credit in the country. This is aggravated by the flight of capital which some estimates put at US $500 million since 1979. Export earnings fell more than 14 per cent in 1981 as coffee prices slumped. Production has been disrupted by numerous guerrilla attacks on farms and businesses while political instability has led to a dramatic fall in earnings from tourism.

Large sectors of the oligarchy might be expected to support the overthrow of Lucas Garcia and his chosen successor in the hope of attracting US economic as well as military assistance. The Reagan administration may also welcome such a move. If it can claim that Guatemala's new government is committed to elections and reform it might be able to persuade Congress to give it military aid.

The role of the United States in this coup was not immediately apparent. The *New York Times* reported soon afterwards that US officials had acknowledged that they knew of plans for a coup as early as January. But even if this is so the United States will have difficulty in controlling subsequent events. The Guatemalan oligarchy is deeply disappointed in Reagan's failure to deliver the military support promised during his election campaign. According to Lionel Sisniega Otero, one of the leaders of the MLN and their vice-presidential candidate in the elections, 'Mr Reagan has too many Carter people in his administration. Maybe his intentions are good, but he has yet to prove them'. The presence of the MLN in the new government will make it difficult for Reagan to persuade Congress that it is genuinely interested in democracy or reforms.

The coup reflects the power struggles within the Guatemalan oligarchy and armed forces which have intensified as the guerrillas have grown in strength and the economic crisis has deepened. Only their commitment to defeating the guerrilla movement at any cost unites these forces. The Reagan administration undoubtedly sympathizes with this aim. Its ties with the Guatemalan right, including the MLN, have been well documented (see p.170 *et seq)*. But unlike in the 1960s, foreign policy-makers in the United States today cannot easily ignore congressional and public opinion. The Guatemalan oligarchy, like its counterpart in El Salvador, is unwilling to make the concessions which would enable Reagan to give it the support he would like to.

The dilemma facing the Reagan administration in Guatemala and El Salvador today is the legacy of over a century-and-a-half of US intervention in Central America. It no longer controls the right-wing oligarchies which it has always backed in the past, the centre no longer exists, and the guerrilla movements gain in strength daily. The United

States still fails to understand the nature of the Central American struggle. It will take more than US military equipment to defeat the popular war now being waged in the region.

Testimony of an Indian Woman

My name is Rigoberta Menchu Tum. I am a representative of the 'Vincente Menchu' Revolutionary Christians, a revolutionary mass organisation that forms part of the 31 January Popular Front. My father was Vincente Menchu, an Indian. For years he carried out a truly heroic resistance to the landowners' constant abuses, until he died, burned alive in the Spanish Embassy on 31 January 1980.

I have experienced in the depth of my being the marginalisation of my race, the taunts and the murders against what is mine, my family, my people.

On 9 December 1979, my 16-year-old brother Patrocino was captured and tortured for several days and then taken with twenty other young men to the square in Chajul. An officer of Lucas Garcia's army of murderers ordered the prisoners to be paraded in a line. Then he started to insult and threaten the inhabitants of the village, who were forced to come out of their houses to witness the event. I was with my mother, and we saw Patrocino; he had had his tongue cut out and his toes cut off. The officer jackal made a speech. Every time he paused the soldiers beat the Indian prisoners.

When he finished his ranting, the bodies of my brother and the other prisoners were swollen, bloody, unrecognisable. It was monstrous, but they were still alive.

They were thrown on the ground and drenched with gasoline. The soldiers set fire to the wretched bodies with torches and the captain laughed like an hyena and forced the inhabitants of Chajul to watch. This was his objective — that they should be terrified and witness the punishment given to the 'guerrillas'.

The whole village was crying, and after a time the people became filled with anger and courage. Their indignation and courage led them to rise up against the army and throw them out of Chajul. Then the people watched over the bodies and gave them a Christian burial.

I am part of these sorrows. All of my people are a part of them; of the government violence; of the permanent war, where kidnapping is an official institution; of the exploitation, oppression and discrimination. I am 22 years old. My sorrow and my struggle is also the sorrow and the struggle of a whole oppressed people that is fighting for its liberation.

We, the indigenous, are massively joining the struggle because we know that it is the only way by which we can free ourselves from the misery, exploitation and marginalisation. We fully understand that this course is the revolutionary participation of the whole people in the establishment of a democratic, popular and revolutionary government.

Selected Bibliography

Many primary and secondary sources have been used in this book. The following is a selected list of the most important and the most readily available for those who would like to explore further particular topics.

Part I — The Eagle Rises

Two good books in Spanish on the socio-economic-political history of Central America are: E. Torres Rivas et al., **Centroamerica Hoy**, Siglo XXI, Mexico 1976, 2nd edition, and E. Torres Rivas, **Interpretacion del Desarrollo Social Centroamericano**, EDUCA, Costa Rica 1973, 3rd edition. A good historical survey of US imperialism is Richard Van Alstyne, **The Rising American Empire**, Quadrangle Books, New York 1965 and on US policy toward Latin America there is: Gordon Connell-Smith, **The Inter-American System**, Oxford University Press, New York 1962 and Alonso Aguilar, **Pan-Americanism from Monroe to the Present: A View from the Other Side**, Monthly Review Press, New York 1968. On the Spanish-Cuban-American war there is the two volume: Philip S. Foner, **The Spanish-Cuban-American War: The Birth of American Imperialism**, Monthly Review Press, New York 1972. A mammoth book on Cuba worth dipping into is: Hugh Thomas, **Cuba**, Eyre and Spottiswood, London 1971; also: M. Kenner and J. Petras (eds), **Fidel Castro Speaks**, Penguin, Harmondsworth 1972. On Guatemala, the North American Congress on Latin America (NACLA) publication, **Guatemala**, 1974 remains essential reading both for this early period and for events in the 1960s and 1970s, also Thomas and Marjore Melville, **Guatemala — Another Vietnam**, Penguin, Harmondsworth 1971. A good study on Nicaragua in Spanish is: Jaime Wheelock Roman, **Imperialismo y Dictadura**, Siglo XXI, Mexico 1975, also NACLA's **Nicaragua**, February 1976. On the growth of US investment during this and later periods see NACLA's **Yanqui Dollar: The Contribution of US Private Investment to Underdevelopment in Latin America**, 1971 and specifically on US investment in Central America: Donald Castillo Rivas, **Acumulacion de Capital y Empresas Transnacionales en Centroamerica**, Siglo XXI, Mexico 1980. On the role of the Council on Foreign Relations in the formulation of US foreign policy see: L.H. Shoup and W. Minter, **Imperial Brain Trust**, Monthly Review Press, New York 1977.

Part II — The Eagle Rampant

A useful compilation of essays on US foreign policy in these years is: A. Mack,

D. Plant and U. Doyle, **Imperialism, Intervention and Development**, Croom Helm, London 1979. An important book on US foreign policy in this period is: Michael Klare, **War Without End: American Planning for the Next Vietnams**, Vintage, New York 1972. There is a useful essay on the Alliance for Progress by D. Horowitz in R.L. Rhodes (ed), **Imperialism and Underdevelopment**, Monthly Review Press, New York 1970. For US policy on agrarian reform in Latin America see: J. Petras and R. Laporte, **Cultivating Revolution**, Vintage Books, New York 1971. On the 'military alliance' there is: Don Etchison, **The United States and Militarism in Central America**, Praeger Special Studies, New York 1975; various NACLA reports: **The US Military and Police Operations in the Third World**, 1970, **The US Military Apparatus**, 1972 and **The Pentagon's Proteges**, January 1976. On CONDECA see the article by John Saxe-Fernandez in I. Horowitz, J. de Castro and J. Gerassi (eds), **Latin American Radicalism**, Vintage Books, New York 1969.

There is a useful article on US intervention in the Dominican Republic as well as other articles on US foreign policy during this period in: James Petras, **Politics and Social Structure in Latin America**, Monthly Review Press, New York 1970. There is a collection of documents on the intervention in: R.R. Fagen and W.A. Cornelius, Jr., **Political Power in Latin America: Seven Confrontations**, Prentice-Hall, Inc., New Jersey 1970. On developments following the intervention see two NACLA publications: **Dominican Republic — Military "Democracy"**, April 1974 and **Smoldering Conflict: Dominican Republic 1965-75**. For more information on US counterinsurgency operations in Guatemala in the 1960s see NACLA's **Guatemala** op.cit., also Roger Plant, **Guatemala: Unnatural Disaster**, Latin America Bureau 1978. Michael McClintock's forthcoming **Dragon's Teeth: The US and Paramilitary Terror in Central America** contains previously unpublished evidence of US complicity in the setting up of death squads. A good introduction to Puerto Rico is: **Puerto Rico: A People Challenging Colonialism**, Epica Task Force, Washington 1976 and more recently NACLA's **Puerto Rico — End of Autonomy**, March-April 1981.

On the English-speaking Caribbean a good historical overview is provided by Gordon K. Lewis, **The Growth of the Modern West Indies**, Monthly Review Press, New York 1968. On the Caribbean bauxite industry see Norman Girvan, **Corporate Imperialism: Conflict and Expropriation**, Monthly Review Press, New York 1976. On Jamaica there is: **Jamaica: Caribbean Challenge**, Epica Task Force, Washington 1979, NACLA's **Caribbean Conflict: Jamaica and the US**, May-June 1978 and **'Going Foreign' — Causes of Jamaican Migration**, Jan-Feb 1981. NACLA also provide a useful study on Trinidad in **Oil in the Caribbean — Focus on Trinidad**, October 1976. A general survey of the Caribbean's dependence on the US economy is: R.W. Palmer, **Caribbean Dependence on the United States Economy**, Praeger Special Studies, New York 1979. For a comprehensive survey of how the United States view the Caribbean see R.S. Crassweller, **The Caribbean Community**, Pall Mall, Lon-

don 1972. On Haiti there is D. Nicholls, **From Dessalines to Duvalier: Race Colour and National Independence in Haiti,** Cambridge University Press, 1980. **Haiti Report** published by the Friends of Haiti in New York is a useful source of information.

A good survey of the Central American economy in the 1960s and in particular the Central American Common Market (CACM) is S. Bodenheimer et al., **La Inversion Extranjera en Centroamerica,** EDUCA, Costa Rica 1974. The CACM is also covered in NACLA's **Guatemala** op.cit., and **Centroamerica Hoy,** op.cit. Donald Castillo Rivas, **Acumulacion de Capital y Empresas Transnacionales en Centroamerica** op.cit., provides an analysis of US investment in the 1970s and a useful list of multinational corporations which operate in the region. It also contains information on the changing role of the banana companies. NACLA's **Del Monte Bitter Fruits,** September 1976 deals with the banana war. A very good book on agribusiness with much relevance to Central America is: Roger Burback and Patricia Flynn, **Agribusiness in the Americas,** Monthly Review Press, New York 1980. On the growth of arms sales during the Nixon presidency see NACLA's **The Politics of US arms sales to Latin America,** March 1975 and Michael Klare and Cynthia Arnson's article in Richard R. Fagen (ed.) **Capitalism and the State in US-Latin American Relations,** Stanford University Press, California 1979. For a good general survey of US military assistance see Michael T. Klare, **Supplying Repression: US Support for Authoritarian Regimes Abroad,** Institute for Policy Studies, Washington 1977.

Part III: The Eagle Retrenches

There are many books which deal with the Nixon shocks and the subsequent crisis in the US economy. Two recent accounts are: Fitt, Faire and Vigier, **The World Economic Crisis — US Imperialism at Bay,** Zed Press, London 1980 and Manuel Castells, **The Economic Crisis and American Society,** Basil Blackwell, Oxford 1980. The New York journal **Monthly Review** has also covered these developments extensively. An important collection of essays covering all aspects of trilateralism is Holly Sklar (ed.), **Trilateralism: The Trilateral Commission and Elite Planning for World Management,** South End Press, Boston 1980. For Brzezinski's own views read his **Between Two Ages,** Penguin Harmondsworth 1971. Another useful collection of essays on US foreign policy in this period is R. Fagen (ed.), **Capitalism and the State in US-Latin American Relations,** op.cit. The report prepared for the US Senate Committee on Foreign Relations, **Human Rights and US Foreign Assistance — Experiences and Issues in Policy Implementation** (1977-78), US Government Printing Office, Washington 1979, lists the human rights legislation prepared by Congress before and during the Carter presidency. On the effectiveness of Carter's human rights policy see Richard Feinberg, **US Human**

Rights Policy: Latin America, Centre for International Policy, October 1980, Noam Chomsky and Edward S. Herman, US vs. Human Rights in the Third World in Monthly Review, July-August 1977, also Noam Chomsky, Human Rights and American Foreign Policy, Spokesman Books 1978. The Hearings before the Committee on International Relations of the House of Representatives, Human Rights in Nicaragua, Guatemala and El Salvador: Implications for US Policy, US Government Printing Office, Washington 1976 provide useful information on those countries.

Information on the Panama Canal Treaty can be found in Panama and the Canal Treaty, Latin America Bureau 1977 and NACLA's For Whom the Canal Tolls?, September-October 1979. Anthony P. Maingot's article, The Difficult Path to Socialism in the English-Speaking Caribbean in Richard Fagen (ed.), Capitalism and the State in US-Latin American Relations, op.cit., provides a good survey of Carter's policy toward the region in his first two years of office. On the Nicaraguan revolution see Dictatorship and Revolution, Latin America Bureau 1979 and NACLA's Crisis in Nicaragua, November-December 1978 and George Black's (forthcoming publication): Triumph of the People, Zed Press, London December 1981.

Part IV — The Eagle Reborn

An interesting assessment of the Carter presidency is: Laurence H. Shoup, The Carter Presidency and Beyond, Ramparts Press, California 1980. Also many of the essays in Holly Sklar (ed.), Trilateralism op.cit. See also James Petras, 'US Foreign Policy: Revival of Interventionism' in Monthly Review, February 1980. The Paris based monthly publication, Le Monde Diplomatique has published some interesting articles on US foreign policy during this period. The article by Alan Wolfe and Jerry Sanders in Richard Fagen (ed.), Capitalism and the State in US Latin American Relations, op.cit., looks at resurgent cold war ideology in the United States. A right wing assessment of the importance of the Caribbean basin to the United States is The Caribbean Strategic Vacuum, Institute for the Study of Conflict, London August 1980. Those wishing to monitor developments in US foreign policy thinking should consult the journals of the main foreign policy think tanks such as Foreign Affairs, Foreign Policy and The Washington Quarterly.

Useful Congressional hearings during this period which also provide insights into State Department thinking towards the region are: Central America at the Crossroads, Hearings before the Subcommittee on Inter-American Affairs of the House Committee on Foreign Affairs, September 1979, US Government Printing Office, Washington 1979; Special Central American Economic Assistance, Hearing before the House Committee on Foreign Affairs, November and December 1979, US Government Printing Office, Washington 1980; Assessment of Conditions in Central America, Hearings before the Subcommittee on Inter-American Affairs of the House Committee on Foreign Affairs, April and May 1980, US Government Printing Office, Washington 1980; **Foreign Assistance Legislation for Fiscal year 1981 (part 6)**, Hearings before the Subcommittee on Inter-American Affairs of the House Foreign Affairs Committee, February and March 1980, US Government Printing Office, Washington 1980. On the right in the United States see the articles by Alan Wolfe and Mike Davis in **New Left Review**, July-August 1981.

Much of the information on more recent events in this book comes from primary sources. In addition to the national press of the countries mentioned there are a number of regular publications which provide up to date information on the region: **Caribbean Insight** (London), **Caribbean and West Indies Chronicle** (London), **Caribbean Contact** (Barbados), **Caribbean Basin Report** (Ottawa), **Latin America Newsletters' Caribbean Regional Report** (London), **Noticias del Caribe** (Dominican Republic), **Central America Update** (LAWG, Toronto), **ALAI** (Quebec), **Latin America Newsletters' Central America Regional Report** (London), **Noticias de Guatemala** (Costa Rica), **Inforpress** (Guatemala), **This Week — Central America and Panama** (Guatemala). For regular information on US foreign policy there are the United States publications: **Newsweek, Time, The Nation** and **Covert Action**. A number of organizations which monitor US foreign policy produce useful publications: **WOLA Update** (Washington Office on Latin America), **CLASP Bulletin** (Caribbean and Latin America Solidarity Project) and the press releases of the Council on Hemispheric Affairs (COHA). The reports of the Institute of Policy Studies, the Center for International Policy and the Coalition for a New Military and Foreign Policy also provide regular information on US economic and military assistance to the region.

Part V — El Salvador: The Eagle's Reckoning?

Two introductions to the country in English are: David Browning, **El Salvador — Landscape and Society**, Clarendon Press, Oxford 1971 and Alastair White, **El Salvador**, Ernest Benn, London 1973. On the 1932 uprising: Thomas P. Anderson, **Matanza: El Salvador's Communist Revolt of 1932**, University of Nebraska Press, Lincoln, Nebraska 1971. In Spanish **Estudios Centroamericanos** (ECA), the journal of the Universidad Centroamericana Jose Simeon Canas, contains many useful articles. Two publications on El Salvador in the 1970s are: **Violence and Fraud in El Salvador**, Latin America Bureau 1977 and **El Salvador under General Romero**, Latin America Bureau 1979. On US policy see: **The Recent Presidential Elections in El Salvador: Implications for US Foreign Policy**, Hearings before Subcommittees on International Relations, March 1977, US Government Printing Office, Washington 1977. NACLA has also published two reports on the country: **El Salvador — Why Revolution?**, March-April 1980 and **El Salvador — A Revolution Brews**,

July-August 1980. On human rights violations since October 1979 there is The Legal Aid Service of the Archdiocese of San Salvador — **El Salvador — One Year of Repression**, Commission of the Churches on International Affairs, World Council of Churches, 1981 and the **Inter-Church Committee on Human Rights in Latin America Newsletter**, Toronto, Canada. A good study of the agrarian reform announced in 1980 is L.R. Simon and J.C. Stephens, **El Salvador — Land Reform 1980-81**, Impact Audit, Oxfam America, Boston Massachusetts 1981.

Useful Addresses

BRITAIN

**Amnesty International —
British Section**
Tower House,
8-14 Southampton Street,
London WC2E 7HF

**Amnesty International-
International Secretariat**
10 Southampton Street,
London WC2E 7HF

Britain-Cuba Resource Centre
76 Sydenham Park Road,
London SE26 4LL

British-Grenada Friendship Society
c/o 4 Windus Walk,
Stoke Newington,
London N16

Caribbean Labour Solidarity
138 Southgate Road,
London N1

**Catholic Institute for International
Relations**
22 Coleman Fields,
London N1

**Committee for Puerto Rican
Independence**
BM-CPRI,
London WC1V 6XX

**El Salvador Human Rights
Committee**
c/o 20-21 Compton Terrace,
London N1 2UN

El Salvador Solidarity Campaign
c/o CARILA,
29 Islington Park Street,
London N1

Guatemala Working Group
c/o Latin America Bureau,
1 Amwell Street,
London EC1R 1UL

Jamaica Action Group
74 Corfe Tower,
Park Road East,
London W3

Liberation
313/5 Caledonian Road,
London N1 1DR

Nicaragua Solidarity Campaign
c/o 20-21 Compton Terrace,
London N1 2UN

**St. Vincent & the Grenadines
Society**
84 Dynevor Road,
London N16

War on Want
467 Caledonian Road,
London N7

UNITED STATES

American Friends of Guatemala
Box 2283, Station A,
Berkeley,
CA 94702

Amnesty International
304 W. 58th Street,
New York,
NY 10019

**Association in Solidarity with
Guatemala**
PO Box 13006,
Washington DC 20009

**Broad Movement of Solidarity
with the Salvadorean People**
PO Box 38735,
Los Angeles,
CA 90038

Caribbean and Latin America Solidarity Project
PO Box 1080,
New York,
NY 10025

Center for International Policy
120 Maryland Avenue NE,
Washington DC 20002

Coalition for a New Foreign and Military Policy
120 Maryland Avenue NE,
Washington DC 20002

Committee for Progressive Salvadoreans
PO Box 12335,
San Francisco,
CA 94112

Council on Hemispheric Affairs
1735 New Hampshire Ave NW,
Washington DC 20009

Ecumenical Program for Inter-American Communication and Action
1470 Irving Street NW,
Washington DC 20010

Friends of Haiti
PO Box 348,
New City,
New York,
NY 10956

Guatemala News and Information Bureau
PO Box 4126,
Berkeley,
CA 94704

Institute for Policy Studies
1901 Que Street NW,
Washington DC 20009

National Network in Solidarity with the Nicaraguan People
1322 18th St. NW,
Washington DC 20036

North American Congress on

Latin America
151 W 19th Street 9th Floor,
New York,
NY 10011

Maryknoll Missioners
Maryknoll PO,
New York,
NY 10545

Religious Task Force for El Salvador
PO Box 12056,
Washington DC 20005

Salvadorean-American Human Rights Committee
PO Box 3982,
Grand Central Station,
New York,
NY 10017

Washington Office on Latin America
110 Maryland Avenue NE,
Washington DC 20002

CANADA

Agence Latino-Americaine d'Information
1224 Ste-Catherine 0. 403,
Montreal,
Quebec H3G 1P2

Amnesty International
English-Speaking Branch,
Box 6033,
2101 Algonquin Avenue,
Ottawa,
Ontario K2A 1T1

French-Speaking Branch,
1800 Blvd. Dorchester Ouest,
4eme etage,
Montreal,
Quebec H3H 2H2

Canadian Action for Nicaragua
1961 Perrot Blvd.,
Ile Perrot,
Quebec J7V 5V6

Committee for Human Rights in
Central America
Box 1178,
Port Alberni,
BC B9Y 7L5

Inter-Church Committee on
Human Rights in Latin America
Suite 201,

40 St. Clair Avenue,
East Toronto,
Ontario M4T 1M9

Latin American Research Unit
Box 673,
Adelaide Street P.O.,
Toronto,
Ontario M5C 2J8

Latin American Working Group
Box 2207 Station P,
Toronto,
Ontario M5S 2T2

List of Abbreviations

AID	Agency for International Development, USA
AIFLD	American Institute for Free Labour Development, USA
ANEP	National Private Enterprise Association, El Salvador
BPR	Popular Revolutionary Bloc, El Salvador
CACM	Central American Common Market
CARICOM	Caribbean Community and Common Market
CONDECA	Central American Defence Council
COPEI	Christian Democratic Party, Venezuela
CRM	Revolutionary Co-ordinating Committee of the Masses, El Salvador
DRU	Unified Revolutionary Directorate, El Salvador
ECLA	United Nations Economic Commission for Latin America
ERP	People's Revolutionary Army, El Salvador
ESF	Economic Support Fund, USA
FAN	Broad National Front, El Salvador
FAPU	Unified People's Action Front, El Salvador
FARN	Armed Forces of National Resistance, El Salvador
FDR	Democratic Revolutionary Front, El Salvador
FECCAS	Christian Federation of Farmworkers, El Salvador
FMLN	Farabundo Marti National Liberation Front, El Salvador
FPL	Popular Forces of Liberation-Farbundo Marti, El Salvador
FMS	Foreign Military Sales, USA
FSLN	Sandinista Front for National Liberation, Nicaragua
IDB	Inter-American Development Bank
IMET	International Military Education and Training programme, USA
IMF	International Monetary Fund
ISTA	Institute for Land Reform, El Salvador
JLP	Jamaica Labour Party
LP-28	Popular Leagues of 28th February, El Salvador
MAP	Military Assistance Program, USA
MLN	National Liberation Movement, Guatemala

288

MNR	National Revolutionary Movement, El Salvador
NJM	New Jewel Movement, Grenada
OAS	Organization of American States
OPS	Office of Public Safety, US AID
ORDEN	National Democratic Organization, El Salvador
PDC	Christian Democrat Party, El Salvador
PNP	People's National Party, Jamaica
PRD	Dominican Revolutionary Party, Dominican Republic
UCS	Communal Union, El Salvador
UDN	Democratic National Union, El Salvador
UPEB	Union of Banana-Exporting Countries
UTC	Union of Rural Workers, El Salvador
WPA	Working People's Alliance, Guyana

Index

Items are listed under the headings of countries and major organizations.

213, 218, 226, 227; Communist Party, 211, 212, 221; CONDECA, 60-1; 1961 coup, 53; D'Abuisson, Major, 179, 222 227, 235, 246; Democratic Revolutionary Front (FDR), 152, 236, 237, 239, 245; Duarte, Jose Napoleon, 75, 134, 148, 211, 216, 226, 238, 239, 246-7, 252; FALANGE, 213, 220; FAN, 235; Farabundo Marti National Liberation Front, 237, 248; Garcia, Colonel Jose, 220-1, 235, 238, 246-7; guerrilla organizations, 212-3, 239-40, 249; Gutierrez, Colonel Jaime Abdul, 220-1, 226, 235; industrialization, 211-2; Majano, Colonel Adolfo, 220, 235, 238; Mayorga, Roman, 221, 223; Medrano, General, 214, 221, 222; Molina, Arturo Armando, 216-7, 218-9; National Guard, 209, 222, 223; National Police, 210, 223; oligarchy, 210, 217-8, 221-2, 223, 225, 232; ORDEN, 68, 212, 214, 215, 216, 217, 220, 222, 232, 235, 241; Popular Revolutionary Bloc, 212; Romero, Carlos Humberto, 135, 218-20; Romero, Oscar Arnulfo, 213, 227-9; Socorro Juridico, 226, 227, 235-6; Treasury Police, 210; Ungo, Guillermo, 221, 223, 246, 249; Unified Revolutionary Directorate (DRU), 236, 237; White, Robert, 156, 184, 226, 239, 249; White Warriors' Union, 121, 213, 218, 220, 222

France: 146-7, 202; and Cuba, 146; and El Salvador, 240, 248; and Mexico, 252-3; Cheysson, Claude, 252; Guadeloupe, 146; Guyane, 146; Martinique, 146

Great Britain: and Belize, 199; and El Salvador, 240, 248-9; and Grenada, 121, 122-3, 155, 163; and Jamaica, 77; Booker McConnell, 94; Commonwealth Caribbean, 24, 81; declining influence, 140-1, 146; Geest Industries Ltd., 121, 141; influence in 19C, 8; Organization of East Caribbean States, 155

Grenada: 121-3; and mercenaries, 159; and Reagan administration, 184, 187, 189, 203; and Socialist International, 152; and US, 128, 135, 155, 163-4; and Venezuela, 148, 149; Bishop, Maurice, 121-3, 159; Gairy, Eric, 121-2; Geest Industries Limited, 121; Grenada United Labour Party, 121; Hurricane Allen, 141, 164, 169; independence, 140; isolation, 145; Mongoose Gang, 121; New Jewel Movement, 121-2

Guatemala: 66-72; agriculture, 42-3; Alejos Arzu, Roberto, 175; and El Salvador, 239, 249; and Israel, 73; and Mexico, 150; and New Right, 175-9; and Nicaragua, 124, 125, 159; and Reagan administration, 184, 192-9; and United Fruit, 16, 28-30; and US, 53, 56, 154; Arana Osorio, Carlos, 67-8, 70, 74-5, 175; Arbenz, Jacobo, 28-9; Arevalo, Juan Jose, 28; Asociacion de los Amigos del Pais, 175; CACIF, 29-30; Christian Democrat Party, 75; Committee of Trade Union Unity, 121; CONDECA, 60-1; Fundacion Guatemalteca por la Libertad, 175, 178; future, 253: German immigrants, 13; Guerrilla Army of the Poor, 253; industrial development, 48; Lucas Garcia, 175, 178, 193, 199; Mano Blanca, 121; massacres, 192; Mendez Montenegro, Julio Cesar, 67-8; National Liberation Movement (MLN), 68, 70, 175; 13 November Revolutionary Movement, 60; oil, 140; ORPA, 253; Rebel Armed

Forces (FAR), 60; Trotter, John, 175-8, 179; Ubico, Jorge, 21, 28; Villagran Kramer, 133; Ydigoras, President, 33, 53

Guyana: 158-9; and AIFLD, 45; and Cuba, 143; and Grenada, 123, 145, 189; and US, 76, 111, 141; bauxite, 24, 77, 78, 94; Burnham, Forbes, 83, 94, 158; emigrants, 82; exports, 80; imports, 81; Jagan, Cheddi, 45, 83, 94; oil, 140; Rodney, Walter, 158-9; Working People's Alliance, 158

Haiti: 89-93; and Dominican Republic, 62, 91, 154; and Reagan administration, 199, 201; and US, 19, 139, 161, 164; bauxite, 76, 77; Duvalier, Francois, 89; Duvalier, Jean Claude, 89, 199; history, 12, 13; Palace Guard, 74; Tonton Macoutes, 89, 91

Holland: 12-13; Dutch Antilles, 79, 146, 164; Dutch Guiana, 24; Suriname, 146

Honduras: 97-8; and El Salvador, 209-10, 235, 244, 249; and Nicaragua, 185-6; and Reagan administration, 184, 191-2; and US, 154, 155, 157, 164; Carias Andino, Tiburcio, 22; CONDECA, 60-1; 1963 coup, 53; Football War, 49; history, 13; oil, 140; Paz Garcia, 186

Inter-American Development Bank: 44; and El Salvador, 218; and Nicaragua, 123, 185

International Monetary Fund: 44, 119; and Carter administration, 110; and El Salvador, 252-3; and Grenada, 189; and Guyana, 158, 159; and Haiti, 201; and Jamaica, 113, 160; and Nicaragua, 125; establishment, 25-6

Leeward Islands: 12

Mexico: and Carter administration, 106; and El Salvador, 239, 252-3; and Nicaragua, 19, 125; and Reagan administration, 171, 184, 193, 203; in 19C, 8, 17; influence in region, 149-51, 152; Lopez Portillo, President, 150; oil, 139, 140, 148

Nicaragua: 117-9, 123-8; and Carter administration, 121, 132, 135; and Colombia, 189; and Cuba, 145; and El Salvador, 212, 240; and Guatemala, 253; and Nixon, 75, 85; and Reagan administration, 193, 203; and Socialist International, 152; and US, 17, 19, 20, 116, 117, 164, 169, 191, 220; and Venezuela, 148; Chamorro, Pedro Joaquin, 119, 123, 127, 133; CONDECA, 60-1; D'Escoto, Miguel, 154, 250; FAO, 124-5; in 19C, 8; industrial growth, 48, 49; National Guard, 56, 61, 74, 118, 123, 126, 127, 159, 185; oligarchy, 13; Pezzullo, Lawrence, 156, 184; Sandinista National Liberation Front, 60, 117, 123, 125-8; Sandino, Augusto, 19-20; Somoza, President, 117-9, 123-8; UPEB, 97-8

OAS (Organization of American States): and Colombia, 189; and El Salvador, 220; and Mexico, 149-50; and Nicaragua, 124, 126-7; establishment, 26

Panama: and Carter administration, 110, 113-6, 121; and El Salvador, 239, 248, 252; and Nicaragua, 125, 126; and Reagan administration, 192; Canal Treaty, 113-6, 132; Canal Zone, 56-9, 60, 97-8, 113-6, 136, 138, 139; independence, 11-12; School of the Americas, 52, 155; Torrijos, General Omar, 97, 239, 248

Puerto Rico: 111-2; and Carter administration, 110; and Jamaica, 160; and Reagan administration, 201-2; and US, 56, 66, 81, 90, 136, 138; in 19C, 10; 'Operation Bootstrap', 49-51, 78; Roosevelt Roads, 23, 60, 136, 138

St Kitts: and Grenada, 145; and US, 148; elections 1980, 158
St Lucia: and Amerada Hess, 139; and Barbados, 155; and Grenada, 145, 159, 189; and US, 24, 156; elections 1979, 135; Hurricane Allen, 141; independence, 140; Labour Party, 158
St Vincent: and Grenada, 122, 145; Hurricane Allen, 141; independence, 140
Socialist International: 152; and El Salvador, 239, 248
Soviet Union: and Carter administration, 168-9; and Cuba, 33, 36, 138, 153; and Poland, 253; and Reagan administration, 182, 184, 240; and Trilateralism, 132, 133; Cold War, 27, 51
Spain: and Cuba, 9; and Dominican Republic, 13; and Puerto Rico, 10; Hispanoil, 140; Spanish-American War, 9-10
Suriname: and Grenada, 159, 189; bauxite, 77; independence, 146; oil, 140

Trinidad and Tobago: 78-80, 149; and Barbados, 155; and Cuba, 143; and Grenada, 122, 145; and US investment, 164; emigrants, 82; history, 12; imports, 81; independence, 76; oil, 139; People's National Movement, 79; Williams, Eric, 79, 149

Union of Banana Exporting Countries (UPEB): 97-8
United Nations: and Mexico, 150; and Puerto Rico, 49; ECLA, 47; UN Committee on Decoloniza-

tion, 111
United States: AFL-CIO, 45; Agency for International Development (AID), creation, 45, and Dominican Republic, 62-3, and El Salvador, 215, 217, and Guatemala, 47-8, 66, 67, 71, 184, and Guyana, 83, and Jamaica, 96, 108, and Nicaragua, 185; Allen, Richard, and Guatemala, 178, and Reagan, 165, 169, 184, ideology, 181; American Institute for Free Labour Development (AIFLD), and Dominican Republic, 66, and El Salvador, 215, 218, 220, 229, 238; and Guatemala, 97, and Guyana, 83, creation, 45; US and Belize, 199, and Caribbean, 136-43, and Commonwealth Caribbean, 23-5, 156, and Cuban revolution, 31-5, and Dominican Republic, 12, 17, 21, 61-6, 112, and El Salvador, 204, 213-50, and Grenada, 122-3, and Guatemala, 28-9, 53, 66-72, 74-5, 192-9, and Haiti, 89-93, 199, 201, and Honduras, 157, 190-1, and Jamaica, 75-8, 95-7, 113, 160-1, and Mexico, 19, 150-1, and Nicaragua, 8, 12, 56, 117-9, 123-8, and Panama, 23, 113-116; Canal Zone, 11-12, 57-59, and Puerto Rico, 10, 23, 49-51, 59-60, 111-12, 201-2, and Trinidad and Tobago, 78-80; Bank of America, 88, 164; US bases in Caribbean, 23-4; Bowdler, William, and El Salvador, 225, 237, and Nicaragua, 125, 127, 135; Bretton Woods Conference, 25, 101; Brzezinski, Zbigniew, and Cuba, 116, 153, and Nicaragua, 126, 135, and Trilateral Commission, 104, 105-6, 108, 133; CIA (Central Intelligence Agency), and CONDECA, 61, and Cuba, 33, 45, 96, 104, 110, 135, 187, and Dominican Republic, 62, 65, 66,

293

and Grenada, 159, and Guyana, 83, and Honduras, 29, and Jamaica, 161, and ORDEN, 214, creation, 27; Committee on the Present Danger, 107, 131; Council on Foreign Relations, and Carter, 108, and Vietnam, 72, description of, 104; counter-insurgency, 52-6, 57, 183; Department of Defense, and Puerto Rico, 138, creation, 27, 57; Dulles, John Foster, 29, 104; Eagleburger, Lawrence, 240, 248; Enders, Thomas, 184, 249, 250; Fontaine, Roger, 171, 184, 187, 239-246; Georgetown University, 170-1; Green Berets, 67, 192; US growth in 19C, 8-9; Haig, Alexander, and El Salvador, 241, 250, and Nicaragua, 187, 203, and Soviet Union, 184, ideology, 181, 182; Helms, Jesse, 181, 182, 246; Hinton, Deane, 244, 248; Hoover Institute, 169-70; Kirkpatrick, Jeane, 171, 175; Kissinger, Henry, and Haig, 181, and Jamaica, 96, and Nixon, 108, 109, 117, 165, and Trilateral Commission, 107, 169, flexible response, 37, realpolitik, 73-4; US marines, in Cuba, 17, in Haiti, 19, in Nicaragua, 19-20; McNamara, Robert, 52, 56, 57-9, 61; Military Assistance Program (MAP), 52, 72-3, 109, 119; Military Sales Program, 74, 119-20, 154, 155, 156; Monroe Doctrine, 8, 27, 105; Moral Majority, 165; National Security Council, 27, 132, 135, 160, 165-81, 183, 184; Pentagon, and counter-insurgency, 52, 183, and Guatemala, 121, and Nicaragua, 135; Pezzullo, Lawrence, 134, 156, 184; Rockefeller, David, 43, 104, 107, 114, 165, 202; Rockefeller, Nelson, 73-4, 165; Roosevelt Roads, 23, 60, 136, 138; School of the Americas, 52, 57, 155; Senate Foreign Relations Committee, 63, 247; Sheldon, Sally, 111, 161; Spanish-American War, 9-10; State Department, and Caribbean, 141, 156, 164, and El Salvador, 209, 218, 226, 240-1, and Guatemala, 29, 116, 140, 179, 193, and Guyana, 94, 158-9, and Jamaica, 160-1, and Nicaragua, 119, 123, 125, 126, 134, 135; State Department 'Dissent Paper', 159-60, 165, 237; Sunbelt, 30, 85-8, 175; Todman, Terence, 110-1, 219; Trilateral Commission, and G. Bush, 165, and Reagan, 181, 182, description, 103-8, failure, 131; Trotter, John, 175-8, 179; Vaky, Viron, 134, 135, 141-2, 220; Vance, Cyrus, and Council on Foreign Relations, 72, 104, and Cuba, 152-3, and Dominican Republic, 112, and human rights, 117, and Nicaragua, 126, and Soviet Union, 106-7, resignation, 133; Walters, General Vernon, 184, 192, 201, 240; White, Robert, 156, 184, 226, 239, 249

United States multinational companies: Alcoa (Alcan), and Dominican Republic, 63, and Guyana, 78, 94, and Jamaica, 76; Amerada Hess, 139, 164; Amoco, 79, 80, 140; Falconbridge, 64-5; Grace, W. R., 24, 146; Del Monte, 84, 97, 98; Gulf and Western, 64-5, 82, 164; Standard Fruit and Steamship Company, 84, 97-8; Standard Oil, 24; Texaco, 24, 79, 140, 164; United Fruit (United Brands), 15-6, 24, 28-30, 83-5, 97-8

United States Presidents: Carter, Jimmy, 107-121, 131-2, 134-6, 152-4, 163, 164-5, 168; and El Salvador, 237, 238-9; and Grenada, 123; and Haiti, 93, 199; and Nicaragua, 125, 126; and

Reaganites, 171, 178; ambassadors, 156; Eisenhower, 29, 33; Ford, Gerald, 107, 108; Johnson, L. B., 56, 73, 74; Kennedy, John F., 37-8, 183; and Alliance for Progress, 41, 51; and Bay of Pigs, 33; and Dominican Republic, 62; and subversion, 51, 52; Nixon, Richard, 101-2, 108, 109; and Cuban exiles, 35; and Guatemala, 85; and Haiti, 89, and MAP, 72; and Reagan, 165; and Watergate, 101; vice-president, 30; Reagan, Ronald, 181-3; and El Salvador, 239-40, 247; and Guatemala, 179; and Honduras, 190-1; and New Right, 165, 168, 170-1; and Panama Canal Treaty, 114; future, 253-6; Roosevelt, Franklin D., 22, 23, 24

Venezuela: and El Salvador, 148-9, 239, 248, 252; and Grenada, 189; and Nicaragua, 125, 127; Accion Democratica, 148; Andres Perez, Carlos, 148; COPEI, 148; Herrera Campins, Luis, 148; influence in Caribbean, 148-9; oil, 78, 139
Virgin Islands: 12, 23

World Bank: and Caribbean, 112, 163; and Grenada, 189; and Guyana, 94, 159; and US, 44, 88, 119; creation, 25; report on Haiti, 91

Imperialism out of Central America

Demonstration
10th Anniversary of the coup in Chile
London Sunday 11 September
12.30 Clerkenwell Green

Public meeting
Holborn Library
Theobalds Road WC1
Friday 9 September 7.30

RCP
Revolutionary Communist Party